Mind the Inclusion Gap

MIND THE INCLUSION GAP

How allies can bridge the divide between talking diversity and taking action

Suzy Levy

unbound

First published in 2023

Unbound
Level 1, Devonshire House, One Mayfair Place, London W1J 8AJ
www.unbound.com
All rights reserved

Typeset by Jouve (UK), Milton Keynes

A CIP record for this book is available from the British Library

ISBN 978-1-80018-235-6 (paperback)
ISBN 978-1-80018-236-3 (ebook)

Printed in Great Britain by Clays Ltd, Elcograf S.p.A

1 3 5 7 9 8 6 4 2

Special thanks to patrons of this book:
Circularity First
Clear Channel
Microsoft Corporation

My grateful thanks to the following people for their
generous support of this book:
Mac Alonge
Claire Hockin
Jeremy Oates
Mark Williams

For the ones who gave me their story
and took me on the journey

Thank you

This has only been possible because of
your willingness to let me in and to work
side by side to build something better

Contents

Foreword

Diversity and inclusion are topics that have always needed a deeper understanding, learning and patience. Recently they have been given more oxygen, a higher priority and increased importance. I know that not everyone shares my view but, personally, I welcome the increased focus on both.

Diversity is a fact. It is all around us: from skin colour, religion, sexuality to upbringing, diversity is endless. Unlike diversity, inclusion isn't a given. Inclusion is an action and acting inclusively takes effort.

Former world-champion tennis player Billie Jean King once said that 'you can never understand inclusion until you've been excluded'.[1] Not only do we need a chance to walk in the shoes of others, we also need to have a solid grasp on why things are the way they are. To get a truer and fuller picture of our present day means we must reflect honestly on the events in our past.

Take, for example, cyclist Lance Armstrong. He was a global superstar and a superhero to many. At the peak of his power, he was accused of cheating and found guilty. A federal inquiry into the allegations of doping concluded that Armstrong's actions were 'the most sophisticated, professionalised and successful doping program that sport has ever seen'.[2] As a result, Lance Armstrong was handed a lifetime ban from the sport and stripped of all his titles and credibility. But that isn't his full story. Lance spent a part of his career battling his own personal challenges with cancer. This spurred him on to raise more than $500 million for cancer research.[3]

How will history tell his story? Is it about the man who cheated his opponents, the sport and adoring fans for self-gain, money and success? Or is this the story of a man who single-handedly raised more money in the fight against cancer than any sportsperson before or since?

We should not omit Armstrong from our history. Instead, I believe we need to tell his whole story, learn from it, and use those lessons to better the future of sport. The same is true for all parts of our history – telling the complete story requires admitting that things aren't simply black or white and knowing that good people can do bad things. We live in a world that requires us to explore the 'grey'. Understanding our world requires context. It requires nuance. And it requires an ability to look at the challenges we face through a kaleidoscopic lens.

Mind the Inclusion Gap does exactly that. It is an incredibly well-researched book with a good balance of facts and opinions. It allows you to sit in the shoes of others and see new perspectives. Some of the reading and learning is uncomfortable. I found (more than once) that a fact or finding astounded me. I had to pause my reading to digest and reflect before turning the page, only to repeat the process throughout!

This book is more than just words on a page: it encourages deeper, more meaningful conversations. It gives us all an opportunity to learn, reflect and, ultimately, urges us to take action.

Not every action you take will be perfect, nor will it be perfectly welcomed, but that doesn't mean your actions are not important. Several years ago, I found myself wanting to be a more vocal and visible ally for women in sport. I had followed and covered women's rugby more closely after retiring from rugby in 2015 and worked as a commentator on my first World Cup in 2017, but I knew I could do more. I love the game but felt nervous to put my head above the parapet and speak out. I certainly wasn't the first – many players had made the transition to commentating before me, but there wasn't really much cross-pollination between the men's and the women's game. I never felt more nervous covering a game than I did – and still do (but to a lesser extent) – when I cover a women's game. What if I get a name wrong? It's something I do in the men's game! What will people think?

I have made mistakes, and I have been publicly scrutinised for them. In some instances, the feedback I've received has been helpful. In others, it has been less so. But, ultimately, it's been okay. My intentions are clear: I want to support and grow the women's game and to make rugby more inclusive for all. I won't (and don't) always get it right, but the path of any ally is not perfect.

There are plenty of good people with good intentions in this space. But intention without impact is fruitless. Knowing what action to take can be a challenge – especially with the rise in how social media and popular opinion shape our world views. *Mind the Inclusion Gap* allows us to pause and asks us to go deeper into the conversation and have a level of introspection about why we think and feel the way we do. The book is not here to convert people but to equip us with more information, and to help us move beyond good intentions.

More than anything, I found this book nourishing. In it, Suzy created a safe space for me to learn. She challenged my thinking without making me feel judged. Reading it has made me feel better equipped, more energised and more ready to engage.

I do hope you enjoy it as much as I have, and I hope you are moved to take action as a result.

Ugo Monye

Introduction

Tuning into current affairs can be an exercise in despair. We are faced with rising food and fuel prices. There are raging fights over gun ownership, abortion and equal rights. Combine that with the consequences of climate change, millions fleeing their homeland to escape violence and war, and a seismic political divide, and you have a cacophony of chaos. Each of these issues is enormous in its own right and the compound effect leaves many feeling powerless. That sense of impotence is so disturbing that, for some, the only solution is to tune out and ignore them altogether.

We live in troubled times, and we face some significant world problems. But we also live in exciting times. Never before in history have we been so close to building a society based upon decency and fundamental human rights. Today, we are having tough (but stimulating) conversations about fairness and equality. We are actively engaging in conflicts that have long been there, but that, for the most part, we were not willing to air or explore.

This exploration is both daunting and exciting. It's daunting because expectations are rising that we must work together to fix what is broken. But deeply divided and deeply entrenched views mean we aren't on the same page about what needs fixing, or how to fix it. It's exciting because underneath all the drama lies opportunity. Opportunity for greater human connection and a chance to understand each other in a deeper, more meaningful way. It's also a chance to do something purposeful, and, if we are bold enough, to entertain the possibility of leaving an indelible mark on this world long after we are gone.

Most of us are curious about diversity, and some would go so far as to call ourselves allies, but very few of us are skilled at inclusion. Instead, we double down on being nice and hope it will be enough. In the absence of inclusion skills, we allow our moral compass and our instincts towards kindness to ground us. But being nice and being inclusive are not the same thing. You can be a nice person, and at the same time, totally ignorant to the needs of others. These very honourable traits may harm as much as they help. The more we lean on our niceness, the more we tend to bypass the messy and uncomfortable in order to avoid discord and disagreement. I should know. I spent most of my early life trying to minimise conflict and help everyone get along. As a result, when I started working in inclusion and diversity, I relied on an overinflated sense of niceness to guide me through. While it was a good starting point, I quickly learned that being nice was limiting; not only did it encourage me to avoid conflict, but it also created a false sense of progress.

I wrote this book to help others move away from being just 'a nice person', to go beyond a superficial understanding of inclusion and diversity, and to enable them to gain genuine insight that leads to meaningful action.

Why are you here?

I suspect if you picked up this book, you're at least curious. Some of you may already be very active in this space. Others may be unsure of where to begin. Whatever your starting point, I hope you find the following chapters a useful tool to deepen your knowledge and increase your compassion. Most importantly, I hope this book enables you to play a part (however big or small) in making our world more equitable, more inclusive, and more joyful to be a part of.

Are we there yet?

Our world is a beautiful, brutal contradiction. We live in a moment where (theoretically) women are empowered to be anything we could imagine. Stay at home and enjoy raising kids. Be a CEO. Be a scholar. Be a scientist. Be an astronaut, an entrepreneur or a teacher. The possibilities are endless. For the most part, women and girls are being released from their social bonds and encouraged to be anything they want to be. As a result, women are increasingly rising to take their place in global society.

But progress is painfully slow. It has been twenty-two years since we saw the first female CEO of a FTSE 100 company. Despite girls achieving higher success rates at school and being more likely to attain higher education,[1] only a handful of women are at the helm of those organisations today. You are more likely to be called Steve than you are to be a woman in that cohort.[2] Women make up 49 per cent of the world population, but just 8 per cent of Fortune 500 CEOs.[3] Male dominance in leadership isn't confined to business. Even in the social sector, where women make up nearly 70 per cent of the global workforce, men are still three times more likely to become the CEO.[4] Although women now hold one in four parliamentary positions globally,[5] political power remains stubbornly evasive. There are 195 countries in the world, but currently only fourteen with a female head of state.[6] Within the G20, the intergovernmental forum which together represent 85 per cent of the world's GDP, nineteen out of the twenty leaders are currently men.

Female empowerment is not yet netting the results we would expect, and it is far from universal. Even in the most feminist of societies, opportunities and outcomes for women of colour are not equal to those enjoyed by white women.[7] Whether it's the bigger gaps in pay and employment, the almost complete dearth of representation in leadership positions, or the life-and-death nature of severe health inequalities (Black women are more than four times as likely to die during childbirth in the UK,[8] and more than three times as likely to die from pregnancy-related causes in the US than their white counterparts),[9] women of colour experience unique disadvantages that white women do not face. The variance in outcomes isn't just a matter of skin pigment; location also plays a key role in how women experience the world today. Research by the World Bank suggests that there are only six countries where women hold 100 per cent of the same fundamental rights that men hold.[10] In fact, there are twenty-two countries where women hold fewer than half of the legal rights enjoyed by their male counterparts. Whether it be the right to drive, the right to work, the right to own property, the right to choose to be a mother (or not), or even the right to choose who you marry – we still have a long way to go in order to achieve universal freedom for women.

In many respects, men appear to have it all. Around the world, men rise to the top of society, leading companies and countries and making a lot of money in the process. But when you look closer, the truth is not as simple as it might seem. Globally, men are more than two times as likely to take their own life.[11] They are also more likely to be lonely. One in five British men today say they do not have a single close friend.[12] From an early age we tell our boys to 'be a man', 'man up', to 'grow some balls' and not to 'be a sissy', but where does that lead us? The global patterns are clear: it doesn't matter what the substance may be – alcohol, drugs, sex, porn or gambling – men are between two and eight times more likely than women to suffer from unhealthy addictions. We ignore men in most of our diversity conversations because they are 'leading' and 'succeeding', but is this really success?

Meanwhile, transgender visibility and the debate surrounding trans rights grows. The conversation can be led by extreme feelings – from freedom to fear, dignity to disgust and everything in between. Most of us grew up in a world built upon a fundamental principle that there are boys and there are girls and there can be nothing in between. But is that really the truth? We were taught that gender and sex are the same thing, and that they are rigid in their form. What if our foundations are flawed? What if gender is something we made up and sex is not as binary as we were led to believe? Is it possible to progress women's rights and trans rights at the same time? Or are the two in conflict? There are more questions in the trans space than there are answers and because so few of us know anyone who is transgender, the chasm of information and experience leaves us wide open to manipulation.

Over the last two decades gay and lesbian rights have been catapulted to the forefront of our collective consciousness. There is no doubt that the rainbow flags which fly high during Pride Month are a sign of increasing acceptance. But despite all the progress, there are almost three times as many countries in which being gay is punishable by imprisonment or death[13] than there are countries which allow gay marriage.[14] Just as we have thriving communities where lesbian, bisexual and gay individuals can simply be themselves, we also have communities where holding your partner's hand will get you shouted at, spat on or physically beaten. It's easy to think that acceptance of same-sex relationships will simply change with time, but progress is precarious, and evidence suggests this is not entirely the case. Even in countries where there is widespread acceptance of the gay community, there is at the same time increasing intolerance. In the first three months of 2022, US state lawmakers proposed 238 anti-LGBTQ+ bills, more than the total number of anti-LGBTQ+ bills proposed in 2018, 2019 and 2020 combined.[15] America's young people show both a higher likelihood than older Americans to be something other than heterosexual, and at the same time show a declining level of comfort with, and acceptance of, LGBTQ+ people in certain situations.[16] Despite many people being more open to same-sex and bisexual relationships, homophobia and hate crimes against the gay community are also on the rise throughout Europe.[17]

Racial equality has been embedded in UK and US law for more than half a century, but the global awakening after US police officer Derek Chauvin murdered George Floyd in May 2020 has thrust racism, and its pervasive reach, into the spotlight. Fifty years after the breakthrough in civil rights, immense gaps remain. People of colour* make up 18.3 per cent of individuals living in England and Wales,[18] and 38 per cent of those living in America.[19] Logic suggests that all else being equal, people of colour should therefore be rising proportionally to the top of major organisations, but they are not. Leadership remains stubbornly white. In the FTSE

---

* You will find that throughout this book, I use the terms 'person of colour' and 'ethnic minority' interchangeably. One is more widely used in the US, the other in the UK. Both are inoffensive and both are imperfect. For more guidance on language, see the Glossary (page 313).

100 index, eleven companies still have all-white boards, and in the FTSE 250, roughly half remain all-white at board level.[20] Within the top three roles across the FTSE 100, only 3 per cent, or ten roles out of 300, are held by ethnic minorities.[21] Despite all the efforts to achieve better racial balance, that percentage has not changed since 2014. In 2022, there are only six Black CEOs leading Fortune 500 companies (or 1.2 per cent) despite Black individuals making up 13.4 per cent of the US population.[22] The numbers simply don't add up.

Brexit unearthed a clear divide in British belief systems and the US political environment has never been more polarised. The current climate is driven by some of our most primal instincts. Protectionism and racism are visible and views on immigration are divided. Some see immigration as a critical tool to drive economic growth. Others see it as the reason hard-working individuals struggle to find meaningful employment. 'Foreigners are stealing our jobs and living off our resources' may seem an extreme view, but declining industries, growing populations and global migration create tensions which are real and unavoidable. Meanwhile, poverty, housing availability and widening social gaps make immigration an easy scapegoat.

And of course, there is the global pandemic. From lockdown to loo rolls, coronavirus has shaped our collective experience for the last few years. It has transformed our ability to live and work remotely, but Covid-19 has not been experienced equally. The pandemic has exacerbated income and health inequalities. The link between lower pay, manual and face-to-face jobs and higher virus exposure is painfully obvious, but visibility has done little to reduce the social inequality gap. Quite the opposite, in fact. The total wealth of all billionaires worldwide rose by $5 trillion to $13 trillion during the first twelve months of the pandemic.[23] It is the most dramatic surge ever registered on the annual billion-aire list compiled by *Forbes* magazine. At the same time US unemployment rates for Black, Hispanic and Asian men rose to nearly double the unemployment rate of white American men,[24] and in the UK, ethnic minorities were not only three times more likely to contract Covid-19, they also were five times as likely to experience serious outcomes as a result.[25]

Why is equality taking so long?

Over the last decade, diversity has gone from an obscure topic to one which, at times, dominates the agenda. From the dinner table to the boardroom, the newsroom to the football pitch, the struggle for equality has become a core narrative of life in the twenty-first century. It's easy to buy into equality at a conceptual level. Regardless of which group they belong to, most people I meet want to live in a world, and work in an organisation, where 'merit' and opportunity are connected, and where fairness reigns. But despite these valid intentions, all the underpinning legislation and the talk about diversity, ine-quality remains stubbornly pervasive.

Why isn't change happening more rapidly? What are we doing wrong? Or better yet, what should we be doing differ-ently if we want to drive different outcomes?

I've been working on inclusion and diversity for almost two decades and I see a number of problems with the approaches we take. The first is that workplace diversity programmes often neglect to cater for the complexity of diversity in the world at large. The exploration of race, ethnicity, sex, gender identity, sexual orientation, gener-ational differences, religious belief systems, disability and mental health presents some of the most human and the most complex issues of our time. Diversity manifests in a multitude of ways outside the workplace and plays a key role in our everyday lives, in our communities and our cultures. But within the workplace, we look at diversity in an extremely limited way.

In addition to being limited in our scope we also fail to answer some of the most fundamental questions which are unearthed by the exploration of diversity. How can we ever hope to address women's equality when we can barely speak about the misogyny, harassment, abuse and sexual violence that happens to women and girls every day? Why does who you love matter outside the bedroom? Should I use the word Black to describe someone, or will I offend them? How much of racial inequality is driven by socio-economic circumstance? How is it possible to be born a girl, but then one day be a man?

In some cases, the logic and need for change is irrefutable. In others, it's much more ambiguous, muddying the way forward. People not only have questions about diversity, they also have questions about the reality of what it might take to achieve inclusion. Are we making diversity too important? Has it become so much of a focal point that we 'do' diversity just to be seen to be doing so? Are we headed to a place where everything is so politically correct that we cannot say what we really feel for fear of upsetting someone? Will the silence that follows, and our inability to talk about subjects upon which we disagree, leave us worse off than the upset we avoided in the first place? Is seeing all this diversity just dividing us even further? Does our focus on helping one group mean we have to limit the possibilities of others? These are all good questions – questions we must lean into, even when we may not always like the answers we find.

Despite the best of intentions, many diversity programmes

drive division rather than cohesion. Programmes which pit women against men, or which exclude the majority from important conversations, have the potential to create a wave of resentment, misunderstanding and anger. When we invite minorities into a room and close the door, we create very important spaces for those individuals to let go and be themselves. But if all we do is put minorities in a room, not only do we risk the creation of echo-chambers, we also leave out one important fact. Minorities cannot fix inclusion. If they could, they would have done it long ago. Those closed doors leave some of the most important agents of change both uninformed and disengaged, especially when we launch well-meaning but overly simplified diversity programmes without pausing to explain where we are headed and what will need to happen along the way. Those of us who aren't in the 'diverse' group need to go on a journey too. Unfortunately, we don't often slow down enough to allow those individuals to take part in the complicated and complex conversations. Nor do we teach them how to fundamentally disagree, and still keep talking about topics that are integral to change. These approaches are part of what I consider 'diversity done badly', and when that happens, diversity professionals like myself have a lot to answer for.

This stuff is complex. I've completed bank mergers, launched new products to market, and ripped out and replaced core technologies for some of the biggest companies in the world. Increasing diversity and creating an inclusive environment which delivers equitable outcomes are by far some of the most challenging and difficult problems I've encountered in my entire career, but these problems are solvable. And no matter how big or how small, we all have a role to play in solving them.

What can I do?

Inclusion is achievable. But to do so, we need more people with strong skills taking part in shaping a future that does more than simply replicate the status quo. From activist to racist and everything in between, we are all playing a role in either promoting inclusion or perpetuating inequality. Most people I meet want to help. They want to be part of positive change, but whether their hesitation is due to being time poor, not knowing what action to take, or because they fear the cost of getting it wrong, they sit in largely passive roles.

Mind the Inclusion Gap is not about beating yourself up if you're not taking the kind of action you aspire to take and if you're not being the kind of ally you aspire to be. It's also not about judgement. This book is about building knowledge, increasing compassion and taking thoughtful action. It's a manual in decency and a culmination of learnings – learnings from both my failures and my successes in leading programmes to increase diversity and inclusion over the last decade and a half. But what's contained within these pages isn't only what *I* have learned. Hearing the voices of those who experience what it's like to be 'diverse' every day is crucial to finding the right approach to inclusion. To help you on your journey, and to solidify your own understanding, I interviewed dozens of individuals – white, Black, brown, living with a disability and without, gay, lesbian, bisexual and heterosexual, male, female, trans, gender questioning and everything in between.

In this introduction I've given you a high-level grounding through a handful of facts. My aim is to answer the age-old question 'How far have we really come?' The answer? Not as far as we would like to think. We have much more to do.

You may have already noticed that while the book is littered with examples and facts from around the world, there
is an inherent British and American bias. I was born and
raised in the US, where I lived until my mid-twenties. The
majority of my adult life and the last eighteen years of my
career have been spent in the UK. These two countries are
my frame of reference. They are where I have experienced my
own journey of discovery around inclusion, but that is not
my only reason for including them. They are also two of the
countries where the conversation about diversity, inclusion,
equality and the future of our world is playing out in a very
visible way every day. If you want to understand whether the
data, and the lived experience, holds true for the country in
which you live, I encourage you to go and find out.

Likewise, there will inevitably be important developments
and stories which are not included in this book – it's impossible to encapsulate all the latest news and events when you
have, at a certain point, to send the manuscript to the printer.
While some things within a book can quickly become out of
date, change at scale does not happen overnight, no matter
how much we might wish the contrary. The overarching
concepts and the lessons included inside *Mind the Inclusion
Gap* are intended to be enduring. I hope you find them a
strong guide as you digest the events happening our world at
the point in time when you read this text.

As you move through the book you will find that there
are two distinct parts. The first five chapters are designed to
increase your understanding of why change isn't happening
faster or in a more universal manner. They will help you
unpick some of the messier aspects to diversity and increase
your ability to see the linkages between it all.

Chapter 1 dives into a brief history of racial equality and
gay rights, looking both at how recent and how deeply

impactful key events were. In **Chapter 2**, we look at the power of social norms and how they both shape and limit the life path of boys and girls, men and women. We also explore why those deeply ingrained gender rules mean that some people feel threatened by the mere existence of the trans community. **Chapter 3** explores how the limited scope which is often given to workplace diversity programmes neglects to cater for the experience 'diverse' individuals have in the wider world. From men's violence against women and girls to the gaping imbalance around who does laundry and domestic chores, we shine a light on some of the parts of our society that we are often too ashamed to face. In **Chapter 4**, we unpick the diversity mess in which we find ourselves – looking at just how divided by diversity we have become as fears of reverse discrimination grow and shifts in cultural power feed the very visible and very politicised 'woke' vs. 'cancel' debate. And finally, in **Chapter 5**, we finish by examining the infighting that sometimes arises between, and within, diverse groups.

You might find these first five chapters particularly bleak. They represent the tough reality of what we need to overcome in order to move forward. But it's important that we lean into the challenge these chapters present. It is only with the knowledge and understanding of these complexities that we can respond in a calm, thoughtful and educated manner – removing the destruction and violence that sometimes surrounds these debates.

Reading these first chapters may raise some questions for you. The most obvious one is, 'Why do it?' If it's messy, complicated, fraught with pitfalls and hard to shift, then honestly, why bother? It's a great question. Personally, I think the prize is huge. Getting this stuff right isn't just about being seen to be doing diversity. It's about living a full life. It's about being connected with others in a way that's utterly thrilling. And, when life is excruciating, as it can be, being connected enough with others to get through. This book isn't just about fixing the shit we need to fix, it's about leaving the world better than you found it and living fully along the way. It's about being able to look at the enormity of the problems we face, problems which can often feel overwhelming, and doing something tangible to make a difference.

If you're impatient like me, you will probably want to jump straight into action. I encourage you not to. These first five chapters are important and lay fundamental groundwork to help prepare you for the second half of the book, where we turn a corner towards taking meaningful action. If we don't understand why the action we are taking today isn't working, it's unlikely that the action we take tomorrow will make any difference.

In **Chapter 6**, I share critical lessons which shaped my understanding of what inclusion actually is, and a few of the basic skills which you need to act inclusively. This chapter includes several very humbling errors and missteps on my part – moments which solidified my learning like only failure can. In **Chapter 7**, we delve into the power of high-affinity, high-intimacy relationships (and by intimacy, I don't mean sexual relationships, I mean authentic and deeply connected relationships in every aspect of our life) which allow us to connect with others who are different. Being aware of how easily our relationships develop, and perhaps more importantly don't develop, is an important part of being skilled in inclusion. **Chapter 8** explores the role which we each can play and the (probable) gap between aspiration and action for most of us, despite our overwhelming desire to be nice. In this chapter, we look at the performative gestures that many of us lean on to signal that we have good intentions (without really having to do any work) and instead, how we can choose a conscious and meaningful role.

And finally, in **Chapter 9**, I have created the mother of all checklists. Only it isn't a checklist, because there are no boxes you can tick. Instead, it is a set of guiding principles to what good allyship in action looks like, first in broad and universal terms, and then in more specific and meaningful actions which are needed for specific groups. I encourage you to use it as a prompt and then build your own.

Chapter 10 is where we say goodbye. In it, I leave you with a few thoughts on bravery, hope and the awesome stuff that lies waiting. Whether you jump into inclusion with both feet, or you dip a hesitant toe in the water, there is something for everyone who decides to use their sphere of influence to drive change. Because allyship isn't just about hard work. It's about joy, wonder and the beauty of human connection, and it's part of what makes this such an interesting life.

At the back of the book, I have included a **Glossary** of terms to help you explore the book's content using a solid platform of language. I encourage you to refer to it as and when you find a term in the book you are unsure of or want to understand in more detail.

My hope is that by the end of reading *Mind the Inclusion Gap* you will have gained a deeper understanding of four very visible and interconnected elements of diversity: race, gender, sex and sexual orientation. You will know more about the history of how diverse individuals in these groups have existed in society, but more crucially, where they stand today. You'll understand the role social norms play in furthering inequality and, even more importantly, the role which you can play in revisiting those norms and rewriting those rules. Not only will you be able to spot the barriers to equality, but you'll also have new skills to address the frustrations, tensions and the growing backlash with confidence.

Some of you may race through the book at breakneck speed. Others may need more time to take it all in. Regardless of your approach, I encourage you to sit with the stories and concepts. Soak them in. Then, take them off the page and test them in the real world. Talk to your friends, family and colleagues. But don't stop there. If you have the ambition and the appetite – and I hope you will – I encourage you to set an intention for the role you want to play and then go and be active in shaping a future which you want to be part of.

Part 1

Chapter 1

The Shadow of Our Past

There is no use crying over spilt milk. It's a phrase I heard often as a child. My mother is a wonderfully pragmatic woman and her mantra of 'no tears – dust yourself off, kid' was a core philosophy of my upbringing. A broken plate? Buy a new one. A skinned knee? Put a bandage on it. A low score on your homework? Study harder next time. A boyfriend who doesn't love you? There are a million other fish in the sea. Her advice was as brutal as it was sensible and built upon one key fact: you cannot change what has already happened, you can only change what is yet to come.

In a book about how we can shape a more inclusive future it may feel odd to start first by looking back at the past, but our past casts a lasting shadow and history has a long, long tail. It does not define us, but it does play a role in shaping who we are and how we behave. Understanding it is essential to breaking free from its influence. And so, our journey begins here – as we go back and look at our history in order to pull forward the learnings which are essential to the challenges we face today.

Exploring racial history

The truth about our past can be uncomfortable, and our racial past painfully so. Exploring it requires us to look at the truth of European empires and forced colonialism, the treatment of Indigenous people all over the world, and the tragic events of the human slave trade.

Slavery ended in Britain in 1833 and in the US in 1865. Although it's been more than 150 years since slavery was a common practice, it's important to understand that neither British nor American abolishment of slavery came from a widespread moral epiphany. America's fight to end slavery required a civil war and British slave owners were forced by the government to free those enslaved. To ease the transition, government officials took out a loan of £20 million, the equivalent of roughly £300 billion today, which it paid to British slave owners to compensate for their loss of income.[1] The already enormous impact slavery had on economic prosperity was then exacerbated as generations of slave-owning families benefited from that money, the final payment of which was completed in 2015. Not one single penny went to those who were enslaved, or to their families, as compensation for their enslavement.

In 1914, European countries controlled more than 80 per cent of the world's land surface through colonised territories.[2]

The British Empire was larger than any other ever recorded in history. Its vast reach was seven times larger than the Roman Empire and larger than the Spanish, French and Portuguese empires combined.[3] The Indian subcontinent, or British Raj as it was called, was one of the 'crown jewels' of the British Empire from the mid-nineteenth century until 1947. While Indian independence leader Mahatma Gandhi had been calling on Britain to 'quit India' for some time, Indian troops and supplies were so sorely needed that Britain agreed to give India full independence after the end of the Second World War in exchange for support.[4] Today, the strong and multi-faceted relationship between the two countries can make it easy to forget that during British rule, an estimated 35 million Indian people died of famine alone.[5]

Though some would argue that colonisation – whether of Native Americans, First Nations, Māori, or Aboriginal Australians – brought better healthcare, literacy and democracy in the places where it occurred, the story of how Indigenous peoples were rounded up, murdered, starved, separated from their families and removed from their homelands is undeniably a grotesque one.

In America, the Indian Removal Act of 1830 authorised the forced removal of 100,000 Native Americans from their ancestral homelands.[6] In Canada, the Indian Act of 1876 created laws which forbade First Nations people from expressing their culture or practising traditions.[7] That same act was pivotal in the creation of residential schools, which were designed to influence Indigenous culture and increase assimilation into white Canadian culture. By 1920, First Nations children's attendance at those schools became mandatory and remained so until 1951.[8] The effect was a forced removal of First Nations children from their families and their communities. Although amendments to the Indian Act in 1951 made such schools optional, the last residential school remained open until 1996. That same 1951 amendment gave Canadian officials the power to remove children from their homes and place them into care or adoption, rather than provide support to Indigenous communities. The 'Sixties Scoop', as it was called, led to the forced separation of approximately 20,000 children from their families.[9] A review into the impact of the removal of children from their families concluded that it had not only exposed many to abuse and sexual assault, it also had the effect of 'cultural genocide'.[10]

> We were always aware of apartheid in South Africa, and segregation in the United States. As Canadians, we were proud of our 'cultural mosaic' and to be honest, we were a little smug that such atrocities occurred elsewhere.
>
> We have only recently begun to fully comprehend the impact of Canada's horrific genocide and treatment of Indigenous Peoples here at home, but it's important we understand its effects reached beyond our borders. The unpalatable truth is that segments of apartheid in South Africa were modelled after the Indian Act in Canada.
>
> My commitment to truth and reconciliation is to learn, unlearn and relearn the true history of Turtle Island.[11]
>
> *Marlise*

Although the brutal events of slavery, colonisation and the forced removal of Indigenous peoples occurred mostly outside of living memory, their legacy extends well into the future. In my work, I see a number of areas where these events continue to have a persistent effect on racial equality:

through widespread racial discrimination, which continued long after slavery and empire were commonplace; through the compound effect of racism on financial and economic attainment; through the strained relationship with police and justice systems; and, finally, and through the continuous reinforcement of racial hierarchy, not only in the way we tell history, but throughout many aspects of day-to-day living.

The direct racism, discrimination and disrespect which existed after slavery was abolished is well documented. 'Jim Crow' laws enforced racial segregation and legalised racism in southern US states for eighty-eight years.[12] Most of us have a fragment of understanding of how skin colour divided access to transport and education in the States (remember Rosa Parks and Brown vs. Board of Education?),[13] but the reality was that race-based segregation extended to churches, playgrounds, parks, restaurants, restrooms and many other aspects of daily life.

Meanwhile, over in Britain, more than half a million immigrants from Commonwealth countries arrived between 1948 and 1971.[14] Those ethnic minority immigrants, along with hundreds of thousands of white European counterparts, would play a key role in rebuilding Britain after the Second World War. Their arrival was not met with a warm welcome. On 22 June 1948, the day before the now-famous *Empire Windrush* immigration ship reached British shores, eleven Labour members of parliament sent a letter to British Prime Minister Clement Attlee suggesting that 'the British people fortunately enjoy a profound unity without uniformity in their way of life, and are blest by the absence of a colour racial problem. An influx of coloured people domiciled here is likely to impair the harmony, strength and cohesion of our public and social life and cause discord and unhappiness among all concerned.'[15]

None of the MPs had ever met any of the passengers on board, many of whom had fought for Britain during the war, and yet assumptions were made that *Windrush* immigrants were largely unskilled, likely to be poor, and likely to be a burden.

> *My dad first arrived in 1958 from Jamaica. He worked as a carpenter to save enough money to bring my mum here in 1962. He arrived as a skilled labourer but had no entrepreneurial acumen. He would not put up with offensive remarks which meant at times he would end up in scraps with people who did not want him here. He was sufficiently good at his craft that I can remember him losing a job in the morning and having another one by the afternoon.*
>
> *My mum took a job as a nurse. They both worked hard to save. The intention was never to stay, but instead to earn as much as they could and then return home. Unlike my dad, my mum nearly always put up, i.e. she would bend and bow to meet local customs as best she could because 'England wasn't our part of the world, and we didn't belong here'.*
>
> Rob N.

Racism was not only prolific, but it was also socially acceptable throughout most of the twentieth century. It impacted immigrants like Rob's father, who had no employment protection and could simply be fired for having black or brown skin, or for refusing to put up with racial bigotry.

It wasn't until 1964, the year before my own mother graduated from high school, when the US enacted its landmark Civil Rights Act, which enforced equal employment opportunity regardless of race, colour, national origin or sex, that segregation ended and legal protection against racism began. It would take four more years for the UK to follow suit. In the UK parliament passed the Race Relations Act.[16] From then on, it became illegal to refuse housing or employment based on race, religion or national origin in the UK. But despite laws in both countries aimed at eradicating race-based discrimination in housing and employment, challenges remained.

That same year, US lawmakers began the first of a series of amendments to the law in order to stop redlining, a practice whereby banks, mortgage lenders, healthcare providers and even supermarkets denied services to or altered prices for residents of racially associated neighbourhoods and communities.[17] It would take more than a decade to root out the practice entirely. Redlining is often seen as an American problem, but there is evidence to suggest similar discrimination existed across Europe. In the UK, housing officers were known to steer ethnic minorities away from 'white' neighbourhoods, and the assessment of 'respectability' played a key role in housing allocations.[18] In countries like the Netherlands, there was still evidence of placed-based discrimination as late as 1999.[19]

Regardless of race or ethnicity, those without wealth find it disproportionately more difficult to create new wealth than those who already have it. When you add in the propensity for racial bias to be at play, wealth creation becomes even more challenging. Redlining systematically blocked Black Americans from obtaining homes. Although the practice has been illegal for more than fifty years, the legacy of racialised neighbourhoods still lives on, as does the impact of the lessened wealth creation. According to *Forbes*, a typical homeowner in a neighbourhood that was redlined for mortgage lending by the federal government gained 52 per cent less (or on average $212,023 less) in personal wealth generated by property value increases than one in a greenlined neighbourhood over the last forty years.[20]

The changes in law were a major step forward, but legal changes had little effect on the lived experience of people of colour. Whether discrimination was direct or, in the case of place-based financial exclusion, indirect, upholding the law proved very difficult. Eventually, the gap between the laws, and the ability of police and justice systems to uphold them, became too much. From London to Birmingham, Liverpool, Leeds and Manchester, communities faced unrest as members of the Black and Asian communities protested against racial injustice. Not only were they not receiving equal protection and support from police when laws were broken, but unemployment was also rising fast and economic opportunity was not being realised.

The 1981 'race riots' in Brixton, south London, led to an urgent need for intervention and, as a result, the UK government commissioned a detailed review of policing which was undertaken by Lord Scarman. The purpose of the Scarman Report was to understand what led to the riots, in which hundreds of buildings and cars were burned and almost 300 police officers were injured. The report had a number of key findings, including that the riots were triggered by a series of specific incidents which caused an eruption of built-up resentment towards the police, that those incidents were exacerbated by impacts of widespread unemployment and racism, and that police were disproportionately and indiscriminately using 'stop and search' powers against the Black community.[21] The report was particularly damning in its indictment of the UK police and the systematic over-policing of ethnic minorities.

Twelve years later, on 22 April 1993, eighteen-year-old aspiring architect Stephen Lawrence was murdered in an unprovoked racist attack in south-east London while he waited for a bus home. The fallout which came after his death left a visible scar on national pride. From the bungled police investigation, a failed trial, the persecution of his family by police and an alleged cover-up to hide what had been done, the case was a catalogue of failures. When the events, and the role the police played in them, came to light, it attracted significant attention from all communities and ultimately led to a second public inquiry of policing. The findings of the second examination were clear. Report chair Sir William Macpherson charged the police with 'professional incompetence, institutional racism and a failure of leadership'.[22] Stephen's story left an indelible mark on the nation and brought to light once again the longstanding problems with how ethnic minorities, and specifically members of the Black British community, were treated by police.

The UK is not alone in having historic challenges between people of colour and the police. In 1992, protests and riots erupted across the US after a jury acquitted four police officers of using excessive force despite them being filmed as they gave Rodney King a vicious beating during a routine traffic stop on a sunny Californian freeway. Today, the challenges faced in American policing have escalated to a point from which many fear there is no return. The Black community holds almost no faith that police will perform their duty without extreme levels of racial bias and have real fears that bias has led to the unlawful killing of Black Americans. Meanwhile, the police community are being asked to perform a near impossible task of reducing crime in a society where gun ownership means their lives are under threat on a daily basis.

Challenges with policing in the UK seem pale in comparison to the gulf between the US police and the Black American community, but they are still shaping our social dialogue. Race relations, and dealing with racism in the policing community, isn't simply a US and UK problem. It's a global problem. In 2020, more than 1,400 cases of right-wing extremism were reported within Germany's police and military.[23] In 2021, six French and international human rights organisations filed a class action lawsuit against the French state for failing to take necessary steps to prevent and remedy ethnic profiling by police during identity checks.[24] The series of racial and systemic abuses in France is so well documented that President Emmanuel Macron was forced to announce measures on how his administration would make police more transparent about wrongdoings.

Issues with policing are not one-sided. Individuals who break the law own their part of the equation. But the way people of colour, and Black individuals in particular, are treated differently when they do break the law, or are made to feel they have done something wrong when they haven't broken the law, plays a significant role in how the world is experienced differently depending on the colour of your skin.

One of the reasons that relationships with police are so highly charged is the depth of impact they can have on a community. The tools they play with literally end up determining life or death. The waves of impact following death are so far-reaching that they last far longer than any moment of discrimination occurring, whether it's within or beyond the workplace, in sport, in housing, in education, indeed in all areas of the lived experience. Racism in those spaces has a negative effect for sure, but it doesn't usually have that life-or-death impact which racist policing continues to disproportionately have on the Black community.

> *What makes it even more complicated is that many*
> *see (and want to see) the police and the justice system*
> *as a bellwether for equality. Of course, we need the*
> *legal protections which have been introduced and*
> *indeed strengthened over the decades, but laws are*
> *built upon testing and case precedent. Racial discrimi-*
> *nation laws have been around a long time, but you*
> *don't see many people punished for breaking them.*
> *Inside organisations, no one had the equipment, the*
> *tools or the lens with which to see racism. And so, the*
> *'test' failed. It was almost bound to.*
>
> *Rob N.*

Although the police play a role in upholding and main-taining the status quo, they are not the only ones to blame for the endemic nature of racism in our society. Financial institutions and employers have an even more widespread impact on day-to-day lived experiences. The systemic imbal-ances in employment and wealth are undeniable.

Our UK data shows that whether we look at pay, overall wealth or property ownership, ethnic minorities are simply worse off than white counterparts and Black households face the biggest deficit.[25] In the UK, ethnic minority unemployment has been at least 70 per cent higher than white joblessness in each of the past twenty years.[26] Black Britons are among the ethnic groups with the highest unemployment rate[27] and are most likely to have a household income below £600 a week.[28] The US Black-to-white unemployment gap is the highest it has been in five years[29] and the net worth of a typical* white family ($171,000) is nearly ten times greater than that of a

---

* 'Typical' in this survey of consumer finance was defined as the median wealth, or the wealth of the household at the middle of a distribution.

Black family ($17,000),[30] which may be part of the reason why Black mortgage applicants are still twice as likely to be denied a mortgage than their white counterparts.[31]

Today's conversation isn't just about the racial inequality of the past, it's about the need for race equity today. Race equity requires us to look at the continued imbalances and disparities which promote race inequality, and work together to systematically remove them. It spans financial, employment, health and educational inequalities, but is also relevant to the stories we tell and the cultural norms we continue to hold.

In recent years, the racist beliefs of British Prime Minister Winston Churchill have come under scrutiny. From quips that Gandhi was 'half-naked', that Palestinians were 'barbaric hordes who ate little but camel dung', or his clear stance on how he felt about the Indian nation – 'I hate Indians. They are a beastly people with a beastly religion' – Churchill's views were well documented.[32] Unfortunately, they were hardly unique. He was a man of the times and held views which were of the age in which he lived. He was indeed racist, but he wasn't alone in his racist views. His are simply more reported than most and, unfortunately, the extreme power and wealth which he wielded meant that his views had an exponentially corrosive effect. We do not need to omit historic figures like Churchill from our past, but when we tell his story as a 'saviour', or the man who stood up to the Nazis, but fail to tell the part he played in the death of millions of Indians or of the white-supremacist views he so vocally espoused, we perpetuate the idea that being racist is something which we are prepared to overlook, as long as you do well in other parts of your life.

When the statue of late slave-trader and British philanthropist Edward Colston was pulled down from its plinth and thrown into Bristol Harbour during the summer of 2020, it caused significant upset. Many individuals felt protesters were trying to erase the past. Others saw it as pure vandalism. Very few paused to understand the implications of the idolisation and visible elevation of a man who made his fortune through human flesh and human suffering. His fleet of ships are estimated to have transported more than 80,000 shackled and enslaved Africans to the Americas in the late seventeenth century.[33] We should not hide our past, but do we need to flaunt it? Are we clear on the implications and impacts such a visual celebration of a slave-trader have on modern Black Britons?

Statues like Colston's remind me of the lengths that Britain will go to in order to erase wrongdoing. Statues like his are an attempt to eradicate the impact slavery had and is still having on my community. We still have not recovered from slavery.

You're taught about it in school, and you question. What part did my people play? How does this fit with the stories my family tell? That questioning leaves me at a crossroads. Do I belong? Should I be angry? Where should my allegiance be?

When I was younger, I was quieter. I wanted to assimilate, but the older I get, the more I question. Why was Florence Nightingale taught in school, but Mary Seacole virtually erased? I should have been celebrating her, but Black history was erased. We were virtually written out of history books. Will the same be true for my children?

Vivienne

It isn't simply statues which we need to question. From high-school mascots to professional sports teams, the appropriation of Native American names, or terms associated with the Indigenous peoples of North America, is widespread in the US and Canada. Although Native American and Indigenous civil rights supporters have been calling for an end to the derogatory practice for more than sixty years, it is only now that professional teams such as the Cleveland Indians, the Washington Redskins, the Edmonton Eskimos and the Kansas City Chiefs are beginning to take notice and change their names. When we reduce human beings to team mascot status, in the way animals often are, it sends a not-so-subtle message that individuals in those groups are less than human. There are consequences to those messages, just as there is a consequence when we continue to elevate individuals like Colston, whose key contribution to society was made possible through expansive human suffering.

> *Statues like Colston's, or names of people like him, are everywhere. That kind of visibility is a constant reminder. It says to Black people, 'This is what we think of you.' It's dehumanising and it's degrading. It makes your experience of the world all the more challenging.*
>
> Michelle

The British Empire was vast, as were the fault lines created by it. The extreme wealth enjoyed by British slave-ship owners and colonists left a legacy, just as the extreme poverty of those being colonised and enslaved left its own indelible scar. It's no wonder that British history drives a combination of pride, shame and guilt. We want to be proud of the mark this tiny island has made in the world, but the reality of what it takes to create an empire means that pride is tainted. It's not just Britain. White European leaders achieved much of their historic wealth and prosperity through violence, power and thievery, and in doing so, they enshrined a racial hierarchy which is so embedded in our society today, we fail to notice its presence.

Whether we are talking about legalised segregation in schools, historic practices of racism in employment or home ownership, or the effects of police practices, our history has a much stronger influence than we like to admit. The impact of these events is not contained within the period of time in which they occurred. They continue to shape us in part because racism didn't go away when legislation made racial discrimination illegal. Structures and belief systems which enable white individuals to rise more easily are still present – though they are less widespread and less visible than they once were, just as the brutal, cruel and inhumane effects of racism have become less visible.

The #BlackLivesMatter movement began in 2014, after the acquittal of George Zimmerman in the death of Black teenager Trayvon Martin, but it was the video footage of the murder of George Floyd by police officers, and the clear lynching of Ahmaud Arbery while he went for a midday jog, that thrust racism, and the global nature of racial inequality, into the light. Discussion about systems which perpetuate white success and racial inequality have created a gaping divide in America. While the reaction in Britain has been more muted (as it often is), the exploration of race is still incendiary in nature. There are many who feel people of colour simply need to stop crying over the spilt milk of our past and use their agency to rise out of racial inequality.

We all have a role to play in the success of our own lives, and people of colour are no different. But to suggest that it is simply a matter of agency, of hard work, or of buckling down on the part of Black, Asian, Latino/a, Indigenous or any other ethnic minority group, lacks an acknowledgement of the facts.

However muted, the racist belief systems of our past continue to have a negative impact on people of colour, both on the opportunities which are afforded to individuals, and on the internal pride and sense of self-worth of those communities. We won't be fully free of our history until we work together to rewrite attitudes and rewire the systems which uphold the deeply engrained racial hierarchy of our past.

Gay rights – a tale of two halves

With rainbow flags lining the streets of our cities and the aisles at our grocery stores, it may seem that we have arrived at a place where sexual orientation is no longer an issue. During Pride season in particular, the support for the LGBTQ+ community is ever-present. We have come a long way in creating a society where gay, lesbian and bisexual* individuals can be open about who they love. British progress is especially notable given that same-sex relations between men in England were not only outlawed for 328 years, but they were also punishable by death until 1861, when the law changed to reduce the punishment to a minimum of ten years in prison. It wasn't until 1967, more than 430 years after it became illegal to be gay, that through the Sexual Offences Act we legalised consensual sex between men in England and Wales – though sexual relations between men were still confined to those over the age of twenty-one and only in the privacy of their own home for some time.[34]

---

* In this section of Chapter 1, the focus is on gay, lesbian and bisexual rights. That is not to suggest the trans community are not part of the broader LGBTQ+ group; they are, but this chapter focuses on laws and beliefs which applied to sexual orientation specifically.

It would take another fourteen years for Scotland to follow suit and fifteen years for Northern Ireland. While it was no longer illegal to be gay, there were still aspects of society which were out of bounds for the gay community – including the military, where, until 1994, personnel who were found to be gay faced the possibility of going to jail.[35]

Although it's never been illegal to be a lesbian in the UK, that doesn't mean that gay women have not faced violence, homophobia and discrimination. Treatment of lesbians is often an extreme version of the treatment women more broadly receive. Lesbians are regularly granted acceptance based on how well they conform to feminine norms, or the strength of their sex appeal to others. Lesbians who are seen to be 'masculine' or 'butch' face more social judgement for bending gender rules. Similar negative judgements faced by effeminate gay men compared with masculine gay men suggest that homophobia and rigid gender constructs are significantly linked.

It is easy to assume that when the law changes, attitudes change too. Unfortunately, this is rarely the case. The law is like a sledgehammer: shifts in policy or law open the possibility for change, creating an immense amount of opportunity, but culture cannot be rewritten as easily as the law can. It takes decades, or in some cases centuries, for belief systems to shift.

As with the laws to protect people of colour from racial discrimination, when laws changed to make it legal to be gay, very little was done to uphold gay rights and to actively support the community. For each move forward, we often face a move backward. In 1988, twenty-one years after being gay became legal again in England and Wales, Section 28 was added to the Local Government Act prohibiting local authorities from 'promoting homosexuality or any form of pretended family relationship'.[36] As a result, any discussion of same-sex relationships in schools was virtually eliminated. The legislation not only prevented conversations, it stopped pupils getting support, and played a huge role in legitimising hatred towards the queer community.

Only through activism and political pressure did things change. In 2000, the armed forces lifted the ban on being lesbian, gay or bisexual and serving in the military. Prior to the ban being lifted, gay, lesbian or bisexual members of the military were dishonourably discharged and sometimes stripped of their medals.[37] That same year Section 28 was removed in Scotland, allowing teachers and local government officials to recognise same-sex relationships without fear of losing their job. The rest of the UK would follow suit three years later, but the legacy of Section 28 will be felt for generations. Not only did the law promote fear about actively supporting the gay community, it also created a vacuum of awareness and education which affected hetero- and homosexuals alike.

The next decade brought a whirlwind of progress for gay rights. In 2001, UK law finally changed to allow gay men the same age of consent for sex as their heterosexual peers. Adoption became legal for gay couples in 2002. In 2003, regulations were put in place which prohibited employers from unreasonably discriminating against employees on grounds of sexual orientation, perceived sexual orientation, religion or belief and age. In 2005, civil partnerships became possible, and by 2014, England, Wales and Scotland had all passed marriage laws to allow same-sex couples the same marriage rights as their heterosexual counterparts – though Northern Ireland did not legalise same-sex marriage until 2020.[38] Gay marriage had a profoundly positive effect on mainstream acceptance of same-sex relationships but also on gay pride.

> *Marriage and civil partnerships were a huge thing. All of a sudden, you started getting invited to celebrations. You started to see positive images of gay people on TV and films, rather than camp clichés. When you move from a cliché to more nuanced and representative images of a community, it matters. It's not to say we can't laugh at ourselves and there aren't eccentricities that can be gently mocked, but you're looking for more.*
>
> *Patrick*

With this increased visibility and acceptance has come a rise in the number of people who identify as LGBQT+. Today, 7.1 per cent of all Americans[39] and 7.4 per cent of Germans identify as LGBT.*[40] Although the Office for National Statistics estimates the gay, lesbian and bisexual population in the UK at 1.5 million (or 3.5 per cent),[41] in a survey where respondents were asked to plot themselves on a 'sexuality scale', 23 per cent of those over the age of eighteen, and a staggering 49 per cent of those between the age of eighteen and twenty-four, chose something other than 100 per cent heterosexual.[42] America's Gay and Lesbian Alliance Against Defamation found similar results. According to their research, eighteen- to thirty-four-year-olds are twice as likely

---

*Throughout this book, there are specific variations to LGBTQ+, the acronym I use when referring to the wider gay, lesbian, bisexual and transgender community. Any variation on the term LGBTQ+, such as LGB, LGBQ+, LGBT, or LGBTI, is an exact reflection of how specific research or a specific piece of data was originally published. The variations are included for the purpose of accuracy.

to openly identify as LGBTQ+ than those aged fifty-two to seventy-one.[43] That kind of change between generations indicates an increasingly open approach to sexual orientation.

> *Our kids are growing up in a different world than the one which we were raised in. Their understanding of diversity is so different to ours. The rate of change has been exponential in the last thirty years.*
>
> *Young people are exposed to an extraordinary amount of diversity. My six-year-old son told me about how they raised a rainbow flag at school last week for the Pride families like ours. Inclusion for the LGBTQ+ community is talked about at primary school; when I was young, there was no link between LGBTQ+ people and schools – the assumptions and stereotypes were horrific. It's a different world he's growing up in. I am hoping that he, and others around him, won't ever know the shame that I still have from my younger years.*
>
> *Shame is often unconsciously created by parents. My family were not blatantly homophobic, but there was an absence of understanding or curiosity. I had always been my mum's little girl and once she noticed I had gay friends, her desperation for me not to be gay was palpable. It was hard for her when I came out as she connected femininity with sexuality; her first response was 'I hope you're not going to cut all your hair off' – because for her, my long hair as a child was my feminine crowning glory.*
>
> *Suran*

Suran's story isn't unusual. Family acceptance and parental love play a key role in the life of any child, gay or otherwise.

Both are critical to helping children successfully navigate what the world throws their way. In the case of gay, lesbian or gender non-conforming children, that can often be shame, isolation and bullying.

Despite all the progress, 80 per cent of the world's lesbian, gay or bisexual individuals remain in the closet.[44] Even in largely open and welcoming societies there are social limitations. Being openly gay in sport, for example, is virtually unheard of for men. It was only in 2021, 101 years after the creation of the US National Football League (NFL), that Carl Nassib became the first active player in NFL history to come out as gay.[45] That same year, Australia's Josh Cavallo became the world's only openly gay top-flight professional football player. In May 2022, English midfielder Jake Daniels joined Cavallo – becoming the second openly gay professional football player in the world and the second ever in England's professional football history. Justin Fashanu, who came out in 1990, was the first – though Fashanu's story is a tragic one. His own brother disowned him for being gay and Fashanu took his own life at the young age of thirty-seven.[46] Though much has changed in the thirty-two-year gap between Fashanu and Daniels, homophobic banners and chants at football matches are still all too commonplace.

The culture of fear and hostility towards gay individuals has meant that some elite sportsmen have waited until after retirement to be open about their sexual orientation. Gareth Thomas, one of the most capped Welsh rugby union players, came out after retiring from rugby in 2011. Since that time, Thomas has received an overwhelming volume of support from fans and players. But not everyone has been as welcoming. Thomas has also received a slurry of homophobic abuse and has even been physically assaulted by a homophobic 'fan' as he walked down the street. With that kind of visible aggression, it's no wonder that one in eight LGBT people avoid going to the gym or participating in sport because of fear of discrimination and harassment.[47]

The almost total lack of openness about sexual orientation within elite male sporting circles sits in stark contrast to the number of professional elite sportswomen who are visible and gay. For example, in the 2019 Women's Football World Cup, there were forty openly gay, lesbian or bisexual players, as well as one coach and one trainer.[48] Locker rooms are often cited as a key reason for continued homophobia in male sport. They can be a vulnerable space, but the acceptance of lesbian and bisexual individuals in women's sport shows that it is possible to navigate nakedness and sexual orientation.

But sport is about much more than the locker room experience. Sport mirrors and reflects our society. It represents humanity at our finest and at the same time shines a spotlight on our flaws.

> *Sport is very attached to gender norms. For men, both sport and masculinity are associated with physical prowess. There is great seduction in being in a lauded and dominant group, which elite men's sport is. It's also full of power and privilege. That comes with practical riches, as well as the benefits of public approval, endorsement and visibility.*
>
> *The enticement of belonging to a group like that can be really strong – but it's a Faustian pact of sorts. To be included in that group, you have a hell of a lot to gain. Conversely, when you are in that group, it means you have a hell of a lot to lose and there is a lot of internal and external pressure to conform. Anything that makes you on the outside, like your sexual orientation,*

makes you vulnerable, and particularly vulnerable in a team sport. You risk losing status and money – as well as being exposed to vicious online attacks and abuse on the terraces.

For female elite athletes, it has been different – partly down to the guts of early trailblazers, who were out about their sexual orientation. In the past, the lack of investment and media coverage also meant less scrutiny and exposure. As women's sport gets more profile, there will undoubtedly be more pressure to conform to society's stereotypes. But I am more optimistic about it remaining welcoming to lesbian and bi athletes. Women's sport is forging its own way forwards and has had to fight for its place. That gives it this edge of being on the outside and wanting to do things better and differently. Elite female athletes are already contravening gender norms with their physicality. Perhaps when you have pushed through one barrier, it becomes a habit, and you know you can push through more.

As a lesbian, I love seeing out, proud, glorious women doing their thing on their terms – that really is being a role model.

Jo

Being open about your sexual orientation is becoming increasingly common in the workplace, but according to the LGBTQ+ advocacy group Human Rights Campaign nearly half of lesbian, gay and bisexual individuals still don't reveal their sexual orientation at work in the US.[49] Despite an openness through school and university years, 62 per cent of UK graduates go back into the closet when they enter the job market.[50] The decision to be open and out requires knowing that you will not only be safe, but that bringing your whole self to work will be a benefit to your career. The evidence currently suggests that being open about who you love still presents an element of risk.

In 2007, Lord Browne became the firstly openly gay FTSE 100 CEO, but disclosure about his sexual orientation was not his choice. Browne kept his sexual orientation a secret for forty years during his career at BP until he was outed by the British tabloids. The number of openly gay, lesbian or bisexual individuals who have led FTSE 100 companies can be counted on one hand, and though they have been warmly welcomed by many, it has not been an easy road. In 2014, Lloyd's of London CEO Inga Beale became the first openly bisexual CEO in UK history and, as a result, she received a deluge of abuse including suggestions that she 'should go and die'.[51]

Compound those very visible experiences with the fact that one in five gay, lesbian, bisexual or transgender employees have experienced verbal bullying from colleagues, customers or service users because of their sexual orientation in the last five years, and it's not hard to imagine why so few individuals are open at work.[52] It takes a certain level of bravery to know that being open about who you love could be a potential threat and choosing to do it anyway. That choice is one that heterosexual colleagues never face.

Today in the UK, there are more than thirty openly gay, lesbian and bisexual UK members of parliament. In fact, the UK has the most gay-inclusive parliament in the world,[53] which sits in stark contrast to the US, where just 0.2 per cent of elected offices are held by openly LGBTQ+ people.[54] Sexual orientation is on the national agenda in many countries, and there have been huge strides in the workplace to encourage lesbian, gay or bisexual individuals to be themselves without fear of discrimination. Britain has made great progress in our own acceptance of the gay community, but we also have a lot to answer for. One quarter of the world's population currently live in a country which once belonged to the Commonwealth, and those countries make up half of all countries that criminalise homosexuality today.

Living in a country where attitudes are changing and where more and more lesbian, gay and bisexual individuals choose to be open about their sexual orientation, we sometimes forget that there is a huge variance in global attitudes towards the community. Today, there are sixty-nine countries which criminalise same-sex relationships, twelve of which have the death penalty as potential punishment for being queer.[55] Criminalisation often goes hand in hand with government-endorsed homophobia, which makes everyday life a significant challenge. The propaganda laws in Russia mean you can physically assault someone for being gay and then be exempt from any legal charges if your purpose is to stop 'gay propaganda' with your actions.[56] In Poland, more than a hundred towns and cities have declared themselves 'LGBT-free-zones'.[57] Even within societies which appear 'open', safety and support are not a given.

The reason our past casts a shadow is because there are always people trying to make it go back. I find it very frightening that there are laws saying you cannot be gay. Those laws make it feel so fragile. They support this idea that it's a 'right' to be gay as opposed to being who you are.

When I went to Singapore on holiday, I was surprised about how I felt upon arriving. I literally sat in my hotel room and cried. I knew about the laws. Every gay person knows about sodomy laws. Although they aren't aimed at you as a lesbian, that is only because they couldn't define sexual acts in feminine terms.

There are many places in the world where anti-gay laws have never been repealed. They simply aren't practised anymore. But you just know that if the wrong people are placed in charge they will be dusted off and used again. It's like a seventy-mile-per-hour speed limit which everyone ignores because no one gets a ticket. Until one day someone does, and they target you. Only this is much more frightening because the consequence isn't just a simple traffic fine.

There are restrictions all over the world about whether you can vote, whether you can drive, how old you need to be to marry ... they restrict certain freedoms. But anti-gay laws are the only laws which are about whether you are allowed to be. It makes you feel sick, and very, very scared. To me, it's as fundamental as having a law against people being over six feet tall or being left-handed. These things are completely innate. They are not a choice – just as being gay is not a choice.

Jan

Jan's fear about the wrong change in leadership representing a threat to gay rights isn't unfounded. Although significant and steady progress has been made in creating equality, safety and pride for the gay community over the last few decades, equality does not come smoothly or uniformly. It requires constant attention and continuously overcoming setbacks. There is no better example of the moves and countermoves than in the case of anti-gay laws in Brunei. In the spring of 2019, the Sultan of Brunei announced that death by stoning would be the punishment for men convicted of having gay sex.[58] At the same time, the punishment for lesbian sex was set at forty strokes of the cane, or a maximum of ten years in jail. After the announcement, people from all over the globe began boycotting luxury hotels and properties owned by the absolute monarch, who is one of the richest individuals in the world. Less than a month later, a de facto moratorium on the death penalty was put in place. The law still exists; it simply is not actively being pursued at present. The moratorium appears to be largely due to global financial pressure.[59]

Meanwhile, in the US, the 'Don't Say Gay' bill passed by Florida lawmakers in February 2022 means that Floridian teachers and educators will be prohibited from any classroom discussions on sexual orientation or gender identity between kindergarten and third grade. Although proponents of the bill believe that it will give parents more control over the classroom, they are also very vocal in their belief that gay and transgender communities are a threat to American moral values. Up until a month before its passing, the bill had required head teachers to inform parents if a student identified as LGBTQ+, regardless of whether or not they felt that parent would be supportive of their child.[60] Currently, there are dozens of other American states with legislation in process to enact similar anti-LGBTQ+ laws.[61] This kind of legislation is reminiscent of the UK's Section 28 amendment introduced in 1988, and a clear example of the two-steps-forward-one-step-back rhythm of equality.

Using historical knowledge to actively shape our future

The last 150 years have been filled with a plethora of wins in equality and civil rights – from equal access to education, the equal right to vote, the right to equal pay, maternity and parental rights, the right to fall in love, the right to live in a world free of discrimination, to the more subtle but equally important changes in representation and decision making. Even in the last twenty years, many important 'firsts' have taken place.

- The first Black female British Cabinet member and leader of the House of Lords (Baroness Amos, 2003).

- The first and, so far, the only woman to be elected by popular vote to lead a G20 country since its inception in 1999, and to lead Germany, Europe's largest single economy (Angela Merkel, 2004).

- The first Black woman to summit Mt Everest (Sophia Danenberg, 2006).

- The first NBA player to speak publicly about being gay (John Amaechi, 2007).

- The first Black American president (Barack Obama, 2009).

- The first woman to win an Academy Award for Best Director (Kathryn Bigelow, 2010).

- The first female executive editor in the 160-year history of the *New York Times* (Jill Ellen Abramson, 2011).

- The first openly gay football player to be drafted to the NFL (Michael Sam, 2014).

- The first openly transgender person to be nominated for, and to win, an Emmy (Laverne Cox, 2014, 2015).

- The first Latina to be elected to the US Senate (Catherine Cortez Masto, 2016).

- The first openly gay woman to lead a Fortune 500 company (Beth Ford, 2018).

- The first Black British author to top UK book charts (Reni Eddo-Lodge, 2020).

- The first woman (and woman of colour) to serve as vice-president of the United States (Kamala Harris, 2021).

- The first transgender member of the UK parliament (Jamie Wallis, 2022).

Firsts are important, but they are not equality. They are the green shoots of equality and represent the potential the future could hold but which is by no means guaranteed. We must recognise and celebrate the many positive changes. But if we aim to move beyond potential to more systemic equality and freedom, we must be grounded in how far we have yet to go.

The events described in this chapter are only a very thin slice of our past. They represent a handful of key moments – most of which have occurred in living memory. Those events, however, be they national scandals or major breakthroughs in fundamental human rights, shaped our collective experience. My intention in sharing this condensed and focused section of history is to highlight both the depth of impact that legal restrictions, social attitudes and world events have had on generations who are alive today and the recency of these things. History doesn't simply end when the clock moves forward. History plays a key role in shaping belief systems and forming part of our moral social compass, neither of which are quick to change.

If I apply this timeline of events to my own family, I know my grandfathers, both of whom were poor and white, worked hard to earn for their families. But I also know that they did not face the same racial barriers that ethnic minority individuals of their generation did. My mother, who is proudly anti-establishment and someone with a self-proclaimed 'naughty streak', would not have got away with even a fraction of the things she did if she had black or brown skin. After graduating from high school in 1965 in San Francisco, she, along with my father, enjoyed being part of the alternative lifestyle which 1960s California was famous for. That's not to say my parents did not work hard – they did – or that we were not poor – we were. But their white skin and my mother's honey-blonde hair and blue eyes were additive to their lives. Race never played a negative role in shaping the experiences or the opportunities of my parents, my siblings or myself. This is the definition of 'white privilege', a term at which many bristle but which simply means that someone's skin colour never held them back in life.

Section 28 legislation effectively neutered any conversation within schools or councils about same-sex relationships and had a significant effect on people my age. It was in place through early school years and well into the time when we entered the workplace, creating a chasm of knowledge and limited exposure to the gay community during formative years. That gap still exists for many British individuals of my generation and is exacerbated by the fact that many of today's children are highly educated in this space. When teenagers come home talking about pansexual and 'demiqueer' peers or are asking to be referred to as 'they', many parents and carers have no idea what their children are talking about, and it can create an element of disconnect and fear.

Exploring our history isn't about wallowing in shame. We cannot ever own the attitudes and actions of our ancestors. But if we fail to see the legacy of tragic, discriminatory and inhumane events, we allow their influence to continue. Those events, and the intergenerational wealth and privileges which many of us enjoy, are not simply contained within the period of time in which they occurred. We don't need to feel bad about our past, but we do need to stand up, take notice, speak out and work together to ensure our history does not limit the possibilities of our future.

Chapter 2

The Strength of Social Norms

'We've begun to raise daughters more like
sons . . . but few have the courage to raise
our sons more like our daughters.'
Gloria Steinem[1]

Social norms are the unwritten rules and standards that govern how we behave. They play a significant role in shaping personal belief systems and shared attitudes, and are one of the key reasons our past casts such a lasting shadow. Gender norms are particularly pervasive. They govern our social existence so firmly that to challenge what it means to be a man or a woman means we are challenging the very fabric of our society. A challenge that, in my experience, is rarely welcomed.

Sex is a classification based on biological differences. It's the distinction we give to babies – the moment when a doctor holds up a child and says 'it's a boy' or 'it's a girl'. For the most part, sex is easy to distinguish because of the physical body parts with which we enter the world. These body parts are what doctors call primary sex characteristics. Doctors assign a child to either the male or female category based on our genitalia, but medically speaking, our sex not only includes our bits and bobs, but also our hormones and chromosomes. The latter make up our secondary sex characteristics.

We tend to think of sex as binary, but roughly 1.7 per cent of individuals have physical attributes that sit outside standard male or female norms.[2] Intersex people, or individuals with disorders of sex development (DSDs), as they are often called, experience a wide range of natural variations to the sexual development of the body. Some are visible at birth. Some only become apparent at puberty. And some are so invisible that we only stumble upon them through specialised testing – which is why individuals can be assigned male or female at birth, only to find out later that their primary and secondary sex characteristics don't line up. It's commonly assumed that being intersex is rare, but the prevalence of those who don't fit neatly into our binary sex construct is roughly as common as red hair.[3]

Setting the intersex community aside, it means that for roughly 98 per cent of the world, our sex will influence all sorts of physiological characteristics. From our physical stature to our bone density, or how and where we grow hair, the internal cocktail of hormones we are fed throughout life means most of us follow a biologically predetermined course – though how we develop even within our sex has extremely wide variations (for example, women can be tall or short, men can carry a lot of muscle or almost none at all). Gender, on the other hand, is a social construct. Unlike sex, gender is entirely defined by society. How you act, the way you look, what you do and, to some extent, who you will become, are all greatly influenced by social codes which begin even before birth.

From the moment a pregnancy is announced, there is an unnatural infatuation with the colours pink and blue. In

America, some parents find out the gender of their baby through 'gender reveal' parties where the sex of a baby is announced through pink or blue cake or guessing games which entail items such as glitter for girls and guns for boys, or wheels for him and heels for her. Clothing, buggies, bedding or cuddly toys – nothing is safe. The prevalence of blue and pink as the colours of choice for children is astounding. But do boys really prefer blue and do girls really prefer pink? Or do we teach them to prefer the colour we associate with their gender?

There is very little evidence that suggests children have different colour preferences from birth. Researchers at the University of Cambridge found that when it comes to children's attraction to colours, shapes and toys, both boys and girls preferred dolls over cars at the age of twelve months.[4] And, up until the age of twenty-four months, both boys and girls exhibited the same generic colour preference, preferring reddish colours over blue ones. As the boys began to grow older, however, their preference changed more swiftly and was exhibited more strongly than the girls' preference. Although boys and girls both preferred dolls over cars at age twelve months, boys developed a growing avoidance of dolls as they aged – suggesting that their aversion to 'girls' toys' was socialised rather than something more innate.

In a similar study, researchers in the US presented children with pairs of small objects, such as coasters and plastic clips, and invited them to reach for one.[5] Each item in a pair was identical to the other except for its colour: one was always pink, the other either green, blue, yellow or orange. The test was designed to determine whether boys and girls showed a preference for choosing pink objects, and at what age such a bias might arise. Girls chose pink at the age of two (but not before) more often than boys did. By two and a half, girls had a clear preference for pink, picking the pink-coloured object more often than you'd expect based on random choice. By the age of four, girls chose pink just under 80 per cent of the time. Their excessive bias for pink began to fade over time, becoming less prevalent in girls at the age of five. As you might expect, boys showed the opposite pattern to girls. At the ages of two, four and five, they chose pink less often than other randomised colours. Their selection of the pink object became progressively rarer, lowering to 20 per cent by the age of five.

Both studies suggest that even when it comes to colour, the social and cultural conditioning our children receive encourages gender-based choices. Just as girls are socially conditioned to like the colour pink, boys are conditioned away from colours, objects or behaviours which are associated with femininity. That conditioning often lasts a lifetime.

Though gender norms have always been a part of our social existence, the extreme prevalence of blue and pink, and the excessive labelling of a toy to be for boys or girls, is a fairly recent phenomenon. In 1970, 70 per cent of toys still showed limited gender markings. Instead, children's toys and clothes came in a rainbow of colours.[6] The prevalence of gender-specific children's items, along with blue and pink gender identification, was largely driven by advertisers in a desire to encourage consumers to buy more than one of everything. Gender-specific items meant parents and children became conditioned to believe that gender was an important lens through which to buy the latest must-have kids' item. As gendered marketing became the norm, so did the deluge of pink and blue. Today, you are hard-pressed to find a shop where toys, clothes and other children's gear are not divided by gender. Pink and blue have even made their mark on items such as staplers, umbrellas, cameras and other items which are unequivocally gender-neutral.

But gendered marketing isn't just measured by the deluge of pink and blue; gender-coded slogans are also a key feature of modern children's clothing. Clothes and toys made for boys idealise action and aspiration, while those for girls idealise appearance and happiness. The messages aimed at little boys are about strength, ambition, power or being a superhero. Meanwhile, girls are targeted with being a princess, being kind, messages laden with unicorns, cute animals or doll-like creatures with big eyes and curvy body features. Those gender norms have lasting impacts on self-belief and on the adults who children ultimately become.

The confines of masculinity

Over the last few decades, we have spent a lot of time talking about the effects of gender coding on girls and women, but we are only now beginning to discuss its effect on boys and men.

In 2019, the Welsh government announced the removal of gender associations from school uniforms. Instead of uniforms for 'girls' or uniforms for 'boys' there is now simply a school uniform. At the same time, retailers have begun to challenge the need for gendered clothing through the removal of boy/girl labels and the introduction of more unisex clothing. British retailer John Lewis also announced they would be removing labels which segregated clothing either for boys or girls and instead would simply move to selling children's clothes, with a focus on fit and sizing. The idea behind the move was to let children choose and to go back to varied options for all. Many supporters felt the move towards gender-neutral clothing was a step in the right direction, but the change has not been universally welcomed. Some parents expressed anger at the retailer's decision: 'This

John Lewis thing is pure shite, my child is a boy and will be dressed as a boy ... rugby tops, polo shirts, jeans, trainers etc.,' read one tweet.[7]

This sort of negative response to boys wearing what is perceived to be 'girls' clothing' is still a frequent occurrence. Vin Diesel, Jared Leto, Billy Porter and Marc Jacobs are among the handful of famous men who have chosen to buck gender rules and wear dresses. The result has almost always been a torrent of abuse – though there are some signs that attitudes towards men who step into women's fashion are changing. During the summer of 2020, British pop star Harry Styles was featured as the first-ever male cover star for *Vogue* magazine. It wasn't the first, or the last, time Styles has worn a dress or clothing considered to be feminine. Each time, there has been a mixed response, with some voicing disapproval and others welcoming Styles' gender non-conformity and the way he challenges what it means to be 'masculine'. It wouldn't be too much of a stretch to imagine that the people who welcome Harry Styles' gender-fluid expression are of a younger generation, while the critics are likely those who grew up with very binary notions of gender.

Last year, an old friend from childhood posted a picture on social media of a man with long hair which was piled on top of his head using a hair tie. The man's hair was very much pulled back in the way I pull my hair back when I am working – the way my hair is at this very moment as I sit writing this book. The caption he added under the photo suggested that 'anyone with a man bun should be punched in the face'. It took me weeks to get over the sinking feeling I had when I read his post. Why would anyone feel the need to violently punish another human being simply for the fact that they have long hair? Why does the notion of a boy, no matter what age, doing something perceived as feminine drive such extreme reactions? These rigid and narrow ideals as to how men and women are allowed to express themselves are steeped in shame and anger – both of which are often projected outwards, towards the person who dares step outside the boundaries.

Clothing, makeup and hairstyles which are considered 'normal' today are a direct reflection of the society in which we live, and the expectations of our current environment. Although skirts and robes worn by men are part of modern-day customs in many parts of Africa, Asia and the Middle East, with the exception of a stag do, a bachelor party or when wearing a Scottish kilt, you are extremely unlikely to see a Western man wearing a skirt or makeup today. When they do, it can require an incredible strength of character to ignore the negative reaction.

The option for men to express themselves through how they look was not always off-limits. In fact, both skirts and makeup were commonplace for men throughout history. Trousers only became more prevalent with an increase in horse riding and through advances brought by the industrial revolution, which made clothing faster, easier and cheaper to manufacture. We are no longer living in the industrial era. Many jobs no longer have a physical component which requires clothing that allows free movement. And yet, I don't know a single man who rides a horse to work, do you? This is despite the irrefutable fact that their design would allow men more space and more opportunity to regulate the temperature of their private parts, skirts and dresses are simply off-limits for boys and men.

These powerful gender social norms may seem trivial, but they form part of a wider pattern of social behaviour. Men who look and behave like women are subject to a deluge of abuse – labelled everything from 'cross-dressers' to 'poofs'. Women cross-dress all the time, but they do not receive ridicule for wearing 'men's' clothing. Instead, women can wear a dress, a skirt, a mini-skirt, shorts, dungarees, a ball gown or even a tuxedo. Social judgement on what women wear, how they do their hair and how they look is less about *what* they wear and more about how *well* they wear it.

The truth is that women are not confined by the same gendered clothing boundaries, but they are judged by their attractiveness in those clothes and how well they tread the fine line between being sexually attractive but not overly so. When a beautiful woman wears a tuxedo or something traditionally masculine or androgynous in style, she is fine. But if she isn't considered attractive, appears too sexual or has a body shape that doesn't conform to contemporary beauty ideals, that woman is likely to come under a lot more fire. Not for what she wore, but for the purity of her character or her failure to present a model appearance.

Men can, in theory, wear anything they want. So why don't more men break out of social norms and wear something different? When I ask that question, I usually receive two answers: it's either because they have never considered wearing anything different, or because they fear ridicule if they do. The social pressure to fit within masculine norms is immense. Not allowing boys and men the freedom of long hair and different cuts or colours of clothing may seem trivial. But when you add the widespread nature of these restrictions, which push men away from almost anything seen as 'feminine', they form part of a much more rigid and harmful narrative. Not only do they limit the freedom for boys and men to explore their sense of self, but they also perpetuate the idea that women are somehow 'lesser' than men.

The hierarchy of the playground

The playground can be a tough place. It's particularly tough when you look or behave 'differently'. From the length of your legs to the size of your head, the colour of your hair to having the 'wrong' trainers or the 'lame' schoolbag, children will find almost any reason to be mean. Even being seen as too keen in class can lead to instant ridicule.

Playground rhetoric around masculinity is no exception. 'Man up.' 'Grow some balls.' 'Don't be a girl.' 'Don't be a fag.' 'Don't be a pussy.' Even in the twenty-first century, they still form a core part of the masculine childhood narrative.

> *If I had a pound for every time I heard the phrase 'man up' as a boy, I would be a very wealthy man. And what does it mean? You cannot cry. You cannot feel. You cannot be you because everything you feel doesn't marry up with those two little words. 'Man up' means you have to hide what's really going on inside.*
>
> *It usually gets said because the men coaching you to 'man up' don't know what to say. They don't know how to support a little boy who is hurting. They, like the men who taught them, don't have the tools to react to your emotion in any other way than to tell you to get rid of it. So, they tell you to man up. That's how, from generation to generation, we hand down these two rotten words.*
>
> Glen

Playground attitudes and banter about 'being a man', 'manning up' or being told to 'stop acting like a girl/sissy/pansy/pussy/fag' may seem unimportant in the scheme of things, but they have lasting, widespread and negative effects. Historic masculinity has a significant enough impact on the development of boys and men that the American Psychological Association has issued guidelines to help psychologists specifically address the effects of widespread masculine ideals, declaring that 'traditional masculinity ideology has been shown to limit males' psychological development, constrain their behaviour, result in gender role strain and gender role conflict and negatively influence mental health and physical health'.[8]

The toxic playground environment we have allowed has a deep impact on the social and emotional development of boys. The consistent and pervasive nature of these types of comments sends a series of subconscious messages to boys and men:

> Pain must be endured.
> Physical connection should come in a punch not in a hug.
> Expressing sadness or fear is something only girls do.
> Crying is for sissies.
> Men who act like women are not real men.
> Being a girl/woman is a bad thing.

These messages encourage boys and men to systematically bottle up their emotions. Eventually, those bottled-up emotions have to go somewhere. For some, the result is an increase in anger – one of the very few acceptable forms of male emotional expression. Layer that increase in anger with testosterone, and you have an explosive match.

It's commonly assumed that testosterone, that stereotypically male hormone, is innately tied to aggression, violence and risky behaviour. But the more we know about testosterone the more we realise that the connection between testosterone and violence is weak. When aggression is more narrowly defined as simple physical violence, the connection between testosterone and violence almost disappears.[9] Why, then, do boys exhibit more violent and aggressive behaviours than women do?

The answer is status. Testosterone makes you want to rise to the top of the social hierarchy. Changes in behaviour associated with the hormone are shaped by changes in social expectations. If violence, aggression or risk-taking are seen as positive behaviours in a social group, men are more likely to act aggressively or violently. Conversely, if aggressive behaviours are seen as unacceptable, or unwelcomed, then the link between testosterone and aggression falls away.

Researchers at the University of Michigan ran an experiment where actors 'accidentally' bumped into and then insulted unknowing men on the street. The experiment was with two groups: individuals from the southern part of the US, where social conditioning promotes a 'culture of honour', and individuals from the north, where such a culture is less strong. The northerners who were bumped into and insulted were 'relatively unaffected by the insult'.[10] In comparison, the southerners, or those from regions where male dominance and aggression were normalised, were more likely to feel their masculinity was being challenged, more upset (as measured through a rise in cortisol), more physiologically primed for aggression (as measured through testosterone levels) and more likely to engage in aggressive and dominant behaviour.

As someone who has both travelled extensively for work and has lived outside of the US for almost twenty years, I recognise the geographic disparity in how aggression is aligned closely to masculinity in some places, and in others, it is almost non-existent. The acceptance of male aggression differs greatly between the UK and the US, and within the

UK, it varies again between Northern Ireland, Scotland, Wales and England. Just as it varies between countries, the difference is also visible between companies. In some of the companies I advise, aggression is closely tied to masculinity and both tolerated and revered. In others, it's considered off-putting and culturally unacceptable.

Testosterone, in effect, makes you want to be king of the mountain. The behaviour it makes you exhibit will be dependent on what being 'king' is defined by, which is why it may come as no surprise that increased testosterone has been linked to the increased need to purchase things associated with status.[11] From fast cars to loud stereos and kicking trainers, testosterone pushes us to buy, and behave, in a way that we believe will increase our social standing. These subliminal messages create a link between femininity and weakness and reinforce an invisible hierarchy where men are at the top and women are less than. Men who choose not to conform are seen as having 'lowered' their status by behaving or dressing in a way which is considered feminine. The effect is not only restrictive to men's happiness, it's also harmful to men's mental health and to women as it perpetuates the idea that they are somehow 'lesser' than men.

Being gay is not a joke

A few years ago, my husband and I were at an annual Christmas celebration with friends. Somewhere between the red wine and the port, the group naturally separated into women on one side of the room and men on the other. It was a jolly occasion. As the volume of conversation increased, and belly laughs were abundant, I heard the men in the group using the phrase 'I'd go gay for you'. It was a conversation meant to express love and intimacy and a way to say 'I love you'. It should have been a wonderful thing to hear, but instinctively, it didn't feel right to me. I decided to be the party pooper and to intervene.

In that moment, it was hard for me to articulate exactly what was wrong with that choice of words other than a gut feeling. They were an entirely heterosexual group. Would they have used the same language if one of their gay friends had been in the room? And regardless of whether there had been gay men in the group, did using the phrase 'I would go gay for you' minimise being gay into something you get to choose on a whim?

That night, one of our closest friends came over and asked me to explain further. It was the first time in our friendship we had openly discussed diversity and I could see that he was genuinely perplexed at the changes happening around what you could and could not say. When I asked him how he thought someone who was gay might respond to hearing their conversation, he blushed, and then said, 'But we didn't mean anything negative by it.'

Malice is a rare intent for most of us. But throwaway comments can be as harmful as direct homophobia if left unchecked. Unfortunately, ignorance isn't a good excuse. Some people use the word gay as a negative term when they want to be clear that something is rubbish. 'Don't be so gay' or 'That's so gay' was once acceptable language. Not anymore. Today, those kinds of comments are known to be both harmful and inappropriate, but 'I'd go gay for you' is not as clear.

Was I right to intervene and stop their fun? I don't know. But what I do know is that when heterosexuals understand the lived experiences of bisexual, lesbian or gay individuals, only then does it become possible to understand how words and actions, however well intended, can cause such harm.

> It was during a particularly bad argument that my brother outed me to my father. He said, 'Your son likes kissing boys.' In that moment, I had two choices. You either deny it, or you make a joke of it. I decided to make a joke of it.
>
> I was inexperienced and in the early stages of coming to terms with who I was. Now that I am an adult, I am in a completely different place. I don't make jokes about it. Being gay is not funny, it's who I am.
>
> Vinod

Men need more ways to share affection with each other, but they also need to know that hugging your mate doesn't make you 'gay'. We need to allow men the freedom to express positive emotions without negatively impacting or degrading others. Men need to hug, to cry, to laugh and to find healthy ways to show love, but they also need to know that men who love men are not lesser for it, and that being gay should never be the punchline in any joke.

Men as nurturers and carers

The social status of a man is still very much tied to what he does for a living and to his career success. The pressure which men still face to provide financially and 'be successful' is immense, which is perhaps one reason why so few men choose careers which are considered feminine. You only need to look at the percentage of male doctors compared to the percentage of male nurses to see how much more likely men are to go into masculine-perceived professions than those which are seen as feminine. In Europe and the Americas, gender balance between male and female physicians is close to 50 per cent, but in nursing, the gender gap is stark. Men make up just 16 per cent of nurses in Europe, 14 per cent of nurses in the US, and just 10 per cent of nurses in the UK.[12]

Like nursing, looking after children is still seen as a 'woman's' role. The percentage of male primary school teachers in England is 15 per cent – an all-time low.[13] One quarter of all primary schools in England have all-female staff.[14] We often associate extremely negative stereotypes with men who want to look after, teach or nurture children. The assumption is that those men are either weak, or their desire to look after children is based on some kind of perversion. The association of paedophilia and men who enjoy caring for children is so prevalent that many men hesitate to put themselves in certain situations and professions for fear of being labelled as such.[15]

In April 2015, the UK introduced Shared Parental Leave (SPL), which, for the first time, allowed parents to share primary care responsibilities in the first year of a child's life. The legislative change was supported by government statutory pay and time off. This freedom meant that after a few weeks of post-birth recovery time for a mother, couples could choose who was the primary carer. Despite the progressive change in law, in 2021 just 2 per cent of eligible parents made use of SPL.[16] Not only has take-up been slow, during the pandemic the number of British fathers taking parental leave dropped to a ten-year low, with only one quarter of eligible dads taking their short two weeks.[17]

Research on attitudes towards shared parental leave suggest that both men and women are interested in taking time off when children are born. So why aren't more couples making use of SPL? Breastfeeding is an influence for some couples when a child is newborn, but not all couples choose to breast-feed, and many who do aren't using it as the exclusive source of a child's nutrition. Other factors which negatively affect the use of SPL include money, workplace culture, worry that time off would negatively affect a man's career and women not wanting to 'give up' or share their maternity leave.[18]

When it comes to money, the ever-present gender pay gap means that for most heterosexual couples it's often financially beneficial for the woman to stay at home as she is still likely to earn less than her male partner. Unless you are lucky enough to work for an organisation progressive enough to provide well-paid parental leave for either parent, you are unlikely to make a parenting decision that leaves your family less financially well off. But money is not the only reason men don't take SPL. The stigma associated with men who choose to be full-time parents plays a big role. When I talk to men about their concerns about taking time off to be the primary carer for their own children, their comments reflect a high volume of social pressure to conform:

> *'I could never take shared parental leave; I would be laughed out of my friend set.'*

> *'I would not be seen as serious about my career.'*

> *'If I took parental leave, I would never live it down.'*

> *'My friends and colleagues would no longer see me as an equal.'*

Those pervasive belief systems mean that a man taking significant time off to look after a child is often frowned upon, just as a woman *not* taking time off is. Today, one third of British people still say mothers of young kids should stay at home rather than go to work.[19]

The issue with fathers not taking the leave on offer is so prolific that even countries which are seen as parenting-progressive, like Denmark and Norway, have had to force couples to be balanced in how they take parental leave by creating large chunks of non-transferable time off for both mothers and fathers. But forcing balance is only one way to instil change. Employers who focus on changing gender-based perceptions of parenting, and root out the stigma[20] and sexism which prohibit men from staying at home to parent, have seen a surge in the volume of male employees who take SPL.[21]

Shared parenting benefits both men and women. Not only does it reduce the impact that being on leave may have on a mother's career, it also enables a father to play a prominent role in the early part of a child's life – a pattern which, once established, is likely to continue beyond the first twelve months of a child's life. Creating a world where men are encouraged to nurture and where parenting is a valid and appropriate role for all sexes will not only open up possibilities for men, it will open up a whole range of opportunities for women too.

Just as with clothing, when men take on roles that are per-ceived as feminine – be it taking care of babies or taking on jobs which are considered traditionally feminine, such as nursing, teaching or human resources – they feel they are low-ering their masculine status.

Research demonstrates those worries may be justified. When men stray away from masculine norms and adopt more 'feminine' behaviours such as kindness, empathy or vulnera-bility, they are often penalised for it.[22] That judgement doesn't just come from men. Women play a key role in perpetuating those belief systems when they use exclusive language around social support systems such as 'mum and baby' groups. This lends itself to the further distancing by some men from their vital role as parents.

Whether it's in our personal or our professional lives, both men and women are punished for behaviours which step outside traditional gender norms. When studying performance reviews, researchers at Stanford University found that women were 2.5 times as likely to receive manager feedback about their 'aggressive communication style', despite there being no evidence that women are more likely to behave more aggressively than men. Men, meanwhile, were seven times as likely to receive feedback for being 'too soft'.[23]

Interestingly, lesbian and gay couples don't appear to be bound by the same societal rules. Over a period of eight years, researchers in Sweden studied leave patterns for both female same-sex and heterosexual couples having their first child to better understand how parental leave was being taken in the country.[24] Birth mothers in same-sex Swedish couples took, on average, seven weeks less parental leave than birth mothers in different-sex (or heterosexual) relationships. Their research suggests that both mothers in same-sex relationships were willing and able to take time off to contribute to childcare in a way that heterosexual couples did not. The increased balance in family time off is just one example of how same-sex couples are able to more easily defy social gendered norms, something which the heterosexual community could both learn from and benefit from.

In a same-sex partnership, it isn't about gender roles. It becomes more about who's stronger, better and more interested. And if we both really hate doing something, then we do it together. There is a shared mentality about everything.

I do the measurements and she does the drilling. I do the laundry and she does the holiday planning. We both do the parenting. One of us does the drop-off, the other does the pick-up. We are both there together for bath- and bedtime. It's what we do as a family.

Most of my heterosexual female friends work, but they are in 'lesser' roles as their husbands are the primary earner. That means they end up picking up the chores at home on top of working full time. It doesn't work that way in our relationship. We expect equality. We expect the other person to show up. There are no gender-based assumptions and there is no default – which opens up all sorts of opportunities. It also means we have to talk about everything. Especially when it comes to things like work and parenting.

We are both highly ambitious in our careers and intellectually curious. We also want to be active and involved parents. Neither of us has a career that is 'more important'. Which means we send our son to nursery full time. We get judged for that – not because we are gay, but because we're both women. There is still an expectation that one of us should be off work caring for him.

Alicia

Over the last few decades, we have spent a lot of valuable time encouraging more girls and women into careers that were once considered just for men. From roles in STEM (science, technology, engineering and maths) to sales, finance and executive leadership, we have begun to address the clear gender imbalances in our professional worlds. It doesn't matter how you cut it: imbalance is imbalance. We have work to do to create a world where men are celebrated when they choose to be a teacher, a nurse, work in HR, in marketing, in the charity sector or at home as a parent. Equality isn't equality if it's just for women.

Is our narrow definition of masculinity harming men?

We have created a society where men rise to the top. In almost every country of the world, men earn more than women do and often claim higher social status as a result. But are they happy? Is all that financial success leading to a fulfilling life?

The evidence would suggest not. For all the power, money and prestige men wield around the world, there is a much darker side to the story of being a man. Rising to the top often comes at great personal cost. Men in leadership positions are more likely than average to be divorced. Despite women being two times more likely to be diagnosed with unipolar depression,[25] men take their own lives at significantly greater rates than women all over the world. Global male suicide rates are more than twice those of female suicide rates and can be up to ten times higher for men in some countries.[26]

When it comes to addiction, men are more likely to suffer from addiction of almost every kind. Globally, men are twice as likely to become alcoholics than women[27] and three times as likely to die from alcohol-attributed deaths.[28] Addiction to drugs and the prevalence of substance abuse disorders are also more prevalent in men than in women. Men make up more than two thirds of those with a substance abuse problem.[29] Problem gambling, or an urge to gamble continuously despite harmful consequences, is 7.5 times higher in the UK for men than for women.[30] Sex addiction also appears to be more prevalent in men.[31] And, while the effects of pornography are only beginning to emerge, there appears to be a sizeable gap between men's and women's porn usage, regardless of their relationship status. In one study, single men who had casual relationships were forty-two times more likely to report viewing pornography at least weekly or more than women who casually dated.[32] And although porn addiction has been less studied than alcohol or substance abuse, it is becoming clear that the negative effects of excessive frequency or duration in watching porn can have serious consequences in real life.

Science doesn't support any link which would suggest that men have a genetic disposition for addiction. Why, then, are men more likely to be 'addicted'? Some research suggests a link between addiction and sociocultural patterns.[33] The strength of our relationships and the depth of our human connections help us avoid harmful addictions, making those without strong relationships more susceptible. While there is not a one-to-one correlation, it's clear that loneliness, isolation and substance abuse are viciously intertwined. When you add in the prevalence of suicide rates and the fact that men make up 94 per cent of prisoners across the globe, you are presented with a stark reality.[34] The world we have created for men and boys is not quite right. There is a darker, more sinister side to how masculinity is playing out.

Creating the freedom to redefine what it means to 'be a man' must be part of the solution. From the playground to the workplace, if we want to reduce the negative effects on men's health and happiness, we must reimagine masculinity. When we afford men a broader version of success, we not only create opportunities for increased happiness and closer human bonds, we also create increased opportunity for women, transgender and non-binary individuals to be valued, and to be seen as valuable in who they are and how they behave.

The 'trouble' with being trans

When our dominant culture allows very little room for men to define themselves and women have had to fight tooth and nail for centuries to create some semblance of equality, it's no wonder that transgender individuals come under such intense scrutiny. If men who display traditional 'feminine' traits challenge the very idea of masculinity, trans individuals blow the doors off the construct entirely. To transition your gender, or have a gender identity which is anything but fixed, challenges the very foundations of our social existence. It flies in the face of the masculine hierarchy upon which our society is built.

Sex and gender are different.* And neither are as fixed or binary as we have been taught to believe. It took me a long time to understand the difference, and even longer to be able to share how and why they are different in a meaningful way. Perhaps it is because I only started working with the transgender community later in my diversity journey. But I suspect it's also due to deeply ingrained beliefs from my childhood. The only association I had with being trans came from either television or the media, both of which painted a

---

* Gender identity (like race and many other areas of diversity) is both complex and varied. It's complex because humans by their very nature are complex, and varied, because the diversity of what makes us each individual, is expansive. The language I've used to describe sex, gender, gender identity and the concepts that underpin trans inclusion in this, and subsequent chapters, is based upon dozens of conversations with trans individuals and my own experiences supporting trans inclusion. Words and topics have been specifically chosen to help create a level of baseline knowledge for someone who is newer to supporting the trans community, but it is important to recognise that as our understanding of sex, biology, neurology, and gender identity evolves, trans inclusive language is also evolving and maturing.

picture of trans individuals as either people to be feared, or people to be mocked.

Gender is a social concept. It is defined by accepted social norms and is so deeply ingrained in everyday behaviours that we tend to see it as an absolute truth. Gender is the cumulative set of expectations for how we, as a boy or a girl, a man or a woman, should act. Gender norms include what we wear, how we look and what roles we assume. Gender varies significantly based on societal context, geography and culture. In our minds, we merge sex and gender, but very few of the gender norms in our society today are based on actual physiological or sexual difference. Even fewer are based on logic.

Many people confuse gender identity and being intersex. They are not the same thing.[35] While there is no exact, internationally agreed definition of intersex, it is an umbrella term used to describe individuals who are born with reproductive or sexual anatomy or physical characteristics that do not fit the typical definitions of male or female. In comparison, transgender individuals are likely to be born with physical attributes that match typical male and female associates, but their gender identity is different from the sex which they were assigned at birth.

Children become aware of differences in the body and differences in gender-based expectations from a very young age. Their curiosity with bodies is fascinating – if not funny. If you have children and they are anything like mine, their understanding of sexual anatomy and gender norms is often expressed as a constant narrative during bath-time or when getting dressed.

> *Daddy has a willy. Albert has a willy. I don't have a willy. Girls don't have willies. Mummy, why don't you have a willy? Mummy has hair. Ewww. Yuck. Mummy*

has hair! Mummy, why don't I have hair? Look at Mummy's boobies. Daddy, why aren't your boobies as big as Mummy's? Will I have boobies?

This comedic routine is sometimes performed in public settings, much to the bemusement of other adults. It is part of growing body awareness and comes with a mix of curiosity, attention and emotion, which evolves at each stage of development.

Simultaneously to this gentle exploration of anatomy, children are being socially conditioned with rigid associations of masculinity and femininity. Our gender constructs include physical aspects of the body; from breasts to penises, young children learn very quickly which aspects make you a boy or a girl. They also learn quickly which physical attributes and behaviours make you well regarded or disregarded. Pink is for girls. Blue is for boys. Boys wrestle and enjoy rough play. Girls don't. Girls can have long hair. Boys can't. Girls wear dresses. Boys don't.

Gender norms permeate our society and are firmly embedded in how we see ourselves and how we see others.

We tie ourselves in knots trying to categorise gender, which isn't real. The world we have created means we feel we need to rigidly classify people in order to feel we can understand them.

Ayla

Don't get me wrong, the mental models that we have to separate sex are useful. They help us explain the world. Unfortunately, those same mental models also constrain our thinking. When people don't conform to those models, we don't know where to place them. This firm implant of gender is in part why it is so hard for so many people to get their head around gender identity. Let's face it, being anything other than one gender, and the same gender for your whole life, is a mind-blowing concept. It's mind-blowing because we live in binary terms. We like the simplicity of either being a boy or a girl, but our rigid view means we see sex and gender as the same thing, with male and female sitting at two opposing ends of a spectrum, with little awareness of the possibility that anything exists in between.

Inclusion can be tricky, especially when it threatens some of our fundamental belief systems. Having someone say that you can be born a girl and feel like you are a boy is so fundamentally different from what we've been taught that it can seem incomprehensible. Contesting something so foundational to our existence is painful. For many of us, our internal notion of gender has never been in question. You cannot explore gender identity without confronting your own view of gender, and where on the spectrum you sit, which is bound to open up some level of personal provocation. I find that parents, for example, can get into heated conversations about gender-conditioned behaviours and, as a result, become particularly defensive about their own parenting. It's as if questioning social norms is an accusation that, somehow, they have 'been doing it all wrong'.

As a society we have often found ourselves at the precipice of new knowledge, unable to accept it. The first astronomer who came to know that the earth was round, rather than flat, was an ancient Greek mathematician, Eratosthenes, who used shadows on the summer solstice at midday at two points in the northern hemisphere to prove the earth was round. But it was not until a wave of discovery voyages in the sixteenth and seventeenth centuries that it would become widely accepted as the truth. What if transgender individuals are the

Eratosthenes of gender? Is it possible that this version of the truth is more accurate than the simplified binary world in which we have been raised?

Expanding our knowledge of the transgender community

Estimating the size of the transgender population is a challenge, not only because of limited data, but also due to limited disclosure. Best guess estimates put the global transgender population at approximately 25 million.[36] The UK Government Equalities Office tentatively estimates the UK transgender population at between 200,000 and 500,000,[37] while US estimates suggest there are 1.4 million transgender adults in America.[38] Though population estimates are hard to pin down due to the number of trans individuals who are not able to be open about their gender identity, what is clear is the growing visibility of individuals who identify as something other than simply male or female.

That growth in the transgender community and trans awareness can make it feel like changes in gender identity and expression are new, but the concept of being transgender appears to be as old as society itself. Glimpses of 'trans' individuals can be found throughout history. From 4,500-year-old texts which document the 'Gala', who appear to have been transgender priests and sex workers,[39] to Jewish poetry from the 1300s[40] or the Native American 'two-spirits',[41] there is significant evidence that trans people, or 'third gender' people, as they were sometimes referred to, have been ever-present. The exploration of gender identity, like many areas of history which happened at the margins, was rarely spoken about and was sometimes erased entirely.

Elagabalus, Emperor of Rome from 218 to 222 CE, is said to have offered money to any physician who could help him to gain female genitalia and to have frequently worn makeup to enhance his looks. After his assassination in 222, the memory of Elagabalus was cleansed and his image systematically erased from history to the extent that even carvings of the former emperor were ordered to be re-carved with new faces.[42]

Michael Dillon, a trans man, is the first known British individual to undergo a 'medical' female-to-male transition. In 1942, at the age of twenty-seven, Dillon was the recipient of a double mastectomy. He was also one of the first to be prescribed testosterone to support his transition. In 1951, wartime pilot Roberta Cowell became the first known British trans woman to undergo gender reassignment surgery. A year later, American Christine Jorgensen travelled to Denmark to undergo a series of operations and complete the transition to life as a woman. Jorgensen rocked the world. Her surgery was by no means the first, but Christine's public life after the surgery, and her willingness to step into the spotlight, meant she was a beacon for transgender communities around the world.

More than half a century later, transgender individuals in the UK earned the legal right to change their gender. The Gender Recognition Act of 2004 provided transgender people with the ability to obtain a Gender Recognition Certificate (GRC) which legally changes their sex recorded at birth.[43] Currently, the GRC requires trans individuals to have medical psychiatric assessments and to have lived for at least two years in the gender they wish to be officially recognised as. Those two years are often the most excruciating time for a transgender person, where they must prove they are 'man' or 'woman enough' to be recognised as such.

At present, there is a heated debate about any move to change that approach. Trans activists would like to see a more dignified and less medicalised approach, where we don't ask the individual to prove they 'mean it' in a very public and often very distressing way. Those opposing a simplified approach to changing gender worry that any form of gender self-identification will open a Pandora's box of issues, including a potential increase in sexually predatory men posing as women simply to gain access to private female spaces. While UK laws protect trans people and afford them the ability to live in alignment with their sense of self, we still have a long way to go. Nearly half (42 per cent) of British trans people who are not living permanently in their preferred gender role fear that living in the open might threaten their employment status.[44]

To my knowledge I will be the first of my 'kind' at work. Will I be the poster child? The diversity example rolled out to show we're inclusive, then relegated to the back rooms. Or will quiet pressure be applied to 'revert back' or leave? Of course, once you make a declaration like this you can't take it back. Coming out is a one-way trip.

How will my colleagues take this? Will I be a curiosity and suffer hurried, quieted conversations when I enter a room or strange looks and stifled laughs? Some already know and are behind me, but theory is different from practice. Will the actual presentation of my new self change their minds?

Maybe gender fluid is a better choice? Surely I'm denying myself again, but maybe it's a better choice. The male me gets to continue to live and the fem part of me gets to be free. The male part of me doesn't want to die. He's fought to get here for 50 years. He's carried

*the secret and all the guilt. The reward for all that suf-
fering and struggle is he ceases to be, he fades to a
memory. History. He doesn't get to fly. For me to
'ascend' and fly free, he needs to fall to his death when
I take that leap. How do I let him just fall? Cast him
off like a worn-out set of clothes and just walk away?
So much of who I am is because of his journey. His
friendships and struggles. By letting him fall, all those
things may also fall with him too, if they're bound too
tightly to who he is.*

*Maybe that's the answer? I need to figure out how
to ease him into this. Celebrate his journey as much
as look forward to my new future. He built the platform I stand on now. It may be his greatest feat of
engineering. The sum total of his toils may also be
his last.*

Heath, prior to transitioning to Sarah D. *

When I met Heath, he was preparing to transition to Sarah.
We talked at length about his hopes and fears around transition. His love of women's clothing and the joy he felt when he
was able to express himself in the way that felt natural were
apparent. Living as he does in a hyper-masculine New Zealand society, I could understand Heath's hesitation to come
out. His fears, both for safety and acceptance, were very
real. Trans fears around discrimination are not unfounded.

---

* Calling a transgender or non-binary individual by the name they used
prior to transitioning is considered 'deadnaming' and can cause offence.
Whether unintentional or malicious, I don't recommend it. In this instance,
it's important to note that Sarah D. chose to be referred to as Heath in
order to help the reader better understand the internal conflict that often
underpins a transition.

American transgender workers face a significantly greater risk of unemployment and poverty than cisgender individuals (those whose gender identity is the same as the sex they were assigned at birth).[45] Only twenty-two US states have legislative protection to prohibit discrimination based on gender identity in employment or housing,[46] and in the UK 89 per cent of employers have no trans-inclusive policies. More alarming is the fact that one in three employers admit they are less likely to hire a trans person.[47]

If gender ideals were not so rigid, if men were allowed more freedom in how they express themselves externally through clothing, hair, makeup, or even in how they behave, would individuals like Heath feel the need to transition? While having the freedom to redefine masculinity and femininity would be hugely beneficial for all (not just for the trans community), it's important to understand that being transgender is about more than just how you look or the clothes you wear. It's about a fundamental sense of self and your ability to find the alignment between what is on the inside and what others see; for many, that alignment may never be possible without a transition of some form.

According to the Williams Institute at UCLA, the percentage of openly trans adults in the US has doubled in the last ten years, from 0.3 to 0.6 per cent.[48] As you might expect, their research also suggests that younger adults are statistically more likely to identify as trans. In a survey on the acceptance and attitudes towards America's LGBTQ+ community, the Gay and Lesbian Alliance Against Defamation found that 12 per cent of millennials (roughly, people born between 1983 and 1999) do not identify with the sex they were assigned at birth or have a gender expression which is different from conventional expectations of masculinity and femininity. In comparison, only 6 per cent of Generation Xers (roughly people born between 1966 and 1982) responded in the same way.[49]

The increase in those individuals who are open about being transgender is not only in those who we would describe as 'traditionally' trans (trans men and trans women); those who identify as gender fluid, genderqueer, gender neutral or non-binary are also on the rise. There are simply more individuals who openly declare they don't identify with the binary construct of gender. When you look at the harmful effects of how gender plays out in our society, one can hardly blame them for questioning its rigidity.

> *Being Heath is like wearing a suit of armour which I've worn my entire life. I had to wear it because if I didn't, I was vulnerable. The thing is, that armour pinches in places and it rubs you raw. It's uncomfortable.*
>
> *Part of that armour was to throw myself into being masculine. I didn't know what I was, but I joined the navy as part of my attempt to prove to myself that I wasn't gay, or there wasn't something 'wrong' with me. I had a successful career in the navy and was part of the bomb disposal squad. I was good enough at it that they gave me the nickname of Robot because I was able to eliminate all emotion. It doesn't get much more masculine than that.*
>
> *When I look back, I know I was a complete dickhead. I had created a shield with my emotions like so many men do. I am starting to reset that. When I am Sarah, I am calm. It's like being in the eye of the storm, or on the side of the boxing ring. Instead of being in it, holding on for dear life as the next wave of punches lands, I have a different view from the outside. Sarah allows me to be me.*
>
> *Heath, prior to transitioning to Sarah D.*

If we are to break open the rigid gender norms, it will make life less confrontational for gender questioning, gender-fluid or non-binary individuals, creating more scope for people to simply be themselves, without fear of judgement, harassment or violence.

No matter how open we are about gender norms, it is unlikely to change the internal disconnect between sex and gender for all trans individuals. Gender dysphoria is a recognised medical condition which describes when someone experiences an incongruence between the sex they were assigned at birth and their gender identity.[50] This mismatch causes great discomfort and often great distress. Gender dysphoria is a rare experience, but that strong and persistent desire to eliminate the mismatch has been described to me as 'excruciating' and 'all-consuming'.

> From the youngest age, I felt desperately unhappy in my own body.
>
> I remember never wanting to be naked, which is unusual, because most kids love being naked. I always wanted clothes on and never wanted to be on display. Naked is when you're stripped away. It's when you are at your most vulnerable. I never wanted to be naked, even if no one was around. I refused to bathe because I loathed getting my clothes off. When puberty was looming, I had crushing anxiety. It filled me with shame, self-disgust, and a level of self-revulsion at my own body.
>
> My dysphoria was crushing. I just wanted to disappear – and to be alone. At least then, I could be the boy I knew myself to be without anyone telling me otherwise.
>
> Gender dysphoria can be so excruciating that you would literally do anything to get rid of that feeling.

When you transition, the changing of clothes can help alleviate that feeling of dysphoria, but it only alleviates the feelings placed on you by society, or how society treats you. When you strip it all away, it's got nothing to do with how you dress. It's your body and your own sense of self.

Jake

In addition to the feelings that your gender is at odds with your biological sex, those who suffer from gender dysphoria also show a strong desire to be rid of or to hide the physical signs of their biological sex, including muscles, breasts or body hair. They also often show a strong desire to be rid of the genitalia of their biological sex.

For most of us we have two elements to our gender identity. There is a sense of self which is constant but evolving – especially as you grow into an adult and know who you are. There is continuity to one's sense of self and an expression of your gender identity, which includes what you want to look like and how you want the world to interact with you.

For some there is a third element, which is gender dysphoria. There is no cure for gender dysphoria, it's just a matter of how well you manage it. The only way I can describe it to someone who has never experienced it is that it's pure anguish.

Being trans isn't an ideal situation. If I could have managed my dysphoria by living as a man, I would have. But that wasn't possible for me, and it wasn't who I am.

Ayla

Not all trans individuals have gender dysphoria, but the effects on those who have it are very real. Jake and Ayla both express a sense of urgency and palpable pain created by the disconnect between sex and gender. It is a condition which, left untreated, can lead to depression, self-harm or even suicide. Whether one is officially diagnosed with gender dysphoria or not, being able to live a life in alignment is crucial. Cisgender individuals simply do not experience that disconnect or misalignment. We might be annoyed by gender norms. We might even be harmed by their limitations, but we don't share the internal discord, or its effects.

Gender transitioning and living in alignment

When an individual decides to transition and live as the gender they feel on the inside, this process is called transitioning. Not all transgender individuals go through a transition. More importantly, not all transitions are visible.

Transitions are personal. For some, a transition may come in the choice of clothing, a change of name or change of pronoun. For others, a transition may include hormones or even surgery. They can be as internal and silent as accepting your own gender identity or as external and visible as exiting the office where you present as a man on a Friday and returning as a woman on Monday morning. There is no one singular solution to living in alignment. The nature of humanity means that it's simply not that prescriptive.

> *When I transitioned, I didn't change myself. I knew who I was, and my internal sense of self had been the same for decades. Instead, I changed my external*

appearance, which changed how others saw me. My transition could have been called complete when I was able to come out and live as a woman. I could finally live as myself even without surgery. But I worried that society would not have accepted me. In part, my lower surgery was more for others to accept me as a woman, not just for me to complete my own transition.

Ayla

Transitioning can be inconvenient. Individuals like Ayla have been very clear with me that being trans isn't ideal, and it's not a decision that anyone takes on lightly. Life would be a lot easier if that internal disconnect between sex and gender did not run so deep. Transitioning is not a perfect solution, but it's also not something we should fight tooth and nail to avoid. Many trans people I've met come to a point where they simply can no longer exist with the disconnect. Transitioning, both socially and medically, alleviates psychological distress and even an imperfect transition is often better than the current reality many trans individuals face.

There is no such thing as a complete transition, but it wasn't until I was into the journey of mine that I felt comfortable with myself and my body. Outwardly, I appeared happy and to be leading a very comfortable life. I was very successful in my career, but as a person, I was unfulfilled. I experienced a complete lack of substance in my life. My transition was bloody hard. But not being able to be who I was, was even harder.

Hannah

Transition can be a challenge for individuals who know the person transitioning. It is not easy to accept that someone who you have always known as John will suddenly become Jane, for example, or that he will become she. Names and pronouns are so deeply ingrained in our language they can seem impossible to change. But women who get married change their name all the time. And, because it's considered a 'normal' thing to do, despite surname changes after marriage being tied to a ninth-century law where women were legally given away as 'property' from father to husband, we accept it, and we adjust. After a few months, many of us cannot easily recall what the individual's maiden name was. In my experience, name changes and pronoun changes for trans individuals follow a similar path if you allow your mind to stop trying to fight you. Sure, you have a few missteps, but your brain quickly rewires if you make a conscious effort to get it right.

A lot of recent media coverage has focused on detransitioning, or the reversal of transgender identification or a gender transition. Detransitions do happen. In my research I found studies which suggested a wide range in the number of transgender individuals who detransition – from roughly 1–2 per cent in the Netherlands[51] to 13 per cent in the US.[52]

What I found perhaps more relevant than the numbers of those who choose to detransition were two clear themes: many who choose to detransition only do so for a period of time, and most detransitions are not driven by internal regret. Instead, external factors such as family or societal pressure, harassment and discrimination are the most common reasons for detransitioning. A recent and widespread study of trans individuals in the US suggests that of the 2,242 individuals who reported detransitioning, more than 80 per cent reported that external factors such as social stigma and pressure from family played a key role in their decision to detransition. Less than one in five (specifically 15.9 per cent) reported internal factors such as fluctuations or uncertainty regarding their gender as a driving factor for their detransition.[53]

At the heart of our inability to process a person's transition lies our own alignment with identity. We tie ourselves in knots trying to categorise people based on the rigid system we've been taught, but most of us have never had to question our gender identity. That's because our sex at birth matches the gender identity we have. If you've never felt that conflict, it's difficult to comprehend why anyone would want to transition in the first place, let alone the steps needed in order to make that transition.

When a colleague or a friend does decide to transition, how we react to their decision is pivotal. If we choose to do so, there are many positive roles we can play to support someone in their transition – from our ability to help trans individuals plan how and when they will transition, to how we will help others around them understand the process, how we create opportunities to ask questions which many are afraid to put into words, and ultimately how we lay a foundation of compassion and respect.

Social norms are holding us back

Our world is indeed gendered, from the pervasive pink and blue at birth, through adolescent years when, in an effort to fit in, girls and boys begin shying away from activities and things which until that point gave them great joy. From adolescence to teenage years and into adulthood, gendered belief systems leave an indelible mark.

These gendered colours, gendered toys and the gendered nature of our playgrounds may seem harmless. But those formative years provide the grounding of our social lives.

Boys are actively coached away from things which are seen to be too 'girly' and not sufficiently masculine. Being a girl is seen as a bad thing. It makes you 'less than'. Our conscious mind might reject these statements, but social conditioning leaves an unconscious imprint of masculine primacy which affects women throughout their entire lives.

Social norms aren't limited to just gender. Norms around race which place white culture and white skin in a position of power and primacy are so embedded into our everyday existence, it's hard to see them. The first inkling I had about the potential for their existence came when a friend gently challenged me on a comment I made about music. We were listening to the radio late one night while working together on a particularly complex piece of client work. It was a song by the band Journey. After I finished belting out the lyrics at the top of my lungs (it was quite late and all of us were delirious from the long hours and intense work), I made a comment about 'what a classic' the song was. My colleague Vince, a Cameroonian man, turned to me and said, 'For you, maybe.' I was curious at his reply and asked him to explain. Over the next hour, he educated me on how 'classic' is situational. 'Classic' means something different for a white American whose parents loved rock music than for someone where jazz is the family truth, and different still if you have Caribbean roots vs. roots in Africa. Assumptions, and the judgements which often go hand in hand with those assumptions, are defined by cultural, ethnic and familial norms.

Heteronormativity, or the mindset that heterosexual relationships are the preferred or 'normal' state, is equally as pervasive. It's part of the reason why gay and lesbian individuals are in the closet – because we assume they are heterosexual unless they say otherwise.

Whether it be the mindset that men must have short hair,

the expectation that an afro or braided hair is 'unprofes-
sional', or the idea that someone's accent makes them more
or less intelligent than another human being, many norms
have consequences. Social programming sits at the very core
of our day-to-day behaviours. If we ignore their impact on
inclusion, we stand very little chance of enabling real change.

Chapter 3

What Happens Out There Matters in Here – the World and the Workplace are Inextricably Linked

'The truth is rarely pure and never simple.'
Algernon, in Oscar Wilde's
The Importance of Being Earnest[1]

In addition to the far-reaching effects of our past, and the deeply embedded social norms which rigidly guide our behaviours, inclusion and diversity outcomes are also limited by the extremely narrow approach we take to diversity interventions, and by an almost total avoidance of the gritty and harrowing aspects of inclusion.

How can we understand how women and men behave in the workplace, if we cannot draw from how women and men behave in the world? How can you talk about race at work, if you can't talk about racism and the far-reaching effects it has on the mental health, resilience and self-worth of people of colour? The same holds true for homophobia, transphobia and violence against the LGBTQ+ community. These are tough subjects because they are ugly aspects of the human race – and unfortunately, they are part of the lived experience of 'diverse' people all over the world.

Take, for example, the women's agenda. Organisations

invest a lot of time and energy to help women rise. From leadership development programmes to maternity leave provision, extra coaching or sponsorship, employer-led interventions to help women into leadership are abundant. But how many employers are willing to tackle how women are treated in the world itself? Our interventions are polite and clinical, and for the most part, we totally ignore two significant external factors: an enormously skewed division of domestic labour and the persistent nature of men's violence against women and girls. When we approach women's existence in a limited way, we should not be surprised when we achieve limited results.

Equality in laundry may not feel important, but the domestic role of every generation of women, in every country in the world, is exponentially greater than the role that men play. Imbalanced ownership of housework and life admin, as well as the exceedingly high social expectations of women as carers, nurturers, parents, friends and pillars of their community, all come at a cost. Yet this work nets women virtually zero income.

In Spain, women do double the amount of housework as men.[2] In India, that figure rises to triple the amount men do.[3] Some may argue that imbalanced division of domestic labour is simply due to the fact that women are putting hours into housework while their partners put hours into employed work. But that argument doesn't hold weight in the UK where, despite seven in ten women being in work, British women carry out an average of 60 per cent more unpaid work than men.[4] Women fought for decades for equal access to employment. As they began to enter the workforce in more volume, men did do more at home. We probably all know at least one family where the woman is the breadwinner and the man takes on most of the unpaid domestic labour. However, these men are the exception. We are still a long way off equality at home. The world outside is moving on, but it's as if laundry and lunchboxes are stuck in a gendered time warp.[5]

The effects of Covid-19 have not helped. Around the world, as the pandemic took hold, women assumed a larger proportion of household duties, including taking the primary role in home-schooling when in-person schooling became unavailable. When UK schools were closed in the lockdowns, 70 per cent of women in the UK reported being mostly or completely responsible for home-schooling.[6] During the same period, researchers found that women with children in the UK, France, Germany, America and Italy were doing one third more unpaid domestic labour than fathers.[7] That division of labour did not get better as lockdowns progressed. In Italy, researchers found that in both the first and second national lockdowns, women took on the brunt of domestic chores even if their partner was able to work from home. For Italian men, the opposite was true.[8] They took on less housework and childcare if their partner had arrangements to work from home. Why do women still take on such disproportionate roles in parenting and domestic life?

One reason may be the undeniable fact that women feel disproportionate social pressure to do so. No matter if a woman works or not, she will be judged for how well her house is kept, how well presented her children are, and how active she is at the school gate, in a way that a man is not. Author Tiffany Dufu suggests this burden on women leads to 'home control disease', where women are conditioned to see an immaculate home as a sign of their self-worth.[9] As a result, women are more likely to do household activities – activities on which men often don't place the same value.

Women are judged in a way that men aren't. Perhaps some of that judgement is unique to the social circles we are part of, but I can see my wife getting stressed about small things. In my mind, a lot of it is trivial stuff. She wants other people to think the house is tidy and that the kids are well presented. Unless it's making sure they have the right kit for PE or being in their school uniform, I don't care what they wear. I genuinely don't see the point. I won't make a big deal about it. I'll just be passive and make a priority call on what gets done and what doesn't.

James

This 'I don't see the point' attitude comes from a position of privilege. Men often don't have to see the point of domestic work, because often their partner will do it anyway, but the view that domestic tasks are not critical isn't the only reason domestic work falls so heavily on women. Many men don't help out because they don't believe the tasks should be shared equally. Researchers in the US found that one quarter of Americans believe that while men and women should be equal in the public sphere, they also believe women should do the majority of the domestic work and childcare. The same study also found that men were more likely to believe differences between sexes were 'natural', whereas women saw them as stemming from 'societal' expectations.[10]

It doesn't help when sometimes women refuse to delegate activities to their partners because they don't believe men will do the task with equivalent quality and attention. US women are two times more likely to feel comfortable delegating tasks to their children than to their spouse.[11] From how nappies are changed to how a child's hair is done, how the washing is hung on the line or how clothes are folded, many women judge the way men do household chores. If we want better balance in the home, men are going to need to step up, and women are going to have to let go and make space for men to do things their way.

The imbalance in household activities continues with civic duties. At the state primary school that my daughters both attend, there was not a single man who volunteered as class representative in the first four years our children were at the school. At school fair preparation night, I noticed more than fifty mothers showed up to support pricing and arrangement of items and to help raise money for a new school playground. Not one father was present. It isn't just fundraising. This imbalance is clear throughout school life. I've been a parent volunteer in the classroom ever since my eldest child started school in 2016 and have only ever met one father volunteering to do the same. Despite the fact that the vast majority of mothers work and despite attempts to pull men in to help out with these activities, volunteering in any capacity to support the school is something men simply don't do at the same rate – unless, of course, it's sitting on a board of governors. Men take on between one third and one half of school board positions in the UK and are more likely than women to be chairs of those bodies.[12] Is it that men don't see value in these community activities? Or do they only see it as valuable when they are leading?

We can argue that part of the problem is women having overly high expectations when it comes to running a household, but if men don't value these roles and feel it's important that they take ownership in getting these tasks done, it is unlikely we will see any change in the balance of domestic and civic labour. To make matters worse, domestic patterns of behaviour often bleed into the workplace, where women put disproportionate effort into nurturing their teams and giving time to diversity and inclusion efforts. According to McKinsey, employees with female managers are 12 per cent more likely to say their boss is providing emotional support. They are also significantly more likely to say their boss is checking in on overall wellbeing and helping to ensure workloads are manageable.[13]

Activities like housework and laundry can seem trivial, but household chores place an enormous emotional and energy burden on individuals and families, just as leading people in a meaningful way at work takes up more time and energy. Gender equality doesn't work when we don't look at all aspects of one's workload. If we want to achieve balance in the boardroom, we cannot underestimate the importance of men playing a more balanced role with domestic chores or civic duties. Nor can we ignore how those behaviours play out in the workplace – including how they inform varying styles of leadership and what individuals see as a 'valuable' use of their time.

Equality and equal laundry are inextricably linked. Whether it be women learning to let go of some of the unhelpful social expectations they have of themselves and the family home, women making space for men to own and do household tasks in their own way, or men seeing housework or emotional leadership as part of their daily role, we all have more to do.

The stuff we don't like to talk about

It's not just the laundry, the dishes and the schoolwork – diversity programmes also neglect to take into account some of the more disturbing realities for women. Sexual and predatory violence against women is astoundingly common. The

World Health Organization estimates that one in three women will be subjected to acts of physical or sexual violence by men in their lifetime.[14] In France, 26 per cent of women have been victims of at least one form of sexual assault in the last year[15] and in Britain, one in five women over the age of sixteen will be sexually assaulted by a man in their lifetime.[16] This is not wolf-whistling, catcalling or even sexist remarks. Sexual assault is when someone intentionally touches you without your consent and can range from the unwanted hand or body part pressed against you on a crowded train journey to the extreme of rape.

Following a wake of high-profile allegations against movie mogul Harvey Weinstein, the #MeToo movement has left an indelible mark across social media, and the world more broadly. Alyssa Milano was not the first women to use the #MeToo hashtag. Nor was she the first to tell her story. But her call for women to share their truth opened up a floodgate. There were 19 million #MeToo tweets within the first year, not to mention millions more on Facebook, Instagram and other social media platforms.[17]

#MeToo exposed widespread harassment and assault. What was in the beginning a call to speak out against highly paid actors and wealthy producers quickly became a release valve for women everywhere. Allegations arose against business leaders, academics, politicians, civil servants and reporters. Supporters of the movement called for individuals to be held accountable for their actions. The deluge of stories and accusations ignited an immediate backlash, but there was enough evidence to bring forward charges in hundreds of cases. For me personally, it opened up conversations with every woman in my life about their experiences. From aunties to work colleagues, the sudden and widespread honesty about sexual harassment and sexual violence being experienced by women lifted the lid on a lifetime of silence and shame.

#MeToo was just the beginning. In 2021, a British university student founded the Everyone's Invited website, where victims of harassment and assault within a school setting can tell their story anonymously. In under six months the site reached 50,000 separate testimonials from secondary school- and university-aged girls.[18] The site's purpose is not to prosecute any specific perpetrator, but instead to provide leaders and educators with a factual account of how school-aged boys are behaving towards their female peers. The truth is not pretty.

In France, #MeTooInceste erupted after the publication of a memoir in which the author accused her stepfather, a high-profile French academic, of having sex with her twin brother (his stepson), who the boy was only fourteen at the time.[19] Although the legal age of consent in France was twelve when the incidents occurred, the case raised some serious questions about the ability for minors to be able to consent to sexual relations. In Spain, women took to the streets after all five men who gang-raped an eighteen-year-old woman were acquitted of rape and handed a sentence for the lesser crime of sexual assault – despite filming the act on their phones and bragging about it to friends.[20] Two key aspects of the defence were the fact that the victim had been seen smiling days after the rape (and therefore it must not have been that bad) and the fact that she didn't scream, punch or kick to stop the rape. Similar protests erupted in Sweden when three men were acquitted of raping a fourteen-year-old girl with a glass bottle. The court ruled that absence of the girl's consent did not constitute rape and the verdict explicitly stated that 'the girl may have kept her legs together out of modesty'.[21]

Stories like these are hard to discuss. Rape is an extremely uncomfortable topic, but it's one we must face into. In

2015, there were 215,000 violent sexual crimes in Europe. Of those reported crimes, 80,000 were rapes and nine in ten instances were women being raped by men.[22] Rape is so widespread that today, one in twenty women in the EU have been raped.[23] Although instances of reported rape are on the rise as brave victims are increasingly speaking out, more must be done to end rape culture and prevent rape from happening in the first place.

We may not like the frenzy which social media creates around a topic, but we can all admit it has a unique ability to galvanise energy and to engage millions in important conversations like these. The pressure it created around men's violence against women led Swedish lawmakers to redefine rape as 'sex without consent' and forced French officials to raise the age of sexual consent from twelve to fifteen years. In Spain, the supreme court overturned the lower court's verdict, ruling that the men had committed rape rather than sexual assault and had their sentences raised from nine to fifteen years each. The case also led to an important judiciary conversation, which the public prosecutor summed up brilliantly when she said, 'You cannot ask victims to act in a dangerously heroic way.'[24]

As the prevalence of talking about violence and harassment has increased, so too has the fear of being inappropriately accused. There is an underlying worry that anyone can simply accuse another human being of harassment, misconduct or sexual violence, and permanently stain the reputation of the accused with only 280 keystrokes. While it is possible that accusations of sexual harassment and sexual violence can be fabricated, fake accusations are rare. In a decade-long study of allegations of rape at US universities, more than nine out of ten accusations were found to be true.[25] The US Federal Bureau of Investigation's data shows a similar trend as only 8 per cent of rape claims are determined to be false after investigation.[26] The vast majority of harassment and rape claims are real.

Fake harassment and rape accusations get a lot of media attention, which is perhaps why men continue to underestimate the level of harassment women face. In a post-#MeToo-era survey on perceptions of sexual harassment, men, on average, underestimated the actual volume of harassment women reported by 36 per cent. The gap in perception was widest in France, Denmark and the US, where, on average, men's belief that harassment happens (44 per cent) is roughly half of what women say they experience (81 per cent).[27]

The volume of men's violence against women and girls is alarming. But unfortunately, it's so pervasive that it's almost part of the furniture. We don't see it because we don't want to see it, even when it's right in front of us.

Trump: Yeah, that's her. With the gold. I better use some Tic Tacs just in case I start kissing her. You know, I'm automatically attracted to beautiful – I just start kissing them. It's like a magnet. Just kiss. I don't even wait. And when you're a star, they let you do it. You can do anything.

Bush: Whatever you want.

Trump: Grab 'em by the pussy. You can do anything.

These are the unaltered comments of the 45th President of the United States of America, Donald Trump, taken from a recorded transcript of an interview.[28] They are *not* hearsay or conjecture. They are a record of his exact words. We live in a world where a man can brag about grabbing women 'by the pussy' and still become president of one of the most powerful countries in the world. Whether we like it or not, we have to acknowledge the fact that when we allow men in positions of power and influence to treat women as something to be owned, conquered or groped, we legitimise and perpetuate assault.

Though Trump's actions may have added to a more widespread occurrence and he should be held accountable for any violence he himself has done, we cannot blame him for all sexual violence against women and girls. That ship sailed long before his time. So did the domestic violence boat. Domestic abuse remains an aspect of our society which is rarely discussed, and yet it affects women in epidemic proportions. Globally, almost a third (27 per cent) of all women aged fifteen to forty-nine have been subjected to physical and/or sexual violence by their intimate partner at least once in their lifetime.[29] Every week in England, two women die at the hands of their partner.[30] These atrocious acts are underpinned by atrocious attitudes. According to the Gender Social Norms Index, 28 per cent of the world (including both men and women) think it's justified for a man to beat his wife.[31] How is it possible that something so prevalent gets such little focus? Why are we so willing to largely ignore the violence men do to women and girls?

On the evening of 3 March 2021, in the middle of a strict coronavirus lockdown, thirty-three-year-old Londoner Sarah Everard was kidnapped by a police officer while walking home from a friend's house. She was raped, murdered, and her body was burned to hide the evidence. Later that year, Londoner Sabina Nessa was murdered as she walked through a local park to meet a friend. Her body was found with clothes removed and more than thirty bludgeon marks from a traffic triangle. When London residents took to the streets in an outcry against men's violence towards women, they were called both 'irrational' and 'hysterical' by some elements of the media.[32]

Women spend their lives making behaviour changes to be safe. From holding our car keys as a self-defence weapon, making sure the door or garage door closes behind us every time we come or go, parking in well-lit areas, never going running at night, varying our route home from work or being careful not to drink too much, we undertake dozens of actions on a regular basis in order to avoid sexual harassment, assault or even murder. Men, on the other hand, rarely have to alter their behaviour. That is not to suggest that men are not also the victims of such crimes – they are. But the relative rarity of sexual assault in men's lives means that it seldom warrants changing everyday behaviour. Sexual violence, harassment and rape don't only happen to women, but these issues disproportionately affect women. It's not all men who harm, but *all* men do need to play a role in eradicating men's violence against women.

Dr Jackson Katz is an American educator, filmmaker and author. In a recent podcast interview, he described why so few men speak up on issues like violence against women and girls:

> So many men who are 'good men', who see themselves as good human beings and are compassionate human beings, if they were honest, would have to say they've never attended a Take Back the Night rally. They've never donated money to battered women's shelters or rape crisis centres. They've never challenged or interrupted other men who are acting out in sexist ways other than if they saw an actual assault in front of them or something. But they didn't interrupt even, you know, jokes that the guys will tell, sexist or misogynist comments that men will make in groups of all men.

Most men have remained silent, and I often say not because necessarily they agree with what they see or that that they are somehow embodying the same belief systems, necessarily, as the man who engaged in that abusive behaviour or talk, but whatever the reason that they don't say anything, and their silence is read as consent or complicity in the enactment of whatever beliefs or behaviours another man or other men are engaging in.

And so, there is this sort of false consensus in certain parts of male culture where guys think that what they're doing is completely acceptable and normative, in part because men who don't agree don't speak up. And one of the reasons why men don't speak up is because a lot of men are afraid of other men.[33]

A lot of men I meet clearly believe in equality. They believe women should be treated with dignity and respect. But with the exception of a handful of men who choose to engage on this topic, most hesitate to call out other men when they behave in a misogynistic or predatory manner. Unfortunately, preventing it requires calling others out – and just like calling out racism, homophobia or transphobia, calling someone out for their misogynistic, sexist or aggressive behaviour towards women presents a level of personal risk.

It isn't only men who need to change if we are to eliminate men's violence against women and girls. Change will require everyone playing their part – that includes parents talking to their sons, sisters talking to their brothers, and so on. Scottish poet Len Pennie describes our aversion to talking about perpetrators in the closing line of her poem 'Am I flirting with you?' when she says, 'look through your people, and recheck your friends list, we all know a victim but don't know the rapist?' We all play a role in either continuing sexual violence, condoning it or preventing it – and if we cannot admit that someone we know has the propensity to rape another, we stand no chance in eliminating it.[34]

It's no wonder that organisational diversity programmes omit subjects like these. Not only do they drum up vulnerable emotions, but organisations also generally avoid taking uncalculated risks. Let's face it, tackling sexual or other kinds of male violence against women is not only unpleasant, it's also individually and institutionally risky. But when we build our diversity programmes on a very narrow view of women's existence, focusing only on finite elements within the workplace and ignoring the truth about how far we still need to go, our equality ambitions are unlikely to be realised. Misogyny and violence against women are ever-present outside of the workplace, and those underlying attitudes towards women will be playing out within the walls and halls of our organisations too.

Men's violence against women doesn't simply impact women in the moment when it's happening, and it isn't just happening outside the workplace. Violence, and our acceptance of it, impacts all aspects of a woman's life. How can it not? Women are coached throughout their lives about the importance of safety, and those daily decisions to reduce the risk of being harmed spill into the broader choices we make.

The reality of racism

When 51.89 per cent of the UK population voted to leave the European Union, the 2016 Brexit vote exposed a Britain divided. Although many who voted for Brexit did so without racist intentions, they played a role in unleashing a wave of overt racism, the likes of which the country had not seen for decades. Those who thought that racism was long gone were proved wrong in a very visible way. But Britain is not alone in racist rhetoric. From the VOX party in Spain, Marine Le Pen and the National Rally in France, the Swiss People's Party or the Alternative for Germany, nationalism is on the rise, and, along with it, overt racism too.

It is easy to disregard racist tripe as something that only a handful of bad people do. But when we look more closely, we can see that overt racism is much more prevalent than most of us would like to think. In the 2017 UK general election, Black female MP Diane Abbott received half of all online abuse sent to female politicians.[35] Female abuse tends to be violent, aggressive and often sexual. The abuse Diane Abbott received was not only violent and sexual, it also contained references to her 'kind', being 'smelly', being a 'monkey' and being a 'black c--t'. The deluge of hate which she and other visible Black leaders face is as disgusting as it is appalling.

Online hate can be so extreme that it's easy to dismiss. It's important to consider that the online world, and uniquely awful places like Twitter, are simply an avenue for beliefs which exist in the physical world. The only difference is that social media permits cowards to hide behind their keyboard with sublime anonymity. The same technology which enables widespread awareness and galvanises positive energy also provides widespread opportunity to send hate into the world. It is the epitome of what could be wonderful about our world, but if left unchecked, it can go horribly wrong.

Racial abuse is still widespread, but who are the abusers? Some people are willing to put their name and face to their racist beliefs, but mostly it comes in anonymous form. It would be easy to think that racism is owned by the uneducated or the unemployed, but there are simply too many racists for that to be the case. Who are they, then? And where do they work? It is important that we understand that these individuals might be members of our own organisation or even on our team.

Racism knows no boundaries, and it isn't confined to social media. When British cricketer Ebony-Jewel Rainford-Brent showed her support for fellow cricketer Azeem Rafiq after he spoke out about experiences of racism in the sport, she received a handwritten note suggesting she had been 'found naked in Africa', and that she 'should leave our country now bitch!'[36] Rainford-Brent, who was born in south London, was able to make light of the threatening letter, but it wasn't the first racism she'd received while playing, and unfortunately, it is unlikely to be the last.

We don't have to like Diane Abbott or agree with her political views, just as we don't all have to be fans of cricket. But it is important that we understand the extent of the racial abuse that people of colour, and Black individuals in particular, are subjected to. It's never-ending. From parliament to the sports pitch, if you have black or brown skin and are visible, that makes you a target for racial hatred. The same isn't true if you're white. Prominent white figures face many criticisms and often they too suffer abuse, but racial abuse is extremely unlikely.

If we believe that kind of shameful and shocking racism is only aimed at celebrities, or those in the public eye, we are mistaken. Racism exists in all parts of our society and affects all kinds of people.

It was just after Brexit. I had gone to a local Waitrose for groceries, and I remember being flustered because the trolley I had picked up had a dodgy wheel. I struggled for some time trying to get it to move and then decided to go back and get a new one when I noticed there was a couple behind me. They were a bit older than me and very well dressed. As I was faffing with the trolley and about to apologise for holding them up, the man shouted at me, 'Fuck off back to Spain – you Spaniard.' Meanwhile his wife just stood there and said nothing.

I remember looking at him in shock. It had come out of nowhere. There were no clues. No pre-warning. No context. I suppose I was also shocked in part because I am not Spanish, but also because they looked posh. For some reason they didn't look like people who would be racist.

It's not like I haven't experienced racism before. At work, I expect racism. I am a clinical psychologist. As a doctor, and as someone who holds a lot of power over a patient, being on the receiving end of racism from patients is often a helpful reminder of what they have been through. A lot of my patients are sectioned. They are taking medication. They are fearful for what's happening to them – and so it's easy to see why they might lash out. I also experience a lighter, clumsier version of racism in social settings. I've been asked what hours I work by someone who assumed I was a nanny when picking up my own son from nursery because my skin is darker than his, or told that lemon sorbet is someone's favourite 'Indian' food from childhood.

Racism in any form is surprising. Usually, I have the ability to laugh it off or to see why someone is behaving the way they are. This time I couldn't.

Ally

Racism is everywhere. So much so that for individuals like Ally, it's become such a norm that she expects it and has learned to live with it. That strategy works, until one day it doesn't, because racism catches you out and, eventually, it takes your breath away.

Although racism is often sharpest when aimed at the Black community, who, in my experience working to combat racism, are subject to more frequent and more vicious attacks, racism affects every person of colour. Whether they be Asian, Latino/a, Native American, First Nations, Indigenous Australian, Māori or from any other minority group, the negative treatment of people of colour and the global prevalence of white-supremacist attitudes is well documented. Like many other forms of discrimination, rooting it out is like a game of whack-a-mole. Just when you think you've made progress, something ugly pops up that you need to attend to. In the US, for example, a steep rise in Asian hate crimes has been recorded since the beginning of the coronavirus pandemic. From the eighty-nine-year-old Chinese American who was attacked and then set on fire in New York, to the mass murder of six Asian women in the state of Georgia in 2021, hate-related incidents against Asian Americans have risen at 'an alarming level'.[37]

Imagine the effect seeing that kind of visible hatred has on your daily life, as well as on your aspirations. It requires an incredibly strong character to see the deluge of racist abuse that visible people of colour receive and still want to put your head above the parapet. Very few of us are strong enough in character to be willing to put ourselves in that sort of racial firing line. To make matters worse, individuals who speak up about racism are often tarnished with the label of being angry. We afford ethnic minorities very few spaces where they can be honest about the racism they face and the anger they feel, but if anger isn't the appropriate emotion when hate mail and hateful words flow freely, then I don't know what is.

Throughout my career, I've been able to be a social chameleon, altering which version of myself I needed to be for the given moment. In predominantly white spaces, I find myself code-switching, which allows me to feel more confident in spaces others may not normally have access to. When I lead conversations on race, it requires a kind of practicality and detachment. I know as a Black woman I can help move things forward, that I can drive a benefit for the whole community, and most effectively when I engage in the dialogue with facts and not feelings.

As soon as you bring emotions in and you move beyond the 'business case for diversity', you end up in – racism – empire – colonisation – slavery – and perhaps even the systematic destruction of Africa. It's not possible then to be detached. Once you let emotions in, you invite in the trope of the 'angry Black woman'. You could be passed over for senior leadership, seen as not right for the executive meeting, the panel, or the stage.

Izzy

Izzy isn't alone. Individuals who raise the reality of racism in open settings have to do so with caution. The potential is too high that their card will be 'marked' and they will be seen as a person who 'causes trouble', is 'difficult' or 'abrasive'. In her book *Real Wins*, Michelle Moore talks about those moments. 'You may find yourself in situations where you think, "I shoulda, woulda, coulda" and spend inordinate amounts of time after an incident wishing you had responded differently.' She sets out three key questions which help her assess whether (or not) to speak up: 'Is it worth it? What are the personal consequences to me? What is the bigger question?'[38]

It's much harder for someone of colour to raise the issue of racism. Speaking up not only requires you to relive the trauma of an incident, but those who are attacked are often targeted because of their vulnerability.

> We ask ourselves these questions ... Why didn't that woman speak up at the time she was harassed? Why did she wait months or years to report it? The reality is that people often shut down in the face of threat, it's a survival mechanism – flight, fright or freeze. People can freeze when traumatic events occur, it's the safest option. That's why we need more people who witness or hear inappropriate banter or behaviour to speak up. This is allyship. The more we all call it out, the more we create a collective energy and the sooner we reach the tipping point of behaviour change.
>
> Suran

This is where allies can play a key role. Not only are we (unfortunately) more likely to be listened to, but we are also often in greater positions of power to raise important issues or challenge behaviours. I know that as a white woman working in diversity, and specifically as a white woman working in the area of racial equality, my lighter, whiter skin affords me extra privilege when I call out injustice. When I challenge a room of senior leaders (who are inevitably over-whelmingly white), my challenge is more palatable and I am more likely to be heard. I also know that when my husband calls out other men for talking over women in meetings or operating in a way that undermines women, he is more likely to be heard than when I do.

Racism, and the narrative that feeds it, leaves a lot of emotional baggage – baggage that many of us never have to carry, but those who do know the weight of. Racism makes you doubt yourself. It makes you question your worth and feel shame about your culture or family. Like violence against women and girls, the impacts of racism are not limited to the moment when it happens. It has a constant presence in our society and in our organisations, which means we need a constant counteraction to its far-reaching effects. Like sexism, misogyny and violence against women, racism cannot be fixed by the group who are experiencing it. It will take those of us who are not subjected to its demeaning, violent or humiliating effects to stop being bystanders and stand up and say 'enough'.

Just because you cannot see it, doesn't mean it isn't happening

The first time someone used the word racism in a meeting with me I could feel myself physically tense up at the term. I can remember the exact moment – the pale walls of the conference room, the stale air of a room with no windows, and the heated feeling I had from hearing the word. I can also remember the searching eyes of the woman who sat opposite me. Sharon was one of my Black colleagues and the lead for our employee race network. She had collated stories and lived experiences from other colleagues in an effort to share with me the reality of what it was like to be Black and work for our organisation and in our industry. It was an eleven-page document which detailed examples of microaggressions and systemic racism.

I am ashamed to say that my reaction upon reading the document was to explain away the behaviours and to defend the company. I simply could not believe that we were 'racist', and because I hadn't seen it with my own eyes, my assumption was that these experiences were 'misinterpretations'. Imagine what it must have been like to be on the receiving end of my rejection. How devastating to have someone explain to you what 'must have been' and make excuses. My own discomfort with the word racism, and my desire for us not to be linked to racist behaviours, blocked my ability to listen, to empathise and to learn.

Part of the challenge in hearing about these behaviours is that they were not as negative as I expected. I was looking for expletives or to see visibly cruel actions. It's not just racism; there are many workplace behaviours which we find it hard to see and to accept unless they are downright disgusting or glaringly obvious. Maybe it was logical that she was asked to take the notes or leave the meeting to get coffee. Maybe the client didn't defer to the white members of the team instead of listening and working with the Latina leader. Maybe they didn't roll their eyes when a gay colleague was talking about his partner. Maybe they didn't sit with their arms folded, with a stony look on their face. Maybe they misunderstood. Maybe they misheard. Maybe ...

If you're an ethnic minority, you know the first thing people will see is not your gender, not what you're wearing, but the colour of your skin. When you have those poor, but subtle responses from others, it makes you question your response to not only that situation, but other situations. Am I just overreacting? Have I made this monster in my head?

There is an estate agent two miles down the road in a predominantly white neighbourhood – incidentally the neighbourhood which I grew up in. You know when you walk in to ask about a property that they are already questioning 'Does this person really have the money?' It's easy to believe you're imagining it. But I know I am not when the agent couldn't even be bothered to call me to arrange a viewing later that week or add me to their property alerts, as he'd said he would. Just as I know that when I shop at Waitrose, I am never asked if I have a Waitrose card. It is such a small thing, but I notice. I expect the 'surprise' that I am there, spending money, and I expect to be thought about and treated differently.

In mostly white areas, when I am with my mum, who is Black, we receive a very different response than when I am with my white husband. I feel this difference in treatment at the estate agent, car showrooms, or even the grocery store. I will still walk into those spaces, but you have to put on an extra set of armour.

Sian

Sian's examples may not jump out at you. If you are reading this and you find yourself thinking, 'But how did you know?' or 'Are you sure they meant it that way?', I suggest you pause for a moment. When we say these things, even if we are saying them inside of our own head, we are in effect saying, 'You don't know what you are talking about – let me tell you what really happened.' We are questioning the individual's basic judgement and their inability to read a situation and overlaying it with our own beliefs and assumptions.

It took me a number of false moves before I learned that through my 'maybes', and my need to explain things away, I was part of the problem. I needed to listen. I also needed to learn that just because it wasn't happening to me, or in a way that I could see it, doesn't mean it isn't happening. Some acts of aggression are visible, but many others are subtle. Some people don't even know they are treating others differently and some people are sophisticated in the way that they disguise ugly attitudes with seemingly logical arguments.

It's time to expand how we approach diversity

Getting to the uncomfortable truths about how the world we have created drives suicide, self-harm, self-hatred, violence and aggression is not to be taken on lightly. Sexual violence and harassment are unpalatable. Domestic chores are just plain boring. Like it or not, the Western social hierarchy of white at the top perpetuates racism and upholds racial inequality. These are heavy subjects with serious implications, but if we continue to ignore them and continue to shape workplace diversity programmes which fit into neat boxes, it is unlikely we will ever succeed in our aims.

Women are adjusting their behaviour outside of work in order to be safe and to be valued. That adjustment will spill into their work choices and workplace behaviours. Being groped in a bar isn't forgotten when deciding how to respond to a louder, taller male colleague who talks over you in a meeting. Nurturing duties which fall to women in the home also often fall to women in the workplace. Just as homophobia on the bus leaves a hangover at the watercooler, racism at the football on Saturday doesn't suddenly abate when you come through the door on Monday. Instead, it makes the white-centred nature of our world even more challenging to accept.

As human beings we live in one world. We have one set of

cumulative experiences. What shapes us is the totality of our interactions, not just those which happen during working hours. The world we live in and the world we work in are the *same* world. They are inseparable and they are irrevocably linked. We cannot change what happens in here if we are not willing to look at what happens out there.

Chapter 4

Our Diversity Mess

*'You can't skip to the resolution without
having the difficult, messy conversation first.
We're still in the hard bit.'*
Reni Eddo-Lodge[1]

Diversity is what makes us unique. At its core, it's what makes each of us different from other human beings, despite having 99.9 per cent of the same DNA. Inclusion is the action we take in order to allow all that difference to flourish, and ensure that regardless of what sex we are, which gender we identify with, who we love, or what the colour of our skin may be, we all have equal opportunity to thrive.

Exploring diversity can create joy, wonder and positive energy. But it's not all sunshine and roses – exploring diversity is also messy. It's messy because there is no coherent answer to what diversity is, where it starts or where it ends. Even the most basic question, 'Diverse from what?', has the propensity to divide. Whether diversity is seen as good or bad is often coloured by our own personal views. Diversity is messy because there are no simple solutions. We are making it up as we go along. Our knowledge and awareness of diversity is evolving as we evolve, which means we often get diversity interventions wrong despite having good intentions. When we overemphasise difference, or we pit one group against another, we have the potential to drive resentment, frustration and division. It's also messy because there are often competing belief systems within, and between, diverse groups.

The path to inclusion requires answering some tough questions. It requires understanding why men, and why white men in particular, do proportionally better than others. To answer the question 'Why doesn't diversity happen naturally?' requires looking at some of our base assumptions. Is it that 'we' are biased? Or are 'they' not good enough?

Most people I meet want to live in a world that is fair and just. Unfortunately, fairness is something in which most of us believe, but of which we remain blissfully ignorant. We tend to question fairness when we feel we are being wronged or treated unfairly, but most of us don't consciously seek to understand if we are contributing to the unfairness of others. Why would we, when the answers we find in this space can threaten our most basic instincts? In order to create a more inclusive world for others, do we have to give up power, advantage and opportunity? In embracing inclusion, do we put ourselves at a disadvantage? If we are in one of the groups who have been advantaged up to this point, is it our turn to sit in the inequality chair?

Unparalleled visibility

Our world has always been diverse, but it's never before been this interconnected; what happens in Manila can be seen, heard and felt moments later in Manchester or Miami. Fuelled by access to technology, and the transparency it creates, social-media-led moments have created unparalleled visibility for inequality. Like it or not, #TimesUp, #MeToo, #LoveisLove and #BlackLivesMatter are transforming our world.

We may not agree with everything being posted, but one thing is for certain – technology has not only transformed visibility, it has also enabled a collective voice that was once almost impossible to capture. We have an unprecedented ability to share our story far and wide and to find others with experiences like our own. But like many things, that transparency at speed is a double-edged sword. The pace at which social media explodes a topic means that facts are simply not checked as traditional media journalists sometimes struggle to keep up with social media's unrelenting speed. Journalists also find themselves in competition for the most clickable story, which means accusations can go a long way around the world before any sort of rebuttal is possible. It also means that small mistakes can end up as career-ending scandals. 'Innocent until proven guilty' is irrelevant if an accusation becomes a near instantaneous 'truth' via forwards, retweets and shares.

What you do or say can now be seen by millions of people around the world. With that visibility comes social judgement and scrutiny like never before. The list of individuals who have either stepped down from leadership positions or have been fired for their actions is growing. The global chairman of Saatchi & Saatchi stepped down after he suggested that women in advertising lacked ambition and were not held back by sexism. Six UK-based bankers found themselves quickly out of a job after they uploaded a film of themselves acting out a mock ISIS beheading as part of a work-sponsored training programme. At a global science conference, a Nobel Prize-winning British scientist shared his feelings about women in the lab: 'Let me tell you about my trouble with girls ... three things happen when they are in the lab ... You fall in love with them, they fall in love with you, and when you criticise them, they cry.'[2] As a result, his academic career has been significantly curtailed.

Social media is cruel and a trial by Twitter happens more swiftly than in any real court. Whether your behaviour is simply inappropriate, purposefully unkind or intentionally racist, sexist or homophobic, transparency means that mistakes now come at a high cost.

> *Ultimately, we need to be talking about these things, but we're not. We're scared of having someone pick up something we've said. We're scared that we will be hauled up into HR. Companies need to make a statement by showing that they uphold values and if something we do inadvertently challenges those values you could 'be' that statement.*
>
> Tim

The fear that Tim expresses about being 'hauled up into HR' is something I hear often – not just from men, and not just in relation to the workplace. It creates hesitance in many settings. Because social media means that any misstep can be captured and shared across the world within minutes, mistakes and moments of poor judgement have the potential to come at a high cost and at any time. The widespread and instantaneous ability for anyone to record your actions means that any stupid behaviour you exhibit in your teenage years (or at any other age) could come back as evidence against your character later on. Those of us who grew up in a time without the potential of our every move being digitally documented lived with a sort of freedom that younger generations do not enjoy. And, if we're being completely honest with ourselves, there are moments in everyone's past which, had they been recorded, shared widely, or shared out of context, would be embarrassing and/or potentially career-damaging.

The power and speed of social media is indeed frightening, but not all of the results are negative. It can bind together voices that might not otherwise have a chance to be heard and create unstoppable momentum on topics which have thus far been impenetrable. Take #MeToo, for example. In the first twenty-four hours after Alyssa Milano's tweet calling for an honest account of the widespread nature of sexual harassment and sexual assault, 4.7 million people participated in 12 million posts on Facebook.[3] Facebook is not an anonymous platform. It binds together people who have shared networks and friendship groups. A significant percentage of people were women sharing personal stories of sexual harassment or sexual assault. Without the collective energy of the movement, many women, myself included, would have never shared their stories. It is simply too risky to be a lone voice on subjects like harassment.

Similarly, #BlackLivesMatter would never have had the same global reach had technology not enabled visibility for the irrefutable truth about the final minutes of George Floyd's life, and had millions of individuals not shared their experience of racism as a result. The wake-up call around police brutality, the ongoing legacy of racism, and the life-and-death reality for Black citizens may have started in Minneapolis, Minnesota, but technology enabled a light to be shone on uncomfortable global truths. Black individuals around the world have less access to jobs, good housing, education, healthcare and unbiased protection from police. There is nothing extreme or radical about wanting to access these basics without the interference of racism.

Through the simple act of visibility, technology is playing a key role in shaping the society of the future. We should be cautious about just how far that role extends, but we should not be apologetic if along with the rise in visibility comes a rise in expectations and accountability.

Equals and partners

The 2018 Presidents Club charity dinner in London made headlines for all the wrong reasons. An invitation-only auction and fundraising dinner for some of the wealthiest men in the country, the Presidents Club dinner had been an annual event for thirty-three years. Instead of making news for the £2 million raised for charity in a single evening, the dinner became known as a hotbed of sexual harassment and inappropriate behaviour after an undercover investigation found that some of the senior men attending the dinner groped female hostesses, exposed their genitals, and repeatedly made sexual and lewd comments to the women serving drinks and dinner.[4]

It's easy to condemn these as the comments and actions of a few. But, on the night in question, somewhere in the auction line-up between lunch with then Governor of the Bank of England Mark Carney, and lunch with then Foreign Secretary Boris Johnson, was a night at a strip club and a course of plastic surgery which was marketed as a way to 'spice up your wife'. In addition, all female staff were required to wear revealing black attire, matching black bra and underwear and high heels, and to sign a non-disclosure agreement ahead of the event to silence them from discussing the night's activities. The forward planning and premeditation gives an indication that the organisers knew and expected some of what was going to happen in the room.

I see all kinds of behaviour in my line of work, but this felt different. When the story broke, I shared my dismay with my husband. His reply was simple: 'Regardless of who is or isn't in the room, any event which doesn't place men and women as partners and equals in the world is not acceptable. Period.' It is impossible for me to summarise it any better.

Several weeks later, the Professional Darts Corporation made the decision to scrap 'walk-on girls'. The long-established practice of women wearing very little clothing escorting male darts players to the stage was abandoned with immediate effect. The move was forced through pressure from broadcasters who refused to show darts competitions if the practice continued. Within a week of the darts announcement, Formula 1 racing decided to call it quits on 'grid girls' – women in tight-fitting clothing displaying the sponsor's logo who escort drivers to and from the track. The historic practice had been part of the Formula 1 Grand Prix for decades, but Formula 1 were clear that the practice of using women in skin-tight Lycra suits with intentionally placed body adverts no longer aligned with their brand values or societal norms.[5]

The two moves were welcomed by many, but the removal of walk-on girls and grid girls was a loss to others. Frustration erupted at both decisions in the same way it erupted at the shutting down of the Presidents Club. What's the big deal with women wearing skimpy clothing and parading around with sponsors' names emblazoned on their bodies? After all, these women know what they are signing up to. If they choose to earn a living in such a way, who are we to judge or to remove their right? If women want to be hostesses at a fundraising event where the male attendees get a little 'handsy', or to wear tight-fitting or limited clothing to promote an event or sport, it's their choice.

Hundreds of young women lost jobs when walk-on girls and grid girls were removed. In shutting down the annual Presidents Club dinner many UK charities missed out on

much-needed funding. Was it worth it? Are these moments
where women are sidelined or sexualised that big a deal? Or
are we just bowing to excessive political correctness?

In many ways, we fear that the measure of what is 'okay'
is changing. In reality, most of this was never okay, it was
simply not visible in the way it is today. And, while these
might seem like inconsequential issues in the greater scheme
of things, they are indicative of what we see as acceptable in
society. If the line of acceptability wasn't continually pro-
gressing, slavery and child labour would still be common
practices in the twenty-first century. Not only is it damaging
when we signal to young women that their role in society is
a submissive one, or one based largely on how they look, it is
also damaging when we send a signal to young boys and to
fully grown men that women are objects to be looked at,
owned and conquered.

Small things influence big things. It may seem insignificant,
but any framing of women as playthings or vessels of pleasure
has the potential to influence a wider set of belief systems and
behaviours. Sexual harassment, rape and violence against
women are not separate, independent events. Anything which
portrays women as being for the use of, or pleasure of, men
can't be considered as being entirely unrelated to sexual harassment, rape and men's violence against women.

Regardless of whether the venue is the locker room, the
classroom or the boardroom, the role we give women matters. If we continue to place women in a peripheral role,
valued primarily for the way they look or what they wear,
they will continue to exist largely in a peripheral role. The
same is true for all aspects of diversity. Whether intentional
or not, if we allow culture to literally be whitewashed, allow
gay individuals to be sidelined or caricatured, or allow disability or mental illness to be something you are expected to

hide or feel shame for, we endorse and perpetuate structural imbalances and social inequalities.

Awareness without empathy has serious consequences

Perhaps there is no better modern-day example of the potentially divisive nature of the diversity agenda than gender identity. There are groups with varying belief systems and views often expressed as polar extremes. Aggressive exchanges play out very visibly in mainstream media, but there is very little mainstream understanding of what it means to be transgender. Very few people actually know someone who is trans, which means very few of us have personal experience to counter anything we might read or see on TV. The debate is littered with emotions such as anger, fear and frustration on both sides.

Anger ...
... at how hard trans individuals have to fight to be accepted and to simply live

... at what feels like an affront to religious belief systems

Fear ...
... as it feels like trans women's rights may come at the cost of (cis) women's rights

... as, along with the rise in visibility of the trans community, violence against the trans community rises too

Frustration ...
... that we are still having to fight so hard for fundamental human rights

... that such a small population can take up so much airtime when there are many other pressing matters at hand

The trans community are sometimes part of the messy debate, but more often than not, trans individuals are not present. They are just trying to keep their head down and live. The debate about their existence, their fundamental rights, and the questions around their morality, mean many trans individuals are burdened by the need to explain themselves in order either to alleviate confusion or diffuse the emotion of others. That continual need to justify your existence is exhausting.

From the well-meaning and 'inclusive without question' folks, to those with more traditional views of gender and everyone in between, exploring gender identity is as tricky as it gets. The debate is so messy that it turns many people off who are otherwise curious and interested. When our wonder and our confusion get put in a box, we get very little chance to challenge the mental models we have. Our level of understanding is basic at best, which can leave us feeling uneducated and uneasy, especially when a topic this complex, emotive and divisive is being discussed.

If you say one thing out of line, you get rounded on. It doesn't matter if you are pro-trans or anti-trans, the behaviour is the same. The refusal of people to listen means it is difficult to have a remotely nuanced conversation with anybody. I have been shouted at by both sides. It doesn't have to be that way.

Elly

Gender identity is difficult on many levels, not least of which is because of the fluid nature of the topic and the pace at which it is developing. It's also difficult because most of us don't have enough confidence or knowledge to unpick fact from fiction in this space. We are largely influenced by media sources to form our opinions and, depending on where our sympathies lie, we are swayed in one direction or another. Unfortunately, most of us are too far removed from knowing someone who is trans well enough to have the thoughtful and nuanced conversation which could move everyone forward.

To make matters worse, the debate about gender identity is intense and quick to escalate. When things turn ugly, those of us who don't have a vested interest in the outcome tend to look the other way. We ignore transgender issues or frame them as a passing fad, hoping they will go away. The irony is that if more people were to engage in the debate with more compassion and thoughtful questioning, we could turn the tide towards calm exploration and processing of emotions. Just by the sheer nature of our presence, we could force a different approach.

We live in a cruel world. If you dress a bit weirdly, you get laughed at. The more 'different' or out of the 'ordinary' you look, the more likely you are to be the recipient of more than just laughs.

Several weeks ago, I was talking to a neighbour out in front of our house. She and I don't know each other well, but we are both middle-aged mothers and I was asking after her young children as I watered the front garden. During the course of our conversation, one of our younger neighbours passed by. They are a gender non-conforming individual who sometimes presents as male, and other times wears a skirt, wears makeup, or sports a bold new hair colour. On this occasion, they had a beautiful new hair shade – somewhere between bright pink and candy-apple red. I complimented them on it, as I often do when we meet on the street. They gave me a beaming smile and then admitted to being worried that the colour was too bright, before continuing on their way. Just as they stepped out of earshot, my middle-aged neighbour turned to me and quipped, 'Well, that was weird.'

Transphobia is the irrational fear of, aversion to or discrimination against transgender individuals and can produce a range of negative emotions and attitudes from discomfort through to hatred, violence and aggression.[6] My neighbour may not be transphobic, but her actions show she's far from inclusive. She had seen our interaction and must have sensed that we knew each other. There was nothing to gain by her comment, and yet she still couldn't help herself. She just had to say something about them.

Today, the trans community has unprecedented visibility. With that visibility comes unprecedented danger. LGBTQ+ organisations around the world are reporting an increase in hate crimes and violence against the trans community. That violence is not only widespread, it's also rising. According to the Human Rights Campaign, 2021 was the deadliest year on record for trans individuals in the US, where at least fifty transgender individuals were murdered.[7] In Britain, two in five trans individuals have experienced a hate crime or incident based on their gender identity in the last twelve months.[8] Perhaps that's why in an EU-wide survey on LGBTI acceptance, 37 per cent of trans individuals in Europe said they are almost never open about their gender identity.[9] It's simply too much of a risk to be yourself.

Awareness of the transgender community is at an all-time high but understanding and empathy lag behind. When it comes to transgender, non-binary or gender-fluid individuals, there are a wide range of emotions and attitudes. Curiosity. Confusion. Befuddlement. Agitation. Aggression.

Anger. Anxiety. Fear. Exasperation. Excitement. Freedom. Hope.

Part of the challenge in dealing with the range of emotions in this space is that there is also almost a total void in confidence around the ability to talk about this stuff. Although gender identity has been transported into mainstream awareness, it has not been transported into mainstream understanding and fluency. If you increase visibility but don't increase the engagement, education and understanding required to reset fixed mindsets, the lack of empathy can have a hugely negative impact on trans individuals.

Because so few individuals know someone who is trans, understanding of the transgender community often stems from what we see on television or read in the media. It does not help that historic portrayal of trans individuals suggested they were people either to fear or be disgusted by. Prominent trans characters in movies have been portrayed as psychotic killers (*Silence of the Lambs*), evil people who hide their gender identity and their intentions (*Ace Ventura: Pet Detective*) and/or sex workers. If the storyline doesn't depict trans individuals as a threat or a monstrosity, it often places a disproportionate focus on the violence done to the trans community, like the story of Brandon Teena in *Boys Don't Cry*.

When the Gay and Lesbian Alliance Against Defamation catalogued trans TV characters over a period of more than ten years, they found only 12 per cent of trans characters were considered groundbreaking, fair and accurate while more than half contained negative representations of the trans community.[10] When the stories we tell of the trans community either vilify or mock, media and television play a role in propagating transphobia, just as they play a role in lowering trans individuals' sense of self-worth and increasing the probability of self-hatred and self-harm.

Although primetime television shows such as *Glee*, *Pose* and *Transparent* are showcasing a broader set of trans role models and telling positive trans stories, these are relatively new additions which are much more likely to be viewed by younger audiences. They do very little to sway the mindsets of generations whose experience of the trans community was steeped in hostility and born from the idea that trans individuals pose a threat to society.

The transgender community are a small portion of the overall population, but today, they are in the spotlight. In 2015, Andreja Pejic became the first transgender model to be on the cover of *Vogue* magazine.[11] That same year, Caitlyn Jenner emerged, making it impossible to ignore the transgender community. Her rise to fame was helped by the exceptional sporting achievements she achieved before her transition (in 1976, Jenner won an Olympic gold medal in the men's decathlon). But it was her willingness to be in the spotlight and share the intimate details of her life, and her transition, that made Caitlyn a trans icon and one of the most visible transgender role models in the world. But Caitlyn is a character who is larger than life. The social media and TV bubble which has surrounded her existence as a trans woman has not always been flattering or kind. In many ways, she is a 'spectacle' more than an individual.

This phenomenon, where members of a diverse community assume extreme caricatures in order to break through old stereotypes, is not new. Individuals seeking change need to be disproportionately visible. Take the intensely camp gay man, for example: in his exaggerated self, he is able to assume a new ability to entertain, to flourish and to skirt the acceptable norms of male conformity. This excessiveness allows him to explore behaviours and break social rules in a way that perhaps a more 'average' gay man cannot. That sort of behavioural exaggeration is not that different from women who adjust their personas in order to 'outman' the men, or hyper-feminise themselves in order to set themselves apart from men.

When we see individuals like Caitlyn Jenner, we become transfixed. As humans, we are drawn to the unusual, the curious and extravagant, which fuels our fascination with reality-TV stars, whether they be cis or trans. This larger-than-life effect means that we are unable to avert our eyes. In our inability to look away, we can no longer deny the existence of the trans community. But eyeballs are not empathy.

Reality TV has the potential to leave us emotionally detached from the people we see on screen. It fuels a darker fascination, and in the context of the trans community, creates an environment where some become interested in gender identity and transgender people, but not always in a gentle or supportive way. It allows us to associate transgender people with the extreme experiences of just a few. To think that a reality-TV star like Caitlyn Jenner represents the trans community is as absurd as thinking that contestants on *Love Island*, *Big Brother* or *The Real Housewives* represent the lives that cisgender people lead. The majority of any community, trans or not, have a much simpler, if not somewhat mundane existence.

It's important to remember that trans individuals are not trans in isolation, just as being gay or being Black is not a singularity. Expressions of gender identity are critical to one's sense of self, but are just one part of the huge array of things which makes us human. Trans people are mostly ordinary people looking to lead ordinary lives free from cameras, limelight and attention. When we strip away all the negativity the world aims at the trans community it becomes easier to see that trans people are just people. And, whether it be finding gainful employment, looking for love, or the desire to have a family, trans hopes are human hopes.

The mask of political correctness

There is a growing worry among some that our world is becoming too politically correct. A fear that, as a result of social 'progress', we will forget how to laugh, lose our ability to call something exactly what it is, or stop saying what needs to be said simply to avoid social awkwardness.

Consequently, when individuals do raise an issue, they can be quickly labelled as either the 'PC police' or a 'sensitive snowflake'. The PC police, according to some, are hypersensitive people who run around making sure no one can say anything remotely funny or offensive. Snowflakes, meanwhile, are individuals so fragile in their view of the world, they would melt if any substantial problem came their way. The assertion from some is that these two groups hold the world in a humourless vacuum and have created an environment where straight-talking people are not able to speak their mind.

Political correctness is blamed for a lot of things, but do we really know what political correctness is? According to the Merriam-Webster dictionary, political correctness is 'conforming to a belief that language and practices which could offend political sensibilities (as in matters of sex or race) should be eliminated'.[12]

If you asked me, based on that definition, whether I would want to be one of the politically correct in the world, or the one calling out the truth or challenging the status quo and giving two fingers to political sensibilities, I would automatically want to be the latter. The sheer definition of the term makes me want to be un-PC and shout from a rooftop about what needs to be talked about. But when we label something politically correct, is it really about offending 'political sensibilities', or is it something more?

Take Danny Baker, for example. The BBC broadcaster was fired in 2019 after tweeting a sketch of Archie, the newborn son of the Duke and Duchess of Sussex, where he depicted Archie as a chimpanzee in a suit. The caption of his picture was 'Royal Baby leaves hospital'. As you might imagine, the original tweet, as well as Baker's dismissal from the BBC, created a hailstorm of commentary. Archie was the first ever mixed-race child born into the House of Windsor. Danny Baker was a career broadcaster who had been employed by the BBC for more than forty years, and to many, he represented a rare breed of working-class individual at the BBC.

The BBC faced huge criticism for the decision to fire Baker. People felt he was being hung by a politically correct, social-media-led jury. When you read through the vitriol, many opposing the decision to fire Baker held a deep worry that Britain has lost its sense of humour and that Baker's sacking was simply another example of 'cancel culture'. He made a mistake and he apologised. So why did he need to lose his job?

Although Baker suggested that he used the picture to represent the circus life that would ensue for a royal child, the fact that he depicted a mixed-race baby as a chimpanzee without considering the unwritten message his cartoon was sending, or the fact that it is incredibly cruel, not to mention thoroughly racist, to portray a person of colour as a monkey, chimpanzee, gorilla or ape of any kind, is astounding. However unintentional he may have been, the effects of his actions aren't that different from those of the white customer at a Wetherspoons pub who, in 2020, used a Covid-19 restaurant ordering app to send a banana to a Black customer at a nearby table. The difference in Baker's case is that his cartoon was seen by millions.

The backlash and rhetoric against 'cancellations' is growing. Cancel culture refers to the practice of someone being publicly outed for their behaviour and the follow-on consequences to their social or professional lives. If you look at the prevalence of articles on the subject, you might think people are being 'cancelled' every day. In reality, while some individuals who previously enjoyed airtime through television, radio or other media have had their platforms removed or curtailed, no one has been 'cancelled' entirely. Freedom of speech does not remove one from freedom of consequence. Many people are being forced to reckon with a mismatch between societal expectations and their behaviour, while at the same time others are basking in the controversy they create and the emotions they stir.

In 2021, several British newspapers featured articles on the fear of cancel culture in comedy. The focus was on a handful of well-known comedians who felt their humour was being curtailed by 'cancelling'. Many were furious about the potential of being silenced or having their work or their access to platforms revoked. The voice that stood out to me most was that of comedian Russell Kane, who said, 'I don't think anyone is saying you can't be offended, nobody is saying that. What we are saying is you can't use hate speech that would prompt a gender-related crime, a sex-related crime or a race-related crime. There's a massive, much needed shift in the conversation round gender, around men's attitudes to women, around consent. Society has moved on.'[13]

Cancelling is often seen as a fundamental block to free speech and as the prime example of political correctness gone too far. The reality is that comedians can still be funny, and be close to the bone, while not being offensive. We don't need to live in a humourless vacuum, but humour that denigrates, humiliates or puts a person at risk is not funny. Asking for accountability when someone behaves in a knowingly racist, homophobic, transphobic, misogynistic or sexist way is not about political correctness, it's about being decent.

Political correctness means many things to many people, but if it means that being aware of and active around imbalances in the world is seen as synonymous with oversensitivity, then we are in deep trouble. The truth is we no longer find the same things funny that we used to. The jokes we once told about women, about Polish, Chinese or Black individuals, and the extremely offensive terms used to suggest someone was a 'spaz', a 'retard' or was 'riding the short bus', were never acceptable. The difference is that today, we will challenge when humour comes at the expense or degradation of another group or individual. If you want to see just how much the world has changed, turn on a 1980s movie or TV sitcom and cringe as you watch how gay people, trans people, individuals with a disability, women and people of colour were portrayed.

Much of the negative rhetoric in this space gets placed under the 'banter' umbrella. When someone says 'it's just banter' what they really mean is 'you can't take a joke!' The words can be playful, but the intention of banter is often not.

Banter is indeed a useful tool. It breaks the ice. It creates bonds. It can be a healthy outlet allowing colleagues or friends a way to escape their current situation, if even for a moment. But banter is often used as a way to put others back in their box or to reinstate a power structure. Put-downs and criticisms become a substitute for affection between boys and men. Banter is used to guard social norms and to make fun of what we don't like. When something makes us uncomfortable, we often use it to mask our own insecurity – usually by making others feel small and humiliated.

In May 2022, Scottish television presenter and journalist Eilidh Barbour caused a storm when she announced via Twitter that she had 'never felt so unwelcome in the industry I work than sitting at the Scottish Football Writers [Association] Awards'. She and several other guests walked out in protest. Some of the online responses suggested that she 'couldn't take a joke', that 'plenty of other women liked it', and that 'she had stayed through the drinks – so she must not have been that offended'. To put Eilidh's walkout in context, the after-dinner speaker not only made homophobic and racist jibes, he laughingly made references about sexual assault to women in the audience and suggested that 'a man knew if he had f----d a woman from Paisley because his d--k would start to itch'.[14]

Sexual assault isn't funny. Calling someone a 'poof' or a 'nap' isn't funny. Nor does it say much about your comedic capabilities when you have to resort to jokes about sexually transmitted diseases. What is particularly shocking is not that a comedian told these jokes. It's the fact that many in the audience couldn't see what all the fuss was about. Instead of working to understand why the after-dinner routine was so offensive, they were working to vilify Barbour for speaking up.

We all like a world where there is laughter. Laughter has the power to heal, the power to lift and the power to renew. It not only affects our mood, it affects our bodies by increasing blood flow through our veins.[15] It improves our emotional health, lowers stress and anxiety, and strengthens the immune system. And if that wasn't reason enough, researchers say laughter also makes us more attractive to others. Perhaps that's why we are so afraid of becoming overly PC. If we lose our ability to laugh, will we lose the ability to bond and play together in a world that is already overly serious?

As society shifts in terms of its tolerance, there will be new boundaries between funny and disrespectful. Being able to make people laugh is a skill. If we want to keep the good stuff that laughter brings, we need to understand where the good ends and the bad begins. Calling out people who use banter to justify being mean, cruel or unkind is an important first step, as is looking closely when people make accusations of 'political correctness' or 'cancel culture', given they have the potential to be used as distraction techniques when we don't want our actions or behaviours questioned.

A growing opposition to diversity

The changes we see across society are being celebrated by many, near and far. Those same changes are also fuelling a rise in animosity, anger and frustration. That opposition is most heavily felt online in the anonymous comment field or with a Twitter spat, but it's also very evident inside the halls of business. It can be signalled through lack of attendance at an event, lack of support for a programme or an accusation of being 'woke' on internal social media channels.

Do we ignore it? Does responding to it fuel the fire? What role does each of us play in helping tease out these tensions? How do we make it okay for people who don't 'buy into' all this focus on inclusion, or don't share the same views, to express themselves?

Google made headlines for all the wrong reasons when employee James Damore's ten-page 'manifesto' pushing back at the company's continuous attempt to get more women into tech and their 'ideological echo-chamber' went public.[16] The paper was dripping with frustration, but it was also littered with facts. Research into gender-based difference was layered through the document along with Damore's frustration about how it felt to be excluded from the diversity programmes Google had aimed at women.

We may never know why Google fired Damore. Perhaps it was his unabashed interpretation of the facts and extrapolations where he made some very damaging assumptions about the capability and aspirations of women. Perhaps it was his suggestion that Google should stop focusing on women and people of colour and look more widely at including those with different political leanings – individuals like him. More likely, it was that he committed his thoughts to paper in a way which led to Google's approach to diversity being put in a very public spotlight.

Damore losing his job had an impact well beyond the walls of the tech giant's offices. From the outside, what many saw was a committed employee speaking out, trying to use facts, raising important issues and contradictions, who ultimately lost his job in a very public way. It sent a message that anyone who openly voiced an opposition to the diversity agenda could be labelled as an organisational traitor, and that in doing so, they could be placing their job in peril.

We are constantly testing the boundaries of what is acceptable. The story of Maya Forstater shows just how complex those tests can be. Forstater made headlines when her employer decided not to renew her contract after she expressed her personal views about the transgender community online. In 2019, she lost an employment tribunal case; the judge who oversaw the case found that 'she [Forstater] will refer to a person by the sex she considered appropriate even if it violates their dignity and/or creates an intimidating, hostile, degrading, humiliating or offensive environment'.[17] This landmark judgement was the first of its kind to test the friction between freedom of speech, and human rights and dignity. But in 2021 Forstater won her appeal against that tribunal judgement. This time, a High Court judge found that despite the cruel nature of her visible commentary, her 'gender critical' beliefs are protected by the Equalities Act.[18]

This space is complex. The ability to speak in a reasoned and factual way, to challenge each other and act without anger, hatred or fear is crucial to our future – both as a society and for the organisations that exist within it. By clamping down on debate, we clamp down on the learning journey and the passionate engagement which has the possibility of changing hearts and minds.

> *A lot of the current cultural rift [around inclusion] has to do with your relationship with change. Change is unsettling for a lot of people a lot of the time. If you don't have a script for what's happening to you, it can surface a lot of emotion. The changes we are going through as a society don't often partner well if you don't have the tools to contain them. We are challenging work things, life things and human existence things.*
>
> *Someone suggesting there are more than two genders, or perhaps even an unlimited number of genders, is provoking. It takes a lot for someone to say, 'you know what, you have a point'. The consequence is having to re-evaluate a lifetime of interactions – all the people you've met, all the ways you've behaved. That's why the most successful conversations on this messy diversity stuff are done in containment. They are done in a non-judgemental way in order to allow us to reshape our relationship with the world – because that's what we're doing: reshaping our world.*
>
> *Ally*

Inclusion means we must listen to all sides of the debate and create space for differences to play out. But inclusion does not mean we have to listen to or accept racism, bigotry, transphobia or hate speech. We don't have to be bullied or labelled as 'woke' for trying to do the right thing, nor do we have to be labelled as 'sexist' or 'transphobic' for having questions. People who are pro-diversity don't always get it right and it's okay to challenge them.

It would be easy to ignore the rise in frustration and simply plough on. But if we do, we risk the growing anti-current to diversity and inclusion festering like a cultural sore. If you can't say it, it disappears underground. And eventually, the infection it creates becomes like a virus which spreads negativity and divisiveness.

There are many people who have real questions, real concerns and a desire to be heard. They often don't have the knowledge or the skills, much less the time, to figure out some of the more nuanced areas of inclusion and diversity. We need to make space for those voices. But we also need to recognise that there is one key difference between someone who is curious or questioning and wants to have a fruitful conversation and individuals who intend to mock or humiliate others. Personally, I don't see a place for those who choose to throw decency out the window. It happens all too often in conversations about inclusion, and increasingly it happens in conversations regarding pronouns or other terms used by the LGBTQ+ community to express their sexual orientation or gender identity. You may not understand or even like the expansion of terms used by individuals to describe their identity, but their identification and their existence doesn't harm you.

Understanding the fear of reverse discrimination

The more emphasis we place on diversity categories, the more fear we can unintentionally create. If success is increasing the number of women in an organisation, does that mean there is no longer a place for men? If we have a focus on giving additional opportunities to people of colour, does that mean I won't get hired or promoted if I am white? As the focus on increasing diversity and inclusion intensifies, many individuals begin wondering what the implications are when they don't tick a minority box.

Fear of reverse discrimination is real. But is it really happening?

The data would suggest not. Change is slow in coming and, in some cases, not coming at all. Not only are the upper echelons of business, media, sport, law and government still dominated by men, those men, more often than not, are white, without a disability and heterosexual.

If we look at senior leadership positions in the US and the UK as an indicator of whether (or not) reverse discrimination is happening in a widespread manner, the facts are clear across multiple areas of diversity:

Race

- Ethnic minorities make up 18.3 per cent of the population in England and Wales but make up less than 10 per cent of the individuals who hold one of the top three roles (chair, chief executive or chief financial officer) across all FTSE 100 firms. That number has not improved in the six years it's been measured.[19]

- There are zero Black CEOs leading any of the FTSE 100 firms, despite Black individuals forming 3 per cent of the population in England and Wales.[20]

- The proportion of white male leaders in the top forty roles across each FTSE 100 company is increasing.[21]

- In the US, people of colour make up 40 per cent of the population. White men have held 96.4 per cent of all Fortune 500 CEO positions since 2000.[22]

- Today, less than 1 per cent of all Fortune 500 CEOs are Black, despite forming 15 per cent of the US population. In fact, you can count the total number in that group on one hand.[23]

Sex

- Men make up 50.4 per cent of the UK population but 92 per cent of FTSE 100 CEOs and 93 per cent of FTSE 250 CEOs.[24]

- Although women now make up 40 per cent of all FTSE 100 'top table roles', female directors in those firms earn 74 per cent less than their male counterparts.[25]

- Men make up 85 per cent of Fortune 500 CEOs.[26]

Sexual orientation

- Estimates suggest that between 3 and 7 per cent of the UK population are gay, lesbian or bisexual,[27] but there have only ever been four openly gay, lesbian or bisexual CEOs in the history of the FTSE 100.

- There are currently no openly gay, lesbian or bisexual CEOs in the FTSE 100.[28]

- In the US, 7.1 per cent of the population identify as LGBT,[29] but just 0.8 per cent of Fortune 500 CEOs are LGBTQ+,[30] and even fewer (only 0.3 per cent) of directors at Fortune 500 companies are openly gay.[31]

Inequality isn't simply restricted to the upper ranks of big business. It exists at all levels of employment. Americans with a disability are still more than twice as likely to be unemployed than individuals who don't have a disability,[32] and although the gap is closing in the UK, individuals with a disability are a third less likely to be employed than those without.[33] Employment rates for transgender American adults show similar patterns. Trans individuals are twice as likely to be unemployed than cisgender adults in America.[34] In a widespread employment survey done by the UK government, 80 per cent of those aged sixteen to sixty-four said they had been employed at some point in the previous twelve months, but only 65 per cent of trans women and 57 per cent of trans men reported being employed in the same period.[35]

Reverse discrimination may happen to some people, but if it was happening in a widespread manner, the number of minorities in leadership positions would increase accordingly – and it isn't. Contrary to popular belief, there is no evidence to suggest that women, or any other minority for that matter, are disproportionately rising to the top and leaving a wake of qualified men behind them. Why, then, does the fear of reverse discrimination persist? I suspect that fear of reverse discrimination is, in part, driven by how we communicate about diversity. The abundance of diversity messaging has significantly outstripped the reality of diversity change. It has created an atmosphere that makes you feel like you cannot be successful if you are male and white.

If we are to reduce the fear of reverse discrimination, we must openly admit the fear exists and engage all groups in open dialogue about the change we seek. Unfortunately, workplace diversity interventions often exacerbate the issue. Because organisations want to be very targeted in their approach, and because they are unsure about how people will feel about the intervention, they have a tendency to run diversity programmes in a secretive way. Programmes and events are often targeted at people in minority groups. Those who aren't invited into the room or onto the programme often hear about it through rumours or second-hand information. To make matters worse, people who are in the room sometimes aren't sure why they were chosen in the first place.

When communication is scarce, rumours lead the communication circuit and divisions begin to grow. Why aren't there training programmes for white people? Why aren't we celebrating International Men's Day? Why isn't the mentoring scheme for everyone, instead of just for lesbian, gay and bisexual colleagues? There are good reasons to have private, focused and trust-based interventions which only include those in the minority group – but when we consistently operate under the radar, even the best intentions can go astray.

Targets are a great example of diversity interventions which have the propensity to create bad feelings in the workplace. Targets make good business sense, especially when the purpose of the target, the plan to achieve it and the support needed to hit the target are put in place. Unfortunately, communication about a diversity target is often limited, as is understanding about why the target is important, how the target makes people feel and what the organisation will (or will not) do in order to achieve it. When we don't talk about things openly, we create a breeding ground for negative emotions. Will women feel the target has reduced their chances of success? Will every new female promotion unwittingly provoke the question from male and female colleagues as to whether or not the individual was chosen because of their breasts or because of their capability? Will people of colour feel they have to work twice as hard to prove they earned their role? Will men worry that their chances of promotion, and ultimately success, are curtailed?

We also need to be practical in our explanation about how targets play out against opportunity. For example, if we set a target of 30 per cent women at a given level, that still means that at least seven in ten promotions or new hires will be men. Those are good betting odds. It doesn't mean men won't get promoted, it means they will have to shine among other men to be chosen. Likewise, if a mentorship programme is aimed at ethnic minorities, it doesn't mean that white people don't get mentorship. What it means is that ethnic minorities are getting formal structures to build mentorship because mentoring isn't happening in the same widespread manner for ethnic minority colleagues in the way it often naturally flows from white leadership to white colleagues.

The frustration which often erupts in an organisation after the announcement of a diversity target is due to the vacuum of information, and an underestimation of the importance of the emotional engagement needed from both those within and outside of the target group. When we address how people feel, we are much more likely to construct a positive path for how we move forward together. Good communication, which focuses on both feelings and data, can circumvent these issues.

Two-way conversations help diffuse tensions, eliminate frustrations and dispel myths. When we engage all of our colleagues in an open and transparent way, we eliminate secrecy and reduce pushback.

Balancing proportionality

One reason we see so much pushback against diversity is due to the fact that it gets so much airtime. We are constantly talking about it and, as a consequence, it can feel like we are giving diversity so much priority that it comes at the cost of other important issues.

There are moments when diversity cannot and should not be the focus. A few years ago, a new client enquired about my support in creating a diversity strategy. They were a business which was haemorrhaging money and about to make more than half of their workforce redundant. They wanted my help to build a plan to increase diversity, but in reality, they needed to focus their time and effort on keeping their doors open. In the end we decided that staff mental health and wellbeing were their priority until they could get the business into a stable financial position.

Just as diversity doesn't need to be the top priority, we should be cautious when it is consistently relegated to the lowest priority, and never prioritised or funded. Take inclusive design for those with disabilities, for example. Inclusive design is often moved to the bottom of the priority list and then subsequently never funded.

When I looked at universities, many of them had different entrances to get to the classroom. It felt isolating and

highlighted my difference – like a stamp on my forehead.
Every day, I would have to separate from my friends and
go around a back way in order [to find a wheelchair
ramp] to get to the classroom. In the end, the university
I chose had thought about it from the beginning. I got to
go in the same way my friends did. It made me feel
valued – which is massively important. When you're not
included and you're not valued, it's really obvious.

   At some restaurants you are taken around the back
through the bins and the kitchen. Because it's not as
frequent or as prominent, it's not considered impor-
tant. Or even if there is consideration, and you do have
a disabled toilet for example, you cannot use it because
there is a table in front or because they have turned it
into a cloakroom. Things like that go unnoticed by oth-
ers, but when you're the one with the disability, you
cannot ignore it.

                                                    Sophie

Unfortunately, Sophie's experience is not that uncommon.
The result of ignoring the needs of people with disabilities is
not only that organisations are woefully unprepared to support individuals in accessing their services, but it also means
they are continuing to perpetuate the norms which fly in the
face of basic human dignity.

A client recently told me that diversity had been on the
agenda at every board meeting for more than a year, but it
was always last on the agenda, and therefore always the
thing that got cut when other issues took up more time.
Diversity doesn't need to be on every agenda, but when it is
we need to have meaningful conversations and take meaningful action as a result.

The inevitability of uncomfortable

If we want to untangle the mess in which we find ourselves then we must dive into the uncomfortable and allow space to explore emotions, questions, frustrations and contradictions. We need many voices to be heard. We need safe places where individuals can work through why they feel the way they do, without fear of being judged or being fired.

When the #BlackLivesMatter movement illuminated the persistent and widespread nature of racism, colourism and anti-blackness, many white friends and colleagues came to talk to me about the gaps in their knowledge and their discomfort about the truths being exposed. Overnight it became not okay to be white and silent. The weight of judgement for being inactive, and therefore complicit, was second only to the fear of saying or doing the wrong thing.

Fast forward two years and the visibility of Black individuals in marketing imagery, in commercials and on TV has skyrocketed as businesses work to address the severe imbalance (and almost total whiteness) that existed previously. That visible inclusion has made many of the same people, including those who were uncomfortable about being called out for their lack of awareness and lack of action, uneasy again. This time that discomfort stems from different reasons. It's now layered with a sense of threat. Even members of my own family have questioned the disproportionate visibility of ethnic minorities on British television, suggesting that 'it doesn't feel like the country they know'. That disconnect is in part because so most people (regardless of which racial or ethnic group which they belong to) live in racially segregated bubbles, which means they are caught by surprise at how ethnically and racially diverse the UK actually is. But it's also driven by a comfort in whiteness, and a discomfort in anything else. When we feel that discomfort, we must pause and reflect. Why didn't we feel the same way when white faces and white voices were disproportionately chosen and people of colour were omitted from these visible spaces?

Although there is a lot of time and attention devoted to race now, it's only really been a mainstream focus since the summer of 2020. It took the visible murder of a Black man at the hands of white police officers to shake us out of our complacency and challenge our complicity. We should not placate or apologise for white discomfort. The same goes for male, heterosexual or any discomfort. Discomfort is part of the process. However, if we linger on discomfort too long and we never turn the corner to harnessing the awareness into energy and action, we risk winning the 'goal' but losing the 'mission'.

Moving beyond the shouty and the divisive

The diversity agenda is not straightforward. If we are going to reduce inequality and crack inclusion, we must explore the depth of our difference, engage in the messy space and let go of the stranglehold that tolerance has on us. We must embrace the conflict and challenge the unspoken social habits which exclude, or even persecute. We don't need to blindly accept all aspects of diversity and inclusion work or be spoon-fed 'liberal idealism' or the 'woke' agenda. But we do need to be honest about the real problems we face and the reality that the answers will not be found by ignoring the messier aspects of diversity.

So how do we disagree and move on? What are the conditions needed to create positive diversity debates?

First and foremost, we must recognise that inclusion is not a one-way street. It takes two. There is an imperative from all sides to play a part if we want to make headway on this mess we have created. Progress starts when we come to the table with the aim of finding a way forward, together.

We also need to plan for the fact that we are all bound to get things wrong. When we do, we need to be ready to receive the feedback with thick enough skin to keep going. I met a senior leader a few years ago who was interested in being an ally and sent an email asking ethnic minority colleagues to share their experiences. During the process, one of her peers suggested she should 'stop being a white saviour'. She confided in me that not only had she cancelled the event, but more than six months on she was still finding it hard to re-engage on the topic of race. Who knows what went through the individual's mind when they decided to call her a white saviour? It's not a particularly helpful comment, but the senior leader's approach may have needed a course correction. If you decide to engage, people may question your intentions, and you need to be able not only to withstand the feedback, you also need to be able to take it on board and keep going.

We also need to give each other the benefit of the doubt even when we choose the wrong words or take the wrong actions.

> *You have to appreciate that someone is willing to be an ally. That they took that first step, even if it was clumsy. It's much better than nothing. With allies, we need a bit of patience and willingness to see their intent, answer questions and help them find the right path to execution. I try to be an ally for other marginalised groups and know first-hand how hard it is to speak out for others when you're terrified of saying the wrong thing or getting backlash. But now there are a*

lot of resources out there in terms of language and
how to make a stand for others in an appropriate way.
Philippa

One of the keys to success in messy diversity conversations is to focus on mutually beneficial outcomes. Most of us can agree on what good looks like. We want to live in a world that is fair. We want to live in a world where hatred and violence are not present. That is a wonderful starting point. When we lose sight of a common goal, there is a higher probability that when we disagree, we simply stop listening. Debates are not debates when they become a contest to see who can shout the loudest about their point of view.

No matter how messy, violence has no place

Madison Marriage, the journalist who went undercover to investigate and break the story about sexual harassment at the Presidents Club dinner, received a wave of support and enthusiasm for her work. She also received a deluge of negative, nasty and violent responses, which took a clear toll on her, emotionally and physically. Caroline Criado Perez, a British journalist who vocally opposed the Bank of England's decision to remove the only woman other than the queen (nineteenth-century prison reformer Elizabeth Fry) from the face of a UK bank note, received similar online hatred. As the campaign she led placed her in the spotlight, Criado Perez came under a barrage of misogynistic and violent threats.[36] Two people were jailed for sending death threats to the campaigner.

Whether it's the removal of walk-on girls and grid girls, women who push for society to be better receive some of the most horrific, hate-filled, misogynistic, violent and vile comments online. Let's face it, women who challenge the status quo are often at the receiving end of all manner of hatred. In my time leading activities to support women's equality, it's been suggested that I must be 'bitter and envious' of (beautiful) women, 'fat, ugly and nasty' or, my personal favourite, 'a feminist fucktard'.

No one should be subjected to that kind of firehose of hate – online or anywhere else. While an easy answer would be to simply suggest that women should either stop engaging in social media or ignore the venom, neither is a very realistic response. Social media, whether we like it or not, is part of the fabric of our modern society. Eliminating women's, or any other groups', ability to engage with others on the platform cuts off a key connection to the wider world. Telling victims to 'suck it up', or to leave online spaces, is not a realistic strategy.

Don't get me wrong, anger is often a positive emotion. It plays an important role and moves things forward in many ways. But virtual anger and the blind fury which is unleashed in online spaces is unhelpful. It obscures and masks the important conversations – stopping progress and preventing others from joining in for fear that they will be the next one targeted.

Whether we are talking anti-Semitism, Islamophobia, racism, sexism, ableism, homophobia, transphobia or something else entirely, violence and intimidation have no place in diversity debates. Freedom of speech does not make way for hate speech. In the UK, it's an offence to use 'threatening, abusive or insulting words or behaviour that causes, or is likely to cause, another person harassment, alarm or distress'.[37] We must have boundaries and be prepared to act when people overstep them.

Chapter 5

When Belief Systems Compete

The exploration of diversity is not always straightforward. There are fears from those in the majority (the white people, the men, the heterosexuals, those without a disability...) that inclusion of others may come at a cost to themselves. But there are also conflicts within, and between, diverse communities. Those conflicts are equally as harmful.

Inclusion requires us to look deeper. It requires us to go beyond the question 'Why are white people rising to the top?' and ask, 'Why are lighter-skinned ethnic minority or mixed-race individuals more accepted than their darker-skinned companions?' Or better yet, 'What role does colourism play in perpetuating racist norms?' Inclusion requires us to understand why a version of feminism which leaves behind women of colour is more palatable than one which lifts all women. It challenges us to interrogate why we feel differently about women who love women than we feel about men who love men or why we treat trans men differently to trans women.

The answers to these questions aren't simple. They require more sophistication and more nuanced understanding of how power, privilege and hierarchy play out around the world.

When religious beliefs limit human rights and the right to be

Religion is one of the more challenging areas of inclusion. In part, it's challenging because organisations are not trying to increase the number or percentage of individuals of a given faith or who hold particular religious beliefs within their organisation. Instead, the aim is to ensure all employees, regardless of faith, have an opportunity to openly practise their faith in the workplace without limitations to their career. It's also challenging because religion, or, perhaps more accurately, specific personal interpretations of religion, can be in direct conflict with women's rights, gay rights and transgender rights. Who wins then?

Before we answer those questions it's important to understand the variance in how faith manifests. Faith is personal, which is why we see a full spectrum of interpretations when it comes to religious texts. Whether it be from the Bible, the Qur'an, the Torah or the Vedas, personal values guide how we translate the ancient texts and what we choose to

promote (or ignore) within those translations. Religious attitudes towards homosexuality, women's rights and
transgender rights vary greatly between faiths and denominations because the personal opinions of the human beings
who interpret these texts also vary greatly.

Even within the same religion, attitudes towards the gay
community can range from acceptance (whether quiet or
vocal), to intimidation, to promotion of gay therapies to 'fix'
what is considered 'broken', to persecution and even to execution. The same is true for women. Within the same religion,
and sometimes even within the same congregation, women
can be elevated as equals or demoted in status and limited to
a very constrained existence. In my experience, faith is
always tinted by one's personal interpretation. We see in text
what we want to see, and our interpretation of faith is
clouded by the belief systems we already hold.

There are some adherents of Islam who believe women
should not be educated and yet, according to Islamic teach-
ings, education is important for all. It is only selective
readings of the Qur'an which would lead you to believe that
women should be prohibited from learning. There are some
members of the Christian faith who see homosexuality as a
sin and would choose to place judgement and restriction on
gay, lesbian and bisexual individuals, just as there are others
who choose to focus on the Bible's teaching 'Do not judge'
and believe any restriction of fundamental freedom of the
gay community is misplaced.

In her remarkable memoir *Educated*, Tara Westover begins
the book with the following statement: 'This story is not
about Mormonism. Neither is it about any other form of religious belief. In it there are many types of people, some
believers, some not; some kind, some not. The author disputes
any correlations, positive or negative, between the two.'[1]

When it comes to religion and faith, I tend to agree with Westover. There are those in every religion, and of every faith, who use it to justify cruelty, acts of violence and even murder. There are also wonderful, joyful and inclusive people in every faith. Religion is simply their conduit to express and enact those personal beliefs.

> *I belong to an ELCA [Evangelical Lutheran Church in America] church that voted to complete the 'Reconciling in Christ' process and make it clear that all are welcome and, having been created in the image of God, are worthy of love and respect. As part of the decision process, we met with many of our community neighbours with differing backgrounds and experiences: lesbian, gay, and trans people, and in some instances the parents of persons with those experiences and backgrounds. All kinds of people came.*
>
> *In my background, I know many confidences of people that I regarded as their personal information and held the information tightly. My thoughts were, prior to going through this process, that their information was between each person and their maker and, accordingly, theirs to share or not. But as we became more open as a congregation, I began to realise that I too could be more open than I was previously.*
>
> *I respect a person's right to their own beliefs, opinions, and yes, even prejudices. But I do not accept the idea that they can use it to harm or judge others. After all, these people and their experiences are part of my life too and I love them as they are (and others can also).*
>
> *Jack*

Like Jack, many people of faith choose acceptance and choose to embrace the LGBTQ+ community, but others condemn exploration of either gender or sexual orientation as sinful. The Catholic Church, for example, opposes same-sex relationships within Christian society. It also rejects both transgender and intersex people and reinforces the idea that genitalia are solely for the purposes of procreation. At the same time, other Christian denominations, such as the Church of England and the Lutheran Church, not only welcome members of the LGBTQ+ community in their congregation, but they have also ordained gay, lesbian and transgender clergy. The discrepancy between the groups shows how widely Christian belief systems vary.

Religious frictions with other aspects of diversity can feel complex but the answer is actually quite simple. Everyone is entitled to their own opinion, but no diversity category has the right to fundamentally limit the life possibilities of another. Just as heterosexual people should not be allowed to define what love is, or how it is measured, expressions of religious freedom need to be tempered when they fundamentally attempt to eliminate or restrict the core rights of another group.

In 2020, I toured the University of Westminster, one of the most ethnically diverse universities in the UK. Within the undergraduate population, people of colour make up more than 60 per cent of the student population. During my tour, the university vice-chancellor proudly showed me the dedicated lockers provided for Muslim women to keep their university textbooks on site. The extra on-site storage is intended to support the women whose families and religious expectations mean that university education is not welcomed. Some female Muslim students use the dedicated lockers to hide their textbooks and educational papers from their family to ensure they can continue learning in secret.

The university leadership were very clear that they were supportive of faith through prayer facilities, ablution rooms and student resource groups, but that support had limits. They would not support any limitation of fundamental rights, or any contradictions to their core values, under the name of religious freedom.

Not all gay people are created equal

The world treats women differently from men, and the gay world is no different. Gender intertwines with sexual orientation in many ways. From the fundamental difference in the basic rights given to gay women and gay men, to the interplay between gay rights and women's rights, the level of social acceptance for women who love women compared with men who love men, and even how open women are to bisexuality in comparison with their male counterparts, the experience of being gay is far from universal.

For starters, it has never been illegal to be a lesbian in the UK or the US. That omission is in part due to lawmakers' inability to define sexual intercourse in female terms. In fact, only forty-four of the seventy-eight countries which currently criminalise male homosexuality also explicitly criminalise same-sex relations between women. That isn't to say women are not persecuted for being gay in those countries – they often are. But gay rights sit in context to other human rights, and in those countries, women's rights are often also severely compromised – leaving women particularly vulnerable to abuse, control and violence. 'Corrective rape', a horrific process by which lesbians and gay men are subject to sexual violence, is sometimes even ordered by parents who aim to 'cure' or 'correct' a child from their same-sex attraction. It's often done to a lesbian by a male cousin, or a family friend, who forces sex against her will.[2]

Even in countries where it is legal to be gay, treatment of lesbian and bisexual women varies significantly. The way gay women are portrayed in films and the media (or in many instances, not portrayed at all) often mirrors social attitudes. Lesbian film scenes tend to be glamorised, hypersexualised and almost pornographic. They have largely been about women but positioned for the pleasure of heterosexual men. *Orange is the New Black* is an example of the changing nature of LGBTQ+-inclusive film and television. It remains hypersexualised, but for many lesbians is distinguished by a subtle change in that it feels as if it's about women *for* the pleasure of women.

In other instances, words like 'dyke' and 'butch' are used, or lesbians are depicted as 'pseudo' men, with an intention to insult or humiliate. Although butch and femme are used as positive and affirming terms by some in the lesbian community, these terms are often used by others to impose heterosexual (and binary) gender norms on a same-sex relationship.

Instead of being satisfied that it's enough for two women to love each other, individuals must be placed in masculine and feminine roles in order to validate and codify the relationship.

The reaction I have from men and women when they learn I am a lesbian is noticeably different. With women, they often ask me more about the person I am in a relationship with, they are curious about me and who I love. With men, often the first question they ask me is who is the man in my relationship. I find it an odd question. It assumes that one of us needs to be a man in order for the relationship to function.

Alicia

There are also differences in the acceptance of gay, lesbian and bisexual people by gender. Women are more likely to act inclusively towards gay and lesbian individuals and show significantly lower levels of prejudice to both lesbians and gay men.[3] Perhaps that is because the aversion we have to men who love other men is steeped in society's belief systems about masculinity.

> *My own uncle is not out. I don't want to bring him out, but I can see that he cannot be who he wants to be. My family know, but no one mentions it. No one says, 'It's okay to be who you are.' We would accept him, but the wider community would be a challenge. It's easier for gay Black and Asian women. You can hide in plain sight. But it's not easy for our men. Being gay flies in the face of the stereotype as to what a 'man' should be. Gay men in our community cause shame on the family and that's something you never want to do in the Black community.*
>
> Vivienne

Within masculinity often lies an undercurrent of anti-femininity. Gay men receive more abuse for choosing to be 'like a woman' as, for some, a man who loves another man is less than a man. That reduction of status (through feminine association) can be seen directly in terms like 'Nancy' or 'Sissy'.

Homophobic language is off-putting and stomach-churning, but what about phrases which are less easy to spot? According to the University of Atlanta, the phrase '#nohomo' has been tweeted more than 14 million times since 2012.[4] Researchers found that, more often than not, #nohomo was not being aimed at gay people. Instead, the majority of users of the phrase were heterosexual males using it to allow themselves to express positive emotional feelings such as desire, affection or friendship. The world we have created for men is so rigid that many men feel they need to explain they are not gay just to be allowed to talk about their feelings in an open setting. Unfortunately, those positive affirmations of male friendship are simultaneously used as a way to put down the gay community.

Bisexual and pansexual individuals often face altogether different challenges from their gay and lesbian counterparts. Not only is there less understanding of what it means to be bisexual, both within the gay and heterosexual community, but in the past there have been fewer people who have openly identified as bisexual than those who have openly identified as gay or lesbian. Today, of the 7.1 per cent of Americans who openly identify as LGBT, more than half indicate they are bisexual.[5]

Bisexual individuals often face personal judgements about their character. Some judgement comes from the assumption that bisexuality is either akin to youth experimentation, and therefore something which one should grow out of, or that bisexuality goes hand in hand with either promiscuity or polyamorous relationships. A frequent bias about bisexual individuals is that their sexual orientation is as a result of 'indecision'. That judgement can lead to wider assumptions about the character of bisexual individuals, leading some to question whether being bisexual is part of a larger inability to be decisive, to follow through or to commit.

Sometimes bisexual individuals find themselves the recipients of intrusive questions, in a way that lesbian and gay individuals often do not.

When people become aware of my bisexuality it can lead to all sorts of intimate questions. 'Do you prefer girls or guys?' or 'What percentage are you?' are two which I frequently encounter. I wouldn't want to discourage people who are learning, but the tendency is to ask more invasive questions when you are bisexual than a gay or lesbian person might be asked.

Sometimes it's because people have never met anyone who is openly bisexual and they are curious. Other times you can feel the questions are more disparaging. It's as if your overall credibility is being questioned simply because of who you love. Although I am quite open about my bisexuality, these types of questions can be challenging when I am already trying to establish myself as a woman in technology.

Katy

Like trans individuals, bisexual people are a minority within a minority. It's easy to assume their experience is identical to that of gay or lesbian individuals, or that their unique needs are covered by the group at large. Unfortunately, that isn't always the case. The gay community can be particularly tough on bisexual individuals. At times, they are not allowed into close-knit lesbian and gay communities because they are not always seen as 'proper gays'. Some gay men even claim that bisexual men are just easing themselves into being properly gay or trying to hold on to a fig-leaf of masculinity by saying that they are still into women.

Making sure bisexual voices are heard rather than erased, and bisexual individuals are embraced rather than rejected, is an important step for broader LGBTQ+ inclusion.

White people aren't the only racists

Racism knows no bounds. It is not confined to any class, nor is it something that only white people do. While white individuals often hold a disproportionate amount of power, and therefore their behaviours have a cumulatively greater effect on people of colour, racist attitudes also exist within and between ethnic minority communities.

> *In several parts of India, there are many forms of acceptable discrimination. The social hierarchy means we place no value in certain roles in society. A cleaner, for example, is treated with almost no dignity. That openness with discrimination feeds into racism. Many Asians see themselves as above the Black community. The hierarchy is clear. It also leads to a separation. Many people feel 'I can rise, but I cannot let others rise as well – there isn't room for us both.'*
>
> *Shipra*

It doesn't matter where you were born, around the world, dark skin is demonised. Colourism, or the discrimination against dark-skinned people, and anti-blackness, racial prejudice aimed directly at Black people, are prime examples of how racism happens both to and within a community.

> *Anti-blackness is deep even within the Desi (those from the Indian subcontinent and their diaspora). It's rife. Many in my community believe stereotypes of Black people that they've seen portrayed in mainstream media and tabloids. They see themselves as 'better immigrants', that are educated and don't turn to crime.*

It is not just here in the UK, anti-blackness and col-ourism exist all over South Asia. Those who do well in Bollywood have lighter skin. They are heroes and her-oines. Those with darker skin are usually portrayed as villains.

Being Asian, I have the privilege of being a 'model minority'. Our community places high social value on academic success, meaning we end up being seen as the 'good' kind of immigrant. There are a lot of oppor-tunities for Asians to create space, but many try to distance themselves from the Black community. We have forgotten, but historically we partnered with the Black community to fight against injustice in this country. As we had to assimilate to survive, we have cut ties in fear that bringing others along will drag us down. Instead of trying to shed off being brown, we need to shut that shit [racism] down and create an inclusive environment.

Niran

All around the world we are sold a narrative that sug-gests white is better and that lighter skin is not only more beautiful, but also somehow connected to a purity in char-acter. Some of that narrative is based upon historic class systems where darker skin was a clear indicator that one worked in the fields, but even in societies where advances in farming technology mean very few humans are needed to work crops, the hierarchy of skin colour still prevails. The global prevalence of skin-lightening products such as Unilever's Glow & Lovely (known until 2020 as 'Fair & Lovely') are an interesting indicator of just how pervasive the 'whiter is better' narrative is.[6] Skin-lightening creams are even sold for the vaginal area, in case your vaginal skin tone is 'having a direct impact on your self-esteem'.[7] Incomprehensible!

Your colour is not in my rainbow

The rainbow flag has been a symbol of Pride for the LGBTQ+ community for more than forty years.[8] It represents the visible colours of the light spectrum and the ongoing efforts to counter the societal shame placed upon the community with feelings of positivity and pride. There is, and always has been, strength and unity within the LGBTQ+ community. Being different is what sets many gay, lesbian, bisexual and transgender people apart. But that unity has not always come uniformly to everyone under the rainbow umbrella.

When you look at the lesbian, gay and bisexual community through the lens of race, there are some startling differences. People living in the UK are half as likely to identify as lesbian, gay or bisexual if they are Black or Asian than if they are white.[9] The reality is many African, Asian and Latin countries are places where being gay is still illegal or widely condemned as a 'moral sin'. Those international attitudes spill over into local ones where, within the UK, gay ethnic minority individuals are less likely to receive support within their own communities.

Acceptance of gay, lesbian and bisexual individuals is sometimes tied to the point in time when immigrant communities came to the UK. Although attitudes are shifting around the world, like many other cultural norms, immigrant attitudes towards gay or trans individuals can be rigidly connected to a specific era. Meanwhile, back in the country from which they emigrated, attitudes and social norms move on without their knowledge.

> *The reality is that, even with my own parents, I live life half and half. I have a life that is out and then one which is in.*
>
> *My mother doesn't know I am gay. My reasons for not telling her are complicated. She's been unwell for many years but that's not the only reason. She's also not accepting of the gay community. It's as if she's stuck in a historical moment. Her view on a 'traditional family' is very strong. She believes that if you are gay, you can't have a family and that gives a person no reason to live. I've even heard her refer to gay people as 'disgusting'. Her views are narrow-minded and of a particular time in India – the moment when she left – but India is moving on.*
>
> *My dad is also Indian, and he knows I am gay. He's met my partner. With my dad, I don't have to hide who I am.*
>
> *Vinod*

In 2005, the first ever Black Pride march took place in the UK and has been an annual event ever since.[10] It has taken years for the broader LGBTQ+ community to accept the need for specific events and conversations which look at the unique experience of gay people of colour. Black Pride is an opportunity not only to celebrate the LGBTQ+ community, but to look at the specific challenges queer people of colour face.

> *Some homophobia stems from the high levels of religion within the Black community. It's how you've been taught*

so you adopt the practice of ignorance. But some of it is
due to the fact that you're already an outsider. You don't
want to associate with someone else who is an outsider,
because you're trying to assimilate. So instead, you shun.
And if you don't shun, you keep quiet.

                                                                Vivienne

It's clear that more needs to be done within all ethnic
minority communities to support gay, lesbian, bisexual and
transgender individuals, but to suggest that all challenges
between race and sexual orientation are one-sided would be
inaccurate. Racism is a stain which affects all aspects of society, and the gay community is no exception. Segregation has
existed in the gay community just as segregation existed
elsewhere.

The Stonewall uprising of 1969, which was a key catalyst
in the gay rights movement, was not an isolated struggle. The
US was in the midst of a civil rights revolution. The protests
between the LGBTQ+ community and police happened only
a year after Martin Luther King Jr had been assassinated and
just months after Shirley Chisolm had been sworn in as the
first Black woman in Congress. Some of the most prominent
figures of the Stonewall rebellion were people of colour,
including Sylvia Rivera,[11] a Latina gay liberation and transgender rights activist, and Marsha P. Johnson, a Black drag
queen.[12] Witnesses suggest that it was Stormé DeLarverie, a
Black lesbian and drag king, who threw the first punch on
that fateful day in June in New York's Greenwich Village.[13]
Although DeLarverie, Rivera and Johnson were among the
founding members of the gay liberation movement, the relationship between the gay community and the trans community,
or between white communities and communities of colour,
has not, by any means, been straightforward.

Despite the clear gender non-conformity of Rivera, Johnson and DeLarverie, trans acceptance by the mainstream lesbian, gay and bisexual community has been a bumpy ride. Trans folks, like bisexual individuals, are a less visible subset of the community and are set apart due to the fact that being transgender isn't about who you love or who you are attracted to. Because trans individuals represent less than 1 per cent of the world's population, and because their difference is not about sexual orientation, transgender individuals often find themselves on the periphery of LGBTQ+ circles.

Recent efforts by Stonewall and the LGBT Foundation (two prominent UK LGBTQ+ charities) to embrace and include the trans community can make it seem that the transgender agenda is being tagged onto something which was meant only for the gay community, but that isn't the case. While gender identity is different from sexual orientation, prominent trans individuals have been part of the LGBTQ+ community throughout the course of the gay-rights struggle. By the time Stonewall and the LGBT Foundation officially moved to include transgender rights in their core purpose, they were outliers. Inclusion of the trans community had already become a standard in America, Australia and Canada.

Stonewall have come under significant fire both for their inclusion of the trans community but also for what some suggest is a blinkered and 'extremist stance' on their approach to trans inclusion.[14] They may very well have made mistakes and been overly rigid in their approach. Unfortunately, supporting trans inclusion, and specifically supporting trans rights to self-ID (which Stonewall do), is a political football. Their decision to become a trans-inclusive organisation has been met with a healthy challenge from some, but more often than not, it means that the Stonewall leadership are at the receiving end of a deluge of hate, which even comes from members of the gay, lesbian and bisexual community. Just as racism isn't owned by white people, prejudice towards the trans community and transphobia are just as likely to come from members of the lesbian, gay and bisexual community as they are to come from heterosexuals when they feel threatened by the increase in trans rights.[15] That's how phobia works. It drives an exaggerated sense of danger or threat about a situation, an object or a person.[16]

When trans women win, (cis) women do *not* automatically lose

As transgender individuals become more visible, and as the number of people who openly identify as trans increases, so does the backlash against the transgender community. That backlash is most often aimed at trans women and can be both extreme and aggressive.

There are individuals who are openly hostile and proudly ignorant as to what it means to be transgender and do not welcome the questions which the trans community brings to gendered ways of life. But not all groups who find trans and gender non-conforming individuals a threat are driven by sheer ignorance. In my inclusion work, I've come across several distinct groups who find transgender rights a challenge: individuals whose interpretation of faith presents transgender individuals as a threat, those who work to end men's violence against women and girls, and a subset of feminists and gay rights activists who see trans inclusion as a threat to feminism and progress for cis women more broadly.

We discussed the wide variance in how the trans community are either welcomed or shunned by religious groups earlier in this chapter. But what about women who have spent their lives picking up the pieces when men have caused great harm to women? They know first-hand the repercussions of sexual violence, rape and the murder of women. For very real reasons, some in this group find it hard to understand how allowing individuals (who they see as men) in bathrooms, changing rooms and other spaces of vulnerability can be anything other than a threat. The reality is that when you spend your days cleaning up the physical and emotional damage left behind by predatory and violent men, it can become challenging to see trans women as anything other than a danger to women. When the media perpetuate the idea of trans women as a threat, it deepens both bias and fear.

One of the most vocal groups which sees transgender rights and gender identity discussions as a threat are the subset of feminists and lesbians who have fought their whole lives to champion equal rights for women. When you work so hard to create a world which is better for women and girls, accepting trans women can not only feel like an erasure of women's and gay rights, it can also feel like a traitorous assault on feminism. These women are often labelled as TERFs (trans exclusionary radical feminists). The term TERF, like all intentionally derogatory labels, does little to move the conversation forward.

I've met more than a handful of cis women who have significant concerns that young women are coached or 'lured' into becoming trans men, either because life as a woman doesn't grant them the rights they covet, or their religious communities see becoming trans as a way to avoid being lesbian. It's easy to dismiss those who fear that trans rights are eroding women's rights, but their fear is real, even if the cause of that fear may be false.

There is no evidence to show trans women are disproportionate perpetrators of abuse towards women. Quite the opposite, in fact. The common enemy is the cisgender male perpetrator of violence, sexual and domestic abuse – not trans women.

When the author J. K. Rowling wrote her open letter to the world to defend her comments about trans individuals online, and, I suspect, to stop the deluge of 'TERF' accusations being hurled at her through cyberspace, many people watching missed the issue. Rowling has one of the most far-reaching online profiles in the world and her letter made a connection between trans individuals and violence to women. The sheer scale of her reach did instantaneous and global harm in connecting the two, despite her claim not being evidence-based.

I love J. K. Rowling's books. It is because of her incredible capability as an author that not only are my children growing up with Harry Potter as a core character in their lives, but they are also growing up with a deep belief in magic. For that, I will be forever grateful.

I also sympathise with Rowling on many levels. I too have come from a poor background. I too have suffered sexual abuse at the hands of a man.[17] But I cannot agree with her suggestion that for vulnerable cis women to be okay, trans women cannot be in the same spaces. I have searched far and wide and cannot find any evidence to suggest that is the case. Not in the UK, not in the US, not anywhere in the world.[18] The evidence I do find is clear: fears of increased safety and privacy violations are not empirically grounded.[19]

> *Women are getting angry because it's [men assaulting women] been happening for so long and when it does happen to us, we get told, 'Well it wasn't that bad', or 'Don't make a big deal about it.' As women, we spend our lives mitigating the risk. Perhaps that's why we see*

girls' spaces as so sacred. It's a place where they can get away from all those things and be free. It's okay for us to want those spaces because we have spent centuries fighting for them.

The challenge comes because some people think men will transition to get at women. But I don't see it and I don't believe it. If men want to get at women, they just do it. And they do it all the time.

Elly

I don't agree with Rowling's assessment of the risk, but I also don't condone the abuse that she received. It's unacceptable. I think she was trying to be vocal about her concerns and honest about her lived experience. Unfortunately, the inferred statement she made that suggested that when trans women win, cis women automatically lose, not only caused a lot of harm for the trans community, but it also detracted from the important focus we need on male perpetration of violence against women.

Conversations about any potential conflict of rights are not easy, not least because of the high emotions the subject tends to create. Women around the world are asking for support in eradicating sexual and violent abuse. Women who have suffered trauma need support – both cis and trans women alike. We need a continued push for women's rights, rather than stopping where we are today, in a place where women are 'almost' equal. At the same time, trans individuals are asking for dignity. They are asking not to be vilified, humiliated or mocked by the media. They are asking for their personal transition process to be less clumsy, less medical and less dehumanising. They are asking for understanding and compassion and to have a say in their own future, rather than have it defined by others.

We can do both. It won't be easy, and it won't necessarily be straightforward. There are specific trans inclusion challenges we must face into. Inclusion in sport, and competitive sport in particular, is one of those issues. I am a woman who has been shaped and enhanced by my relationship with sport. I was not a natural athlete by any means. My father often joked about my having 'two left feet'. I was clumsy in everyday athletic activities, but he would have been the first to tell you that if you give me enough time to figure my way round a court, with a ball, or on a field, I will eventually find my way to success. Participation in sport has given me much of the deep confidence I have today. Not because it was easy, but because it wasn't. Sport taught me that if I kept going, I would eventually get there.

I am also a cis woman who is passionate about both fairness and inclusion, and someone who has been actively working to change the women's sport landscape. We need widespread and immediate focus on increasing women's sponsorship and funding, increasing TV/print/digital news coverage, achieving equal pay, creating decent facilities, protecting against trolls, and removing sexualised sporting kit. We also need visible stories and role models who showcase to the world what a healthy muscular body can be. Trans women's inclusion in sport is showcased as an urgent problem, but there are many other pressing issues which have more widespread impact on women's and girls' participation in sport. We do need to solve it, but when someone jumps in on the 'trans women in sport' debate but isn't willing to show up for any of the other issues facing girls and women in sport, we should question their intentions. They aren't here to support women; they are here to block trans women.

I do see the frustration that the participation of trans women in competitive sport creates, as well as the dent it makes in fairness. I also see the importance of inclusion in sport for any individual. Sporting bodies are finding their way in this space. They have a tough gig. They must balance the science behind physical development by sex, the unique aspects of each sport, keep a focus on personal safety – especially where body contact is involved – and create a fine balance between inclusion and fairness. We don't have a perfect solution yet, but the science is evolving to give us a better picture. The way forward will require working together and adjusting if we get it wrong – as we inevitably will. Working together is only possible when we stop seeing the trans community as a threat.

Women have been redefining their role in society for millennia. If we can create the right conditions to have calm and considered conversations in this space, we can find a positive way forward, and not accidentally make trans rights a monumental distraction from the inclusion and treatment of women in society more broadly. There is space for both women's rights and trans rights, but we have to aim to find it.

Feminism is an ongoing quest to ensure all women are treated equally and fairly. As soon as any kind of feminism cuts out or starts to remove Black women, women of colour, religious women or trans women, it ceases to be feminism.

Feminists have been fighting not to be defined by their body, and instead be recognised for their mind. It's ironic that those who are behind the anti-trans movement are saying trans women aren't women, because of their body.

Trans people are not delusional. We are very well aware of what we can change and what we cannot. I

*know I still have an XY chromosome, and that will
never change. But I also know that chromosomes are
irrelevant. There are an infinite number of versions as
to what being a woman is. Women are redefining those
parameters every day. If I'm not woman 'enough' to be
a woman, you have a very narrow definition of what a
woman is.*

Hannah

The road forward will not be easy. It will require new
levels of calmness and conscious conversation as well as a
change in attitude on all sides. In order to explore transgender inclusion in the depth we need to, we must let go of the
belief that if trans people win, someone else loses. We must
also be mindful that the mantra of 'some people are trans,
get over it' isn't entirely helpful. It is challenging to move to
immediate and unconditional support of the trans community without looking at some of the fundamental frictions
that unconditional support creates.

Trans positivity and trans pride are crucial elements of
any constructive path forward. If our aim is to get past the
current lack of understanding, the misinformation and the
twisted emotions, we must take a different approach. We
must create an environment where asking our awkward
questions, hearing the life stories of transgender individuals,
and balancing fears and emotions which arise in the cis community with data and evidence, simply become part of the
way we move forward together.

The bathroom block

The bathroom and changing room debate is at the heart of many anti-trans arguments. Which facilities should a trans person use? Should it be the bathroom of their birth sex or the bathroom of their gender identity? If we allow trans individuals into the bathrooms of their gender identity, are we placing members of the cis community at risk?

Bathrooms serve a basic human need. They are a private place to pee, poop, change a tampon and make sure we feel and look ready for the outside world. Gender aside, very few of us are comfortable talking about or sharing the experience of what goes on in a toilet. Bodily functions are simply not for public display.

Both bathrooms and changing rooms are also a place of unique vulnerability. A place where we can literally be caught with our pants down. For some, sharing a bathroom with a trans woman increases their sense of vulnerability. They worry that allowing trans women access to women's bathrooms and changing rooms will result in increased violence against women. This is in part due to experiences in the past where cis men have behaved inappropriately, vulgarly or with violence towards women.

If you have experienced sexual violence or predatory behaviour, enclosed spaces such as the bathroom can be a particularly exposing space, but the assumption that trans women pose a risk to cis women must not go unchecked. There is no evidence to suggest that trans inclusivity in public facilities such as restrooms and changing rooms increases the predatory threat to cis women. Unfortunately, fear and perception remain so high that more than 300 US organisations which support victims of sexual or domestic violence have come together to oppose anti-transgender initiatives and challenge the myth that providing transgender access to restrooms and changing rooms is a threat: 'As rape crisis centers, shelters, and other service providers who work each and every day to meet the needs of all survivors and reduce sexual assault and domestic violence throughout society, we speak from experience and expertise when we state that these claims are false.'[20]

Vulnerability in this space isn't one-sided. When it comes to bathrooms, the group most likely to fall victim are transgender individuals. The Williams Institute at UCLA completed a study on gendered restrooms in America and found that 70 per cent of trans or gender non-conforming respondents reported being denied access to the bathroom or being verbally harassed when attempting to use the facilities.[21] Ten per cent of transgender individuals also reported being physically assaulted in public restrooms. Even more gruesome is the fact that many trans individuals find themselves victims of sexual assault in those confined bathroom spaces. A Harvard study of teenage trans experiences found that 36 per cent of transgender or non-binary students with restricted bathroom or locker room access reported being sexually assaulted in those facilities in the last twelve months.[22]

> *Bathroom segregation has happened at many points in history. Bathrooms in America were segregated based on the colour of your skin. That segregation was never about white rights, it was about bigotry. Years later, heterosexual men didn't want to share bathrooms with gay men, but it wasn't about bathrooms, it was about bigotry. Those that promote the idea that trans women are a threat to cis women in the bathroom or the changing room are doing the same thing. It's just bigotry. And it isn't fact-based. The person most*

> *likely to come to harm in a bathroom is a trans person,*
> *but they would have you believe it's the other way*
> *around.*
>
> *Jake*

While the trans debate is much more than a bathroom debate, it is important we work out our bathroom issues. At a basic level, we all need safe spaces to pee; trans women and cis women are no different in this respect. We also need changing rooms at the pool, in clothes shops, and at the gym. While there is no evidence to suggest that allowing transgender individuals access to bathrooms increases the risk to cis-women bathroom users, we cannot deny the fact that sharing these personal spaces does cause anxiety for some individuals.

Today the bathroom debate has become a fight about who is 'more' vulnerable, trans women or cis women. That debate doesn't help anyone. It hasn't helped that when facilities are adapted to be trans-inclusive, the change is often done without the accompanying conversations and support to understand why these facilities are so important. It also doesn't help when we don't consider the total bathroom experience. Short cubicles offer very little privacy, regardless of who is in the toilet next to you, whereas bathroom designs that include more self-contained spaces would certainly reduce vulnerability for all parties.

We don't often talk about mixed-sex changing rooms when it comes to transgender debates, but in countries like Germany, Austria, Switzerland and the Netherlands public changing areas where individuals are not separated on the basis of sex are common. There are even occasional occurrences at local pools and changing rooms at retailers in the UK. Seeing the bits and bobs of others is normalised instead of being sexualised in those scenarios.

To move beyond where we are today, we need to recognise the emotions which arise, and help people through to the other side. Some people may never want to share a bathroom or a closed space with a trans person, but with better facility design, increased privacy and/or supervision in restrooms, more open conversation about the basic needs of all parties, and more time to adapt, the discomfort that many now feel will fade away. To make that transition, we must challenge perceptions, bring facts to the fore, and work together to fight the real threat to women's safety – predatory men.

How young is too young?

Since its creation in 1989, the UK's National Health Service gender identity service for children has seen exponential growth. Less than one hundred individuals sought support in the first year, but in 2016, more than 1,400 girls and 616 boys accessed the service.[23] Today, thousands of children remain on the waiting list for support.[24] It is not entirely clear as to why girls are seeking gender identity support at greater rates than boys but there are a number of theories. The first is that girls are more likely than boys to seek treatment for anything mental-health-related. In addition, girls who are seeking to change their gender are met more often with acceptance. When you live in a world where men are at the top of the pyramid, the desire to be a man can be seen as a desire to have an upgrade in status. On the other hand, when a boy chooses to transition to live as a girl, he is seen as downgrading his social status. As a consequence, he is less likely to be accepted, more likely to be noticed as different, and more likely to be labelled as 'weird' than a girl who chooses to transition the other way.

The steep rise in children seeking support on gender identity raises a whole host of questions. When are you old enough to make life-altering decisions about your body? At what age does referring to yourself as the opposite sex or enjoying gender-role swaps during imaginative play move from childhood exploration to the emergence of gender dysphoria, or a disassociation with one's sex at birth? If we allow for such role play, are we somehow contributing to gender identity confusion? Will the choices our kids make today have permanent consequences for their future? Is trying on a new gender a bit of a fad? Will kids grow out of it, like last year's fashion? At what age do we simply say 'I believe you'?

There are a lot of questions and a lot of emotions in this space, as well as a lot of ridicule from individuals who portray trans children as deluded or being somehow guided by 'woke' parents who want to create trans children.

It is true that we have seen exponential growth of young people who identify under the trans umbrella. Many people assume the increase is due to the fact that more people than ever before are transgender. However, a more likely answer is that growth in visible trans individuals has been created by a more accepting cultural atmosphere which allows those who have a gender and sex disconnect, or those who feel they don't fit neatly on the binary gender spectrum, to explore their gender identity in a more public way. In her highly compelling and well-considered book *The Transgender Issue*, Shon Faye suggests that 'This is a perilous misunderstanding of the reality; in fact, there aren't greater numbers of children asserting a trans identity than there were in times past. There are simply more children who feel able to talk about it openly and seek support and advocacy from their parents.'[25]

Common sense also suggests that the rise in children who

identify under the trans umbrella is partly due to fact that kids today have better tools and language to talk about things which existed previously but were not allowed to be discussed. There are also a growing number of children who don't buy into the historic gendered bullshit in which my and previous generations were steeped. Being transgender, queer or non-binary allows them to give two fingers to the outdated aspects of our social constructs.

> *Trans individuals used to have to hide. My older peers kept it a secret because it was the 'done' thing. It was binary then. People haven't changed, but how we express gender, how we are allowed to deal with gender and sex conflicts, has changed. Most trans people pick the road which is less traumatic – stay who I am in misalignment, or transition – because you had to pick. The rise in transgender individuals is not because people have changed, it's because our framework is changing. We weren't allowed to have those honest conversations. We should be allowed to talk about it, if not celebrate it, and include trans into our structures. We can all learn and benefit from this.*
>
> *Ayla*

Many trans individuals say they, like their lesbian, gay and bisexual counterparts, have known from early adolescence. Others don't become aware of the conflict between the sex they were assigned at birth and their gender identity until a much later age. Given the variance as to when individuals begin to feel the conflict, it makes it challenging to know the difference between playful experimentation and something much more fundamental.

As our awareness of gender identity grows, and our access

to more widespread support grows, our worries also grow. We worry that allowing children to openly explore gender identity is creating a disproportionate number of non-binary or transgender children. We worry that if being trans is something that gives you attention at school, children could be drawn to changing their gender identity and possibly making decisions with irreversible lifelong consequences, which they later regret.

> *Children are different than grown-ups. I do have worries about trans kids because I remember how hard it was to be a kid. Children are much more likely to be influenced by group think. Things which seem cool, like self-harm for instance, can spread like wildfire.*
>
> *As someone who struggled with my own burgeoning sexuality and puberty and wished desperately to escape from my problematic body to become more androgynous (or rather more immature) – it disturbs me. Children's thoughts and opinions and beliefs can change so fluidly.*
>
> *Elly*

I know a lot of individuals like Elly. Individuals who worry that being overly flexible with gender exploration will create more long-term harm – for our children and our society at large. Parents make decisions which contradict the desires of their children all the time. We force them to eat broccoli and other vegetables, despite daily protests. We force them away from TVs, iPads and other devices and encourage them to go outside and play. We coach them towards music, sport, languages and other activities that they don't see the point of until later in life. We contradict and overrule our kids regularly, because, as parents, sometimes we do know better, and some decisions they may live to regret.

But there is an important distinction between asking your kids to eat their broccoli and trying to limit their exploration of gender or sexual orientation. Exploring gender isn't inherently unhealthy. And, although we as parents may guide our children throughout their life, we don't get to choose who they become or who they love.

> *You have authority as a parent. You choose what they are playing with and who they are seeing. You get to lead on many things with your child. But when you are making decisions about a child's identity, they are the authority. You cannot choose how they identify, or how they see themselves. You can give love and support. You can care about their feelings, but you cannot tell them what to feel.*
>
> Jake

We get to choose a lot as a parent, but we don't get to choose who our children will become. Self-understanding, self-care and sense of self are some of the most important things that our children ultimately own.

Decisions around gender identity are critical to positive self-development. According to UK LGBTQ+ charity Stonewall, more than 80 per cent of young trans people have self-harmed and one in ten trans pupils have received death threats at school.[26] In a 2021 German study of psychological distress among trans adolescents, 50 per cent had experienced suicidal thoughts, self-harm and bullying.[27] Bullying and humiliation of transgender children is very real. Unfortunately, the perpetrators are often adults and even the parents of the trans child who want to shame the child back into gender conformity. If we create a world where we don't help, are we adding to that harm? When someone is emotionally and physically unwell from the gender–sex disconnect which they experience, no treatment is a poor option.

When it comes to supporting children, gender specialists are guided to look for 'consistence, persistence, insistence, and history of gender nonconformity'.[28] They work with parents to create a supportive environment that lets kids lead the process of establishing their own identity. That 'let them be' approach feels logical to me. For some children, the playful gender-swapping games are just that, playful games. For others, the disconnected sense of self, and disconnect between how they feel and how they live, is no game. Our challenge as adults, parents and carers is to help children through what is a tough developmental journey at the best of times. Teenage years can be excruciating regardless. Mental health is a real issue for all children, not just transgender children – even more so with the rise of social media and social expectation.

Helping our children figure out what is real and right for them, through all stages of development, is critical. Some will identify as trans as teenagers. For some, exploring gender non-conformity is part of the exploration of modernising social norms, but that doesn't mean we should automatically dismiss their choice as something they are doing just to be 'on trend'. Nor should we assume that every child who seeks specialist support from a gender identity clinic will emerge from the process reaffirmed as transgender. Many children seek out support, which they are given, and ultimately find better alignment between their gender and the sex they were assigned at birth. We don't hear about those cases as they are less 'media worthy'.

Unfortunately, there is a lot of misinformation about what supporting a child means. If a child is younger, and they want to change their name, play with different toys, or wear a dress, letting your child feel safe, feel heard and able to express themselves is the most important thing you can do.

People jump to conversations about puberty blockers or surgery. Supporting a child isn't really about those things. It's really about listening, hearing, taking it seriously. It's also about not thinking or hoping it's just a phase. It may be, and they may change their minds, and that's okay. But it's also okay if it's not a phase.

We have to be realistic – everyone has hopes and dreams and expectations about the future for their children. When things don't go to plan, it takes a while to get your head around it. You will feel emotion, and likely a sense of loss of what could have been. But it's important we don't project our own sense of disappointment, of shame or secrecy on your child. Just because your child is queer or trans doesn't mean your dreams die, it just means you need to reimagine them.

When it comes down to it, supporting children who are questioning is really all about saying 'I love you'.

Jake

There are a lot of considerations to supporting a child who is gender questioning, but what I am struck most by is the importance of unconditional love. Family, friends, teachers and medical professionals all play a role in helping gender-questioning children live a fulfilling life. While we may not be entirely sure about what to do, our support and our unconditional love matter.

There are no easy answers in this space, only careful and considered choices, which is why most gender clinics have a purposely slow process in order to ensure there is ample space and time for self-exploration and conscious decision making. There will be questions and choices, but for young children *none* of those choices will include surgery or interventions which are known to be irreversible. Gender-identity youth support is geared towards helping a child manage their mental health and allow them the freedom to choose a more permanent physical transition when they become an adult.

Up until the point of puberty, support for children is purely social and can include changing names, pronouns, clothes or hairstyles. At the point of puberty, some children may choose to take puberty blockers, which are intended to help a child to manage their mental health. According to the NHS, the Mayo Clinic and other widely trusted medical organisations, the physical effects of puberty blockers are considered reversible. They simply pause puberty – which can resume once a child stops taking blockers. Although little is known about the long-term psychological effects of taking puberty blockers, not supporting a child who feels an unresolved fundamental sex and gender disconnect can also have serious long-term mental health consequences. Parents and doctors are constantly facing decisions about what the most positive path forward is likely to be for a child.

It isn't until the age of sixteen (and with parental consent) that children in the UK[29] or US can consider cross-sex hormones or, in very rare cases, surgery.[30] Those cross-sex hormones are only given after a thorough clinical review with parents and children to ensure both patient and parent are fully informed. Because of the level of irreversibility, surgery is only done when all other interventions have failed to alleviate a person's gender dysphoria. The phrase 'first do no harm' comes to mind when I consider the balancing act of treatment for children who are in their late teens, but not yet fully fledged adults.

This is a complicated and emotive space. There are many individuals with real worries about the long-term health for children if we get gender treatment wrong. But despite all those worries, very few people I meet have done any research to see what treatment is available to children, what the process is for support, and whether or not treatments given to young people are reversible or not. If we are genuinely worried about irreversible consequences of transitioning, why don't more people support the concept of non-binary? It isn't the only answer, but it would certainly allow some children to find their path, and avoid some of the challenges presented by a binary transition.

Aiming for a win-win

Looking at the totality of the issues we face, along with the complexity of competing belief systems, can make inclusion seem impossible. Simple solutions which don't take into account the complex nature of human emotions, or the wide range of personal motivations in this space, are unlikely to work. But if we wallow in the complexity we risk getting lost in a never-ending sea of disagreement. So how do we lean into these divergences and still find a positive path forward?

First and foremost, we must recognise that these disagreements and frictions exist around the fringes of the diversity agenda. Though these disagreements can be quite visible, when we look at them through the lens of proportion, we can see that they sit on the periphery. We don't need to be mesmerised or held back by them, but we do need to be prepared, and have thoughtful ways in which we can engage, when they do emerge.

Secondly, when tensions arise between groups, we need to take accountability if we played a role in causing them. For example, when organisational leaders and diversity professionals created a 'women's' agenda, but it only worked for white women and did not embrace, support or seek out the unique experiences of women of colour, we underestimated the complexity of the problem. Let's be honest, most of the diversity agenda from the late 1980s until very recently sits in that exact space. Instead, we need to create environments for white women and women of colour to work together – to become allies for each other, and to address the unique and shared challenges different groups of women face.

And finally, we need to aim for the win-win. These competing belief systems make us feel that, in order for someone to win, someone else has to lose, but that doesn't have to be the case. When we root out misogyny and violence against women, men win too. When we break open what it means to be successful and help men find aspects of life that give them joy, passion and make them feel alive outside of work, we free men from a race to the top of the leadership pile. That freedom creates more space for women. It also means more men doing laundry. When the trans community rips up the rule book on what it means to be a man or a woman, we free up cis men and cis women to do the same. The win-win of inclusion is there for the taking, but we will only be able to seize it when we stop treating diversity as a zero-sum game.

That isn't to say that inclusion is a win for everyone all of the time. It isn't. When we unpick the structures that perpetuate discrimination, individuals who benefit from those systems of power will inevitably lose something, but they won't lose everything. But if they were the ones who disproportionately received jobs, were granted coveted roles or enjoyed easier access to leaders, they will have to work harder. They will have to shine brighter in order to stand out in a world which doesn't automatically elevate them ahead of others.

This book is in two parts. The first chapters were created to provide you with a strong foundation in some of the most complex diversity issues of our time: sex, gender identity, sexual orientation and race. These four are the primary focus areas for the book. Other subjects such as age, faith and religion, mental health, parenting, caring, class, socio-economic status, neurodiversity and disability are mentioned in a cursory sort of way. That is not because they are not important – they are. It is simply because there isn't enough space to cover everything in a meaningful way.

I chose these four areas of focus because they create some of the highest levels of hesitation in people. If we can find a way forward with these emotive and complex elements of diversity, we can find our way through anything. I also chose these four because, despite how different they are, there are clear overlaps and joins. Some people call this intersectionality. Intersectionality means that no person experiences the world through just one dimension, and diversity is no different. It's impossible that your experience as a man is not shaped by your experience as a white, brown or Black man. Nor is your experience not guided by whether you are a man with or without disability, a man who is gay or a man who is heterosexual.

But the connection I see between these subjects is more than intersectionality. It's about how we approach diversity with a focus on behavioural understanding. Because many of the issues are the same, regardless of the group, though they may manifest in a different way. The 80-20 rule, which is so often applied to give focus on the important and meaningful, applies here. It doesn't matter what the diversity characteristic is, in my experience, 80 per cent of the concepts are the same. Roughly 20 per cent is unique to that group only. Whether we are talking about social norms, how history casts a long shadow into the future, the limited approach we take to workplace diversity, or how we understand and create inclusion, much of what we need to do as an ally is similar, despite each group being different. I've explicitly written the book through that shared lens, rather than looking at each group individually, to help you understand the common elements of inclusion and allyship.

I hope that you have reached this point in the book with a deeper awareness and deeper empathy, but also with a deeper hunger to know what you can do differently to make the world a fairer, more inclusive place. If so, the next chapters are intended to help solidify your understanding of inclusion and to help you choose a meaningful and active role in the future.

Part II

Chapter 6

Lessons in Inclusion

*'It isn't enough to talk about peace.
One must believe in it. And it isn't enough
to believe in it. One must work at it.'*
Eleanor Roosevelt[1]

We make an assumption that people know what inclusion is and how to do it, but can a person simply act inclusively if they choose to? Is it a matter of mindset? Or does inclusion require something more? In my experience, it helps to start from a place of curiosity and empathy, but inclusion requires more than intention. It requires both knowledge and confidence, and the gap between the inclusion skills we have and the inclusion skills we need is sizeable.

That skill deficit means that when it comes to inclusion and diversity most of us are making it up as we go along. In a fast-paced and attention-seeking society, most of us know enough to get by but very few of us have a genuine depth of understanding. And why should we? There was no course at school on race relations, no syllabus for reversing the effects of unconscious bias, combatting homophobia or spotting everyday sexism. In the workplace, where diversity training is most likely to be found, we often cram training into short e-learning modules. But how effective is an online course at helping us change behaviours in a space which is complex, fractious and underpinned by deeply embedded social norms?

Skills in inclusion are sorely needed. But such skills are rarely invested in, which means we often stumble upon inclusion by accident, rather than by design. My own inclusive skill journey began with a surprise awakening in 2009 and it's still ongoing. I used to think I was 'inclusive', but the reality is I had no idea what inclusion even was. How can anyone be good at something when they don't fully understand what it is they are trying to be good at? The following chapter includes some of the most significant lessons I've learned about inclusion. These are my own personal 'ah-ha' moments. They are moments which changed my understanding of inclusion. They made me a better leader, a better colleague and a better friend. Each one represents a specific moment in time, and an inclusion skill I developed as a result.

Lesson 1: Inclusion is not the same thing as being 'nice'

We make a big deal about diversity, but not a big deal about diversity capability. And, in the absence of skills in this space, we allow our instinct to be nice and our moral compass of kindness to ground us. It turns out that those very honourable traits may harm as much as they help. Don't get me wrong, being nice is a good start, but on its own it isn't enough. In a world fuelled by social approval, most of us want to be liked, if not loved. We don't want to offend or be insensitive. We want to see both sides of the argument. Being nice to everyone allows us to assume an element of neutrality. Neutral is safe – and in this space we can avoid the uncomfortable.

I get the desire to be nice. Choosing sides is not fun. It can be disruptive and upsetting. The fact is that people who champion diversity can be annoying. Trust me, I am one of them, and even I have the propensity to annoy myself. We are annoying because of the passion we have for the subject. We are annoying because we cannot let it go, and sometimes it seeps into almost every aspect of our lives; talking about racial inequality, social injustice, suicide or sexual harassment is a great way to kill a dinner party buzz.

For many nice people, the nature of the debate creates fear and indecision. Because we lack experience of being anything else other than 'nice', we opt out of conflict and refuse to take sides. Most of us are willing to sit this one out and hope for the best. Unfortunately, our silent complicity plays a crucial role in enabling inequality and driving division. The complexity of the world we live in today and the growing divides in our society suggest it will take more active participation on our part.

Most nice people I know hold a deep belief that inclusion will just happen – that if we simply double down on being nice, it will be enough to change the historical imbalances which continue to exist. Tell that to the girl who has just been married off at the age of eleven. Or to the mother of the boy who has just taken his own life because the abuse he received for being 'feminine' was too intense to bear. Tell that to the ethnic minority candidate who has not had a single call-back, despite having a stellar CV. Or to the Muslim cricket player who has just been held down in the locker room and had alcohol poured down his throat. More importantly, tell that to your older self who looks back to consider the positive impact and legacy you created in your lifetime.

As annoying and uncomfortable as calling out inequality can be, when we look back on history, most of us would like to be on the 'right' side of any moral conflict. Our desire is to be on the side that stopped Hitler's Nazi regime, the side that tore down apartheid, the side that fought for equal and human rights. But will we be on that side if we see equality as someone else's job? Or will we be seen as the bystander, the one who was willing to look the other way?

> *It's hard to challenge people. I have a few moments in my life where I regret not speaking up; some of them were almost twenty years ago, and I still regret not saying something.*
>
> *Yesterday, I had a fallout with my mum about my nephew. A few months ago, he told the family that he's bisexual. My mum told my wife she was surprised that we have told our children about his bisexuality. She's worried about what other people will think, and even said 'he might still get a girlfriend'. I had to say to Mum, you shouldn't care about what your friends think, or what your sister-in-law thinks, you should be asking yourself, 'What will my grandson think?' Will he think 'My grandmother supports and loves me' or will he think 'Is my gran trying to hide who I am?'*
>
> *I followed up with my mother today to take the emotion out of it, show we're in this together and to make sure she doesn't do something that she might later regret.'*
>
> Tim

To play an active role in inclusion, we need to jump into the uncomfortable. This conversation between Tim and his mother is a great example of what that discomfort can look like. We must be prepared to ask questions which may offend. These questions won't kill us, and neither will the inevitable course correction if we get it wrong. We may be embarrassed, but we will live to see another day. More importantly, we will grow from the mistakes made and from the lessons learned. If we are to carve a path forward, we must be prepared to see inequality and do something about it. It's time to move beyond the passive role that being nice affords us and take an active role in building a future which doesn't just replicate the power structures and social problems of today.

Lesson 2: Why the 'I don't see . . .' strategy creates a gap between intention and execution

When it comes to diversity, most of us are making it up as we go along, which is why we rely so heavily on good intentions. But what happens when there is a chasm between your intention and your execution?

'I don't see colour' is a good example of the visible gap between intention and execution. Singling out a person for the colour of their skin or their ethnic heritage can feel uncomfortable. Rather than describe someone as Black or Asian, I hear individuals using almost any other descriptor in order not to 'see' race. The person with the long hair. The one with the red coat. The guy with the shorts on. The one who works in the IT department. People will go to great lengths in order not to describe someone by the colour of their skin.

I get it. Their aim is not to see colour in the first place. At first glance it seems like the right kind of thing to aspire to. If we don't see colour, then we inherently treat everyone as equal – right? Unfortunately, there are several problems with the 'I don't see colour' strategy. First and foremost, to ignore colour is not only to ignore the diverse beauty of our physical bodies, but of our ancestry and so many things which have shaped us as well. Black and brown skin is beautiful. It's also different from white skin.

Secondly, ignoring colour is naive. If you ignore colour, you can ignore the fact that skin colour shapes our lived experience. The colour of your skin has the potential to affect whether a security guard follows you around to try to catch you stealing, whether a line manager gives you a second chance, whether the person interviewing you feels an affinity with you or not. Race and ethnicity have an effect on a number of life outcomes.[2] Whether it be the probability of school exclusion,[3] lower wealth, reduced home ownership,[4] poorer health[5] or less employment,[6] there is a clear link between race and opportunity. The fact is, the darker your skin, the worse off your life chances will be.[7]

That doesn't mean that agency and hard work do not play a role. They do. But what it does mean is that even when you work hard, even when you use your agency, you aren't likely to receive the same benefit or the same chances as someone who does the same, but has lighter, whiter skin.

> *I understand the intent behind not wanting to see colour. As heroic and well-meaning as it sounds, not seeing colour means you don't see me. You don't see my blackness. Being Black is a visible reminder of my Nigerian heritage. There is no closet I can put my black skin into. I live with being Black every day. I live through the positive aspects of being Black as well as the negative. If you don't see my colour, you don't see my experience. If you don't see my colour, you don't see my struggle. If you don't see race, you don't see racism.*
>
> Tolu

One of the reasons that white individuals don't see colour is because the colour of their white skin has never had a negative effect on their lives. White people get to be oblivious to the benefits of whiteness when living in a pervasively white (Western) world, with white teachers, white leaders, white role models and white media. The same is not true for Tolu, or for anyone else who has black or brown skin.

The problem is not when we see someone's colour, when we notice someone is gay or that they have a disability. The problem is what we do when we see that characteristic. We don't need to define anyone by their difference, but no one wins when we try to pretend it doesn't exist.

> I get all sorts of well-meaning responses when people try not to 'see' my disability. Sometimes they even come from my friends who have known me since well before the accident. They are trying to say, 'We love you, we don't see the chair', which I appreciate. But I need you to see the chair because it affects my life. If they tell me 'there will be steps to get to dinner, but we have it sorted', then I know it will be okay. Even telling me there is a downstairs toilet means they've thought about me. When they don't see my chair, they don't think about how to include me, and then I have to deal with those kinds of problems on my own, which isn't what I need.
>
> Sophie

When Sophie described her experience to me, she was very open about the fact that her wheelchair creates all sorts of different responses from different people. Some adults avoid looking her in the eye in order to try not to see her chair, but children almost always see it. Their curiosity and openness mean that they even sometimes want to touch it – a choice which inevitably causes a visible reaction from their parents. Some yank their child back, scolding them, but others take it as an opportunity to lean in and engage. You can imagine which one leaves Sophie feeling more valued and more seen.

A few years ago, a good friend called me to ask for advice. During a visit to their local park, her two-year-old daughter had just announced loudly enough for everyone to hear, 'Mummy, look at that chocolate lady,' when referring to a Black woman walking towards them in the park. I could tell by her reaction that my friend was mortified. Red-faced, she had quickly steered her daughter away. It's hard to know what to do in these situations, but as adults we add our own worries and issues into what is already an unsure situation. My friend meant well, but the problem with a parental reaction like that is it adds negative emotion to what could have been a positive experience. Children's wonder is ever-present and it's hugely positive. Their ability to spot the difference is not yet tainted by social boundaries. A simple 'Yes, and isn't her skin beautiful' would have done the trick.

If you are someone who wants to see beyond difference and aspires to see others as equal, I encourage you to see the whole person in front of you. Take in both the brilliant and the beautiful, as well as the challenges they might face as a result.

Lesson 3: Out is not one moment in time

I used to think that coming out was the moment someone plucked up the courage to tell their parents and friends that they are gay, lesbian or bisexual. That couldn't be further from the truth. Being out isn't one singular moment. It's a continuous state of decision making to not hide who you love and who you are. Out is never done. Coming out is the choice you make in every future moment and with every new person you meet. You can be out one moment with one person, but with the very next person you meet, you are no longer out until you choose to share. Those choices are sometimes based on whether you feel you will be safe, whether you will be accepted, or perhaps whether or not you may ever meet the person again in your life. Some choices are simple, natural and swift, and others require more thought.

> *You're constantly weighing up the pros and cons of being yourself. Sharing in any circumstance, for me, requires consideration. Sometimes you end up telling someone you're gay because you feel that if you don't correct their assumptions about you, then somehow you are lying.*
>
> *I was in a long taxi ride recently, and the taxi driver was very chatty. He asked me questions about my wife and my kids. On the fifth time he referred to my wife, I gently began to refer to my husband, hoping he would pick up the subtle change in my language. It took me twenty minutes of intensely thinking about whether or not to tell this person whom I would never again see in my life. This is one small example, but when you amplify all the daily choices you have to make, it's a lot of invested time and energy.*
>
> *John*

John is one of the most confidently open gay people I know. I've seen him speak on stage about his experiences of being gay in such an accessible way that there are queues of people (most of whom are heterosexual) waiting to speak to him when the event is over. Hearing him recall this moment, and the level of internal challenge which arose, it was clear that he hadn't intended to tell the taxi driver over the course of the long journey. But with the continued persistence of the driver, he began to feel a sense of disingenuousness and questioned his initial decision not to share. That simple choice was suddenly made more complex.

It doesn't matter how big or small a role someone plays in your life and it isn't necessarily correlated with how long or how well you know them. Coming out is a constant decision to be yourself. You may be out in the widest sense of the word, but because we live in a largely heterosexual world (or heteronormative world), lesbian, gay and bisexual individuals who have decided to be open about their sexual orientation must choose when the appropriate moment is to share their story. At work, that moment is even more important because the consequences of outing yourself to the wrong person can be career limiting. Perhaps that is why even in the most socially progressive countries, only 40 per cent of employees are fully open about their gender identity or sexual orientation at work.[8]

One solution could be to tell someone from the very beginning, but let's face it, no one wants to be an 'oversharer' when you meet someone new. Finding the right time to reveal your sexual orientation means gay, lesbian and bisexual individuals have to manage a list of those who don't know and those who do.

> You don't want to lead in the first moment you meet someone with, hi, I am 'gay Rob'. I live in a liberal and open society; that would, frankly, be a bizarre and unnecessary thing to do. But at the same time, as a

manager and teammate, I want to be open about who I am. I find that sharing some aspects of your personal life is hugely valuable to build a trusting relationship with my team. And my relationship and sexual orientation, whilst not 'all defining', is a huge part of that. If you leave being yourself and sharing that you are gay to too late in a relationship, there comes a point where it's incredibly surprising for the individual. If you wait too long, it ends up being an unhelpful surprise. Instead, you are constantly looking for a natural opportunity or opening, or enough time to go by in a new friendship, work or social setting, and then you share your story.

Being in that state where I've not yet had the moment to slip in the 'he' when referring to my partner, or finding some other way to mention it, feels awkward. It's like a niggling feeling, an elephant in the room of my head, which sits there until I've got it out. But at the same time, finding the right moment to be yourself takes time. And so, I keep a list in my head. Of people I have told. And of the people I have not. And it's not like I have had a bad reaction, but simply that I need to make sure I know who I have and haven't told and eventually manage that list so that I can simply be myself and relax.

Rob C.

Rob's list of who knows and who doesn't know is something that I, as a heterosexual person, have never had to manage. That fine balance of when to stay silent and when to be out requires continuous judgement of a situation. It's more than just answering the question 'Will I be safe?' Has enough time passed? Has too much time passed? Will my news be received positively or negatively? Will this make our relationship awkward? Is now the right moment? These judgements require a constant assessment of the environment and continual editing up until the point at which you decide to be yourself. And in some cases, afterwards as well. Sometimes there can be a tail of awkwardness or embarrassment after you do disclose that you are gay, which can require ongoing management.

All this decision making uses up precious time and energy. When you are bisexual, the process of coming out has its own nuances. Often bisexual individuals may find themselves in a relationship with someone of the opposite sex. During those moments, they are to some extent 'passing' as heterosexual. When bisexual individuals then change relationships or share their sexual orientation, the coming-out process can be more challenging for others to understand. To some, it feels like a contradiction or a lie, because being out isn't static when you are bisexual. It can mean that bisexual individuals face different types of questions and different challenges from those that gay or lesbian individuals face.

Last year, I received a call during work where I learned an ex-girlfriend had passed away. Although I was currently in a relationship with a man, whom my team knew, my ex had been a big part of my life. My team was incredibly supportive when they heard the news. The following day I received flowers from a client with a card which read 'So sorry to hear about your boyfriend.'

The assumption that my ex was a man was logical. I had never told anyone at the client that I was bisexual. But as messages of support continued to pour in from the client team about my 'ex-boyfriend', I couldn't help but feel disingenuous to her memory. It hadn't felt relevant to tell my clients about my sexual orientation up until that point, and I especially didn't feel up to raising it on top of processing the news I had received. As a result of not telling them, no matter how much my clients tried to support me during this difficult time, it left me feeling disconnected and like I was lying, and it seemed too late and too awkward to correct them.

Katy

Katy was in the midst of processing the news and the emotions surrounding the death of someone she had loved deeply. Those feelings are challenging enough, but Katy's grief was intensified by the added internal conflict around authenticity and the importance of being true to herself, as well as to the people around her.

Coming out is a constant decision for gay, lesbian, bisexual or trans individuals, but it isn't just a LGBTQ+ thing. Coming out is something that people with non-visible disabilities, with mental health challenges, those who hold religious beliefs or those who choose to visibly transition, all face. Coming out manifests differently for individuals and diverse groups. Do I just be myself, or is it more palatable, safer and just plain easier to fit in with the 'norm'? Will I ever meet this person again? Is this (my sexual orientation, my faith, my gender identity, my disability) the thing I want them to know first about me? If I am not open, am I living authentically? These are just a few of the questions individuals face. That need to be true to who you are, but also to balance both personal and professional safety, is complex.

Imagine standing on the edge of a platform, high in the sky. The wind in your face, you can feel it rustling your wings and you know that all you need to do is let go and jump. Freedom awaits, as does the ability to soar and swoop. Others have done it and you see them soaring and hear their words of encouragement. You know it's there, just waiting for you. But . . .

What if you're not ready? What if the wind doesn't lift you up? What if you've messed up and this isn't the right thing to do? What if you jump and you just fall? Once you jump you can't come back to the edge and pretend it didn't happen. There is no rewinding the clock. This jump is a one-way trip.

I've spent forty-five years hiding from myself and these thoughts of change. Or was it forty-five years preparing for this point in my life? I'm terrified.

Am I prepared for the price I'm going to have to pay? Do I actually know what that price will be? I've assumed that some friends will not hang around. Whether they just fade away or explode is yet to be seen. Because this emerging person has taken their friend away. Will their own insecurities drive them away?

Heath, prior to transitioning to Sarah D.

Heath shared his thoughts with me as he prepared to come out publicly and live openly and fully as Sarah. For much of his life, Heath had been editing. In LGBTQ+ terms, he had been in the closet, hiding his love of women's clothes, his desire to reshape his body and his need to find internal alignment. Heath had been shaping who he was to fit into the masculine mould the world had carved for him. But as he stood on the verge of transition and prepared to let go of all the editing he had been doing, his sense of anxiety was palpable. If I stop editing, will people accept me for who I am? Can I accept me for who I am?

It was the autumn of 2009 when I first came to understand that coming out is a never-ending journey of choosing to be yourself. I had just taken ownership of the diversity agenda at my company. It was a moment I will never forget and a lesson which I can never unlearn.

Prior to that moment, I had believed that I had been acting inclusively. But I hadn't really. I had led dozens of different teams and although I considered myself inclusive, my assumption was that being kind was sufficient. I had never consciously created space for people to come forward and be themselves or altered my behaviour in any way. I didn't understand that there were things I could do in order to make it easier for LGBTQ+ and other diverse colleagues to choose to be themselves. From language adjustments as simple as the insertion of the word partner instead of husband and wife, to clear and visible signs that I believe love is love, regardless of which gender or body your partner has, I had never taken purposeful action to make it easier for my gay, lesbian, bisexual or transgender colleagues to be themselves.

Coming out is a personal choice. Some people may never choose to come out and that's okay. We do not need to force anyone to be out, but we must recognise that people are more likely to be out when they know they will be okay. It takes both physical and psychological safety. Making the decision can be simple and easy. But it can also be more complex and require an immense amount of bravery. Whether we are aiming to create inclusive environments in our homes, for our family, for our friends, or in our workplaces and for our teams, we need to understand the actions to take which support the coming-out process.

Lesson 4: We are all editing – some more than others

Several years ago, I attended a multi-day authentic gay and lesbian leadership course. The goal of the course was to explore what authenticity means within the LGBTQ+ context. My role as the sponsor for the course was to be in the room at key moments for the fifteen colleagues who were there to explore the connection between their sexual orientation and their ability to lead authentically. I'll be honest, I wasn't initially keen on having training specifically for my gay, lesbian and bisexual leaders. I didn't see the point in separate leadership courses for diverse groups, but what I experienced in the room transformed my thinking about sexual orientation and about inclusion in general.

While the majority of the fifteen were already open at work about their sexual orientation, there were several colleagues in the room who were out in their home lives, but in the closet at work. Others were out at work, but in the closet in many other aspects of life. Almost no one in the room felt that they could bring their whole selves to work.

As I listened to their very personal accounts of the extent to which they all had been editing, downplaying and limiting the amount that they shared about themselves at work, I was moved to tears. Never in my life had I realised that we live in a world which is, for the most part, designed for heterosexual people. Husbands with wives. Men with women. Boys with girls. If you don't fit that norm, the extent to which you have to adjust, to adapt and to edit yourself to fit in is immense.

As a heterosexual person, I have never had to consciously consider if it was safe for me to hold my husband's hand in public. I have never had to adjust how I respond to the question 'How was your weekend?' in order to be sure I was not upsetting anyone, or to be sure I was safe. I have never had to use non-gendered pronouns to describe my partner. I have never worried that someone would not accept me for the sole reason of who I love. I've never had to worry about where I could go on holiday with my partner, or where I could go on a work assignment and be both emotionally and legally safe to be myself.

It's not only gay people who are editing. We all edit. In a desire not to be seen as different, we all adjust before we enter the workplace door. Ethnic minorities adjust their style in order to fit into what is, for the most part, a white Western working culture across Europe and the US. Women edit to fit into masculine norms. Individuals with a non-visible disability hide their dyslexia, their prosthetic leg, or their hearing aid. Those who have mental ill-health often cover and pretend they are okay.

In a study to determine the extent to which employees edit or 'cover' at work, researchers assessed thousands of employees on four dimensions:

- Appearance (how they look at work)

- Affiliation (avoiding behaviours associated with stereotypes)

- Advocacy (the extent to which they feel they can stick up for one group)

- Association (the extent to which they avoid association with members of their group)

The groups most likely to cover their difference were those who are most likely to be under-represented at work.

Eighty-three per cent of lesbian, gay and bisexual employees surveyed reported they covered in order to fit in at work. Seventy-nine per cent of Black employees and 66 per cent of women covered. Even 45 per cent of straight white men felt they needed to hide their authentic selves at work in order to 'get on'.[9]

It turns out, we are all editing. Unless we possess an uncommon ability to be exactly the same person in all aspects of our life, most of us will have a slightly different flavour of ourselves that we show to our parents, our siblings, our university friends or our co-workers. What a work acquaintance or client knows about us is inevitably different from what our loved ones know. Many people choose to keep their personal lives private. But this isn't about privacy. This kind of editing is about safety and acceptance. In our world, some people are more safe and more accepted, which is why some people are editing more than others. The time, energy and emotion an individual spends in order to edit are often directly proportional to how inclusive and safe we have made their environment. The more inclusive we are, the less time, energy and emotion individuals need to spend altering who they are and how they present.

If you haven't consciously thought about creating an inclusive workplace, chances are that your ethnic minority colleagues are editing more than their peers, and the depth of their editing is likely to be significant. Code-switching, as it is sometimes called, means people of colour are having to adapt their language, their mannerisms, the way they dress or how they wear their hair. For some individuals, cultural norms in the home are so different that when they enter the workplace, they have to reframe the way they speak to elders, how they deliver challenge, or whether or not they seek eye contact.

In certain settings, and in particular in West Africa, there is a deference to parents and elders. In the Nigerian Igbo community for example, when a younger person meets an older person, they go to the floor and literally lie down and wait until they are invited to get up and say hello. What that means is that in cultures of deference, conversations are generally more uni-directional. And in a situation which is potentially serious or contentious, eye contact is seen as dissent. Instead, you look straight down, you listen, you show by your body language that you are taking it in.

My dad was quite liberal. At home, you could have strong debate, but in social settings, even with him, you needed to observe social norms, which means that even though I was encouraged to challenge him at home, I still need to be cognisant of the situation. In one setting those behaviours make you seem respectful. In another, they make you seem diminished or 'less than' to white leaders or white peers. You have to understand which is the correct response, instead of having a default way of operating.

Vince

What is the cost of covering so much of who you are? Some people are so used to editing to fit in that they simply don't notice the changes in themselves as they enter the workplace. But for others, the extent to which they feel they need to modify in order to get on means the workplace can be uncomfortable. A Black colleague of mine once described our workplace culture as being like an 'itchy sweater' – something which you can tolerate if you have to, but you are desperate to get home and change out of.

A very visible example of workplace editing is the conformity and alteration of African hair to make it look more Western. With the exception of a small number of industries such as music or the creative arts, Black individuals have long been expected to have white-looking hair. It's only now that school and workplace policies which discriminate against or restrict individuals from showing their natural African hair are starting to be challenged.

Hair may not seem that important, but it's part of a broader profile of white culture being the dominant culture, white beauty being the only beauty, and white norms as 'the' norm. With each change or edit a person makes, they give away a piece of themselves. If you check who you are at the door, what are you left with on the other side? It's incredibly hard to be authentic if you're constantly morphing your natural way of being in order to fit it.

Lesson 5: People perform better when they can be themselves

Whether we call it editing, covering or code-switching, it's all assimilation. The process of assimilating is driven by basic human instinct. Groups have been essential to survival throughout all of human history and our ability to edit ourselves in order to fit into a group has always been a key tool for survival. Looking different, speaking differently, or behaving in a way that sets you apart can mean that others perceive you as a threat. Being visible and being different has always been an extremely vulnerable place to be.

If you have a workplace culture where being gay is openly discouraged, staying 'in' will feel like a matter of survival. If you have a workplace where sexual orientation is not really discussed, chances are your lesbian, gay and bisexual colleagues might not feel unsafe, but they are probably having to do quite a lot of editing. When you create a workplace which openly embraces gay, lesbian and bisexual individuals, you remove a lot of the emotional baggage and energy that gets wasted in the 'decision to be yourself' process, and at the same time, you add positive energy into the mix. That positivity helps create greater pride and greater opportunity for more trusted relationships to emerge as a result.

> *Building relationships is key. For years I was careful as to who I came out to, and rarely told clients for fear of jeopardising a critical relationship (in the eyes of my company). However, whenever I got over my fear and signalled my sexuality through referencing my wife or discussing our workplace commitment to the LGBTQ+ community, I rarely faced the backlash I thought I would. In fact, quite the opposite. By sharing a bit of myself with people, I earned a level of trust that I hadn't previously had. This led to closer relationships, deeper conversations and, in some instances, clients coming out to me who had been in their 'workplace closet' for their twenty-year career.*
>
> *Alicia*

The positivity effect isn't limited to sexual orientation. The same is true of all aspects of diversity. If you create a workplace where honest conversations about physical and mental health are welcomed, it supercharges how individuals feel about their work and their employer.

> *Several weeks ago, I had a meeting with two colleagues who are part of our mental health initiative at work. We*

did a check-in at the start; each person got a chance to talk about how they were feeling. When it came to me, someone asked me a question about what I'd done on the weekend and the opportunity to tell them how I was really feeling was lost. On that particular day, I was feeling isolated and lonely. I'd not been in the office, and I had been working from home a lot. I wanted to talk to them about how I was feeling. I wanted to get it out. I decided I had to do something. At the end of the meeting, I simply said, 'I don't feel like I got the chance to tell you how I really am,' and they gave me the space to share. The outcome was really good. They checked in on me for days afterward. We arranged to meet for a coffee in the office.

Old me wouldn't have done that. I would have bottled it up and managed it privately. It really is uncomfortable when you bottle it. You go away feeling like you haven't been seen and that no one is listening. That isn't necessarily true, but it feels that way inside.

Being honest about how you're really feeling isn't easy, but I'm getting better at it. Being able to be myself and be truthful when I am not well increases my sense of belonging. The company I work for isn't perfect. My boss isn't perfect. But he and the company have created an environment where I can say 'I am not okay' without fear of being judged or that information being used against me.

Chris

Chris's story is about mental health, but it's also about so much more. Human beings are always assessing threat, safety and the potential for harm. When our brains perceive a threat, our sympathetic nervous system takes charge. That 'fight or flight' response wakes up our body through a near-instantaneous rush of cortisol, allowing us to focus on the immediate and urgent thing in front of us and to ignore any other unnecessary inputs.

Why is the ability to be yourself so important in the workplace? Studies which prove a positive link between increased diversity and increased organisational performance are widely available. The evidence around the 'value' of diversity is enormous.[10] But there is also mounting evidence that suggests if you have diverse teams but do not have an inclusive or 'safe' environment, all that difference can hinder performance. Diversity without inclusion has been linked to lower revenue, lower performance, increased conflict, lower morale and slower decision making.[11] That's because it takes time and energy to work through cultural, behaviour and attitudinal differences and get to a place where diverse teams are high-functioning.

Command and control environments are highly effective when you need to get things done quickly but you don't want people to think too much about what they are doing. Those kinds of environments are exactly the kind that hand our body over to our sympathetic nervous system so that we can focus on the immediate threat. Unfortunately, that same environment reduces our ability to think widely, broadly and more freely. That's because heightened anxiety and stress (the kind you get when you don't fit in, feel on the periphery, feel your work is being overly scrutinised, etc.) are linked to lower working-memory capacity, and reductions in creativity and cognitive processing.[12] Those abilities are not deemed as critical when you're either fleeing or fighting, but they are key to professional performance as well as many other aspects of life.

The 'assimilate to fit in' approach has a short-term

positive effect on workplace productivity, but it isn't conducive to creating affinity or enhancing innovation and creativity. When we create an environment where we lower concerns for safety, we reduce the amount of energy spent on decision making to be oneself, and create positive energy. Relationships between people who are different become more human and more authentic and as a result, we create an atmosphere more conducive to diversity of thinking.

> *Last year, my new finance lead shared a story about her weekend, in which she subtly talked about her female partner. I could tell she was sounding me out for my reaction. I didn't want to make a huge deal about it, for fear of making her decision to come out as anything other than normal, but I wanted her to know that I had heard. I decided that the next time we spoke about life outside of work, I would ask about her partner. It worked. She began to share more and more about her partner, and over time, her level of comfort has increased. She is now open to all our colleagues in the office.*
>
> *Anthony*

Each of us plays a role in creating an environment that enables others to bypass that safety response, to let go of all the energy it takes to edit, and to simply be themselves. You don't have to over-egg it, but consciously signalling acceptance and then positively embracing someone's decision to be themselves creates a cycle of positivity.

Lesson 6: Merit is not the great equaliser we make it out to be

In more than thirty years of work, I have never met anyone who wanted to be judged on the colour of their skin, their age, their disability, or whether (or not) they have breasts. In fact, the desire to be judged on your own merit rather than your diversity category is ubiquitous. Unfortunately, there are a number of problems with that ideological view.

The first problem is our lack of agreement as to what merit is. Many people use merit interchangeably with hard work and talent, without pausing to consider the implication. Merit, and the concept of meritocracy, was popularised in 1958 by British sociologist and politician Michael Young.[13] In his satirical book *The Rise of the Meritocracy*,[14] he cautioned readers on the dangers of using merit as a great equaliser. Merit, as Young saw it, was the system used by those in power to ensure they remained in power. In his book, Young warned that if we continued to promote, select and elect people based on 'merit', we would continue to see an all-white-male-elite-Etonian society, until the point at which a major political and social revolt would occur. His prediction might be bemusing if it wasn't so painfully accurate.

According to Merriam-Webster, the noun 'merit' is defined as:

a) a praiseworthy quality: VIRTUE
b) character or conduct deserving reward, honor, or esteem: *also* ACHIEVEMENT
c) the qualities or actions that constitute the basis of one's deserts[15]

When merit is used as a verb it becomes 'to be worthy of, entitled or liable to' and is closely linked with both 'earn' and 'deserve'.

Within the ideology of merit, there are a few potential falsehoods at play:

- That merit is a factual thing, a skill/talent/worthiness which is *universally* agreed

- That merit is not obscured by feelings or beliefs

- That everything which prepared someone to succeed was merit-based

We see merit as an independent universal concept, but merit is skewed by what an organisation or an individual deems to be worthy or deserving of praise. If we associate merit with commitment, long hours or results, then each of those is worthy of merit. If we associate expediency, decisiveness or swift action with merit, then each of those is worthy of merit.

Just as merit is influenced by the things we value, so is our judgement of who is the 'best' person for the job. You can see that most commonly play out in workplace performance management and appraisal. More often than not, you will still find that historically associated masculine behaviours and masculine tendencies are rated more highly than historically associated feminine tendencies and feminine behaviours. Take a moment to look at the following lists:

Courageous	Gentle
Independent	Empathetic
Assertive	Sympathetic
Risk-taking	Nurturing
Individual	Team
Metrics-driven	Emotive
Confident	Organised
Results-oriented	Structured
Point of View	Collaborative

Which side would you most closely associate with success within your organisation's performance-management system? And, if you had to choose one gender, which list would you associate with men and which list would you associate with women?

In my experience, the list on the left will most often be associated with traits that are highly valued in performance assessments. It will also align with historically associated masculine behaviours, whereas the list on the right will be aligned with traits historically seen as feminine. Many organisations will say that they value those traits equally. But do they? The behaviours on the right are less likely to be associated with top performance rankings. When organisations rate traditionally masculine behaviours higher than they do more feminine traits, merit is no longer performing an important balancing act, but is instead tipping the balance in favour of those who display masculine characteristics.

A few years ago, I was helping a client who had uncovered a number of diversity challenges, including the fact that they were systematically under-promoting their women and systematically over-promoting their men. In fact, they had not promoted a single woman above manager level in three years and more than a hundred promotions. Either the women were underperforming, or the organisation had a broader problem in how they were assessing their women. In my experience, it's usually a bit of both.

In our discussions about the issue, the senior leader who looked after business development shared with me that all of his men had met or exceeded their sales targets. His senior women, however, had not met their targets. He felt they were spending too much time nurturing members of the team and on internal organisational activities, and as a result, they had all received lower performance ratings than their male counterparts. He was genuinely perplexed and unsure how to proceed. I asked him a simple question to stimulate thinking. 'You've reduced ratings of your women for not meeting their sales targets, but have you reduced ratings for your men for not spending time nurturing the people in your organisation?'

As we discussed the answer, it was clear that he was frustrated that his women were spending too much time trying to get the internal organisation right, and not enough time out there selling to clients. It was also clear that he had not considered that all leaders should be playing both an external sales role *and* an internal leadership role. Our expectations of men and women in the workplace should be balanced. Women absolutely need to perform the core delivery of their day job. Men also need to spend time investing in people, coaching, team cohesion and driving positive workplace culture. If either group are not doing their fair share of business nurturing or business delivery, we need to call it out.

Biased workplace expectations are not limited to masculine or feminine social norms. Within the workplace there are also often expectations of extroversion or a bias towards a more Western or American approach to leadership where 'having a point of view' is valued as much as, if not more than, the substance within that point of view. Merit is not independent, nor is not universally agreed, which is why it has the propensity to uphold a dominant culture by denying people who don't fit that mould. Because merit is simply what we, as an individual or organisation, place value upon, unless we choose to redefine merit to take our organisation in a different direction, it plays a key role in enabling and perpetuating the status quo.

Lesson 7: Privilege and fairness are not friends

The ideology of merit is often intertwined with the ideology of fairness. Many of us have a deep belief that if you simply work hard, you will be fairly rewarded. But we don't live in a fair world and there is no tangible evidence to suggest that hard work is the only key to getting out of poverty, or to achieving equality. Hard work plays a role, but is only a piece of the puzzle. For example, if we tell someone with a disability that they simply need to work hard, when perhaps they cannot see, cannot hear, are unable to walk, or suffer from depression, that advice is not only unhelpful, it is also unlikely to be unactionable in some cases.

Fairness and merit are noble concepts, but they lack grounding in the reality of the way the world works. Is it merit if your parents could afford a tutor? Is it merit if you went to a private school? Do you lack merit if you had no parent, nanny or other adult to help you with your homework? Is it merit if your parents could afford the time and money to allow you to play sports, learn to play a musical instrument or follow your artistic talents? Is it merit if your family connections helped you secure a work placement? Is it merit if you had to take the immediate and best-paying job to alleviate the pressure of student loans – forgoing the job you really might have excelled at?

Much of what we consider to be merit-based is actually driven by privilege. Unfortunately, there are very few words which make us recoil in the way the term privilege does. In my experience, the moment a conversation about privilege starts, defences go up. The doors slam shut and openness evaporates.

> *Shame and guilt have historically driven my emotions around privilege. The inference is that you have something you didn't earn ... whether it be plaudits, wealth, status or something else. The assumption is that privilege somehow gave you an unfair advantage. When someone points it out, it's usually not news to you. If you're anything like me, there is a voice in your head which has been telling you about your privilege for some time. All the other person is doing is voicing what you already know.*
>
> *But that voicing is an exposure of something pretty fundamental. Whether it's about race, socio-economic background or sexual orientation (many of which overlap, by the way), the notion that what you have is not somehow down to something you have done or earned, means you can either get pretty defensive or overly apologetic.*
>
> *Jo*

Suggestions of privilege can feel like an accusation. It's as if you are in possession of something you haven't earned. Privilege is associated with words like entitlement. It suggests a lack of hard work or perhaps even laziness, which isn't necessarily the case, but if you admit to having privilege you then have to admit that your achievements aren't the sole and direct result of your own effort. Accepting privilege as a concept means you have to accept that you will inevitably have had some (often invisible) help along the way – help which others did not. Privilege and hard work have little bearing on each other. You can work incredibly hard and be privileged, just as easily as you can be privileged and not work hard at all.

One of the responses I often see in conversations about privilege is that people who have it like to disown it. 'I never asked for this privilege' is a way to explain away any residual guilt and create distance from your privilege. Whether you knew about it or whether you asked for it is irrelevant. Privilege is still an advantage regardless.

It has taken me a long time to understand what privilege truly is and to unpick my own emotional reaction to the word. Privilege in its widest sense means that you didn't have to. You didn't have to think about. You didn't have to react to. You didn't even have to be aware of.

White privilege is not having to worry about how someone will react to the colour of your skin. It's not having to be the only person of colour in a meeting, year after year. It's not having to keep all the receipts when you're shopping because a security guard will inevitably ask you for proof of purchase. Male privilege is never having to be at the receiving end of sexualised catcalls when you're walking down the street. It's not being felt up on public transport, at a bar, or at the corporate Christmas drinks. It's not worrying about your safety in every park, in any wooded area, at any time after dark. Heterosexual privilege is never having to refrain from sharing about your personal life. It's never having to manage a list of who knows and who doesn't. It's not worrying about whether a client, a boss or a colleague will reject you, and your work, for the sole reason that they don't like who you love. Privilege is never having to not hold your loved one's hand for fear of verbal or physical violence.

Privilege is not a universal position. One can have privilege of race and at the same time lack privilege of sex. Or, have the privilege of sex but lack the privilege of socio-economic status. We all have areas of our lives where we benefit from a position, just as we all have areas of our lives where we are on the outside, and must endure what the world throws our way, regardless of how unfair it might seem. The conversation about privilege can quickly move into debate about whose disadvantage was more pronounced.

When people begin to argue about who had it worse, it can lead to a sort of 'oppression Olympics'. It's almost, as if, by proving you had some level of disadvantage, it eradicates any privilege you had in the first place.

I know I am a privileged person, despite having a disability. I have privilege as a white woman, but I also have privilege within my disability. I am an elite athlete who competes for my country. Even something as basic as my wheelchair is a privilege. My sponsors pay for a state-of-the-art chair. I have a strength and conditioning coach who helps me to adapt, to grow, and to get the most out of my body, despite being in a wheelchair. The average person in the disability community does not have the same chair, the access to a coach or many of the things I have. It's a luxury.

But even my privilege gets stripped away. The most frustrating thing is having my independence taken from me. It happens when I cannot get on a train or cannot go up or down steps, but it can even be as

simple as the pans in my kitchen. Short-handled pans
mean I cannot even boil pasta or cook for myself.
When the environment around you creates barriers –
that's when privilege is taken away.

Sophie

In Sophie's world, a lack of privilege can be something as basic as not being able to cook your own dinner because the pan handles are so short that it's impossible not to pour boiling water in your lap. As a person who has the privilege of not having a disability, I have never worried about the length of pan handles, the gap on the train platform, or the steps to the bathroom. I've also never been forced to use an entrance which is different from my friends to get into a restaurant. Nor have I ever felt the indignation as I wheeled myself through a back entrance amid the bins in order to get to my table because there is no wheelchair access through the front.

In order to get over the wall of defensiveness, we need to admit the truth about privilege. It isn't something you earn, or something you work hard for, nor is it something you asked for. Whether you like it or not, privilege simply is. Once we accept its existence, we can get to the more important debate. If I am privileged, what is it that I can do? How do I exchange my personal advantage for collective good? Is it possible to use my privilege to lift others up?

I benefit from a lot of privilege. I absolutely have white
liberal guilt, then I get guilty about the guilt. You can get
consumed by your own stuff in this space. It's a vicious
circle until I tell myself, 'Shut up, this isn't about you'.

If someone names the privilege that I have, it's not
a failing on my part. Privilege is not my fault, but the

issues it generates are real. In accepting that, I get to let go of the energy used up in being defensive or apologetic. By acknowledging and owning it, I can then move on to a position of personal responsibility. Then I can pay attention to someone else and listen to their experience rather than be caught up in my own. It also allows me to be a bit less awkward ... instead of being focused on whether I am going to say the right thing, or worried about my public-school privilege, I can let go of my stuff and see the other person. It's only then I am freed up so that we can work together on common goals.

Jo

Discussions about privilege have gone astray if all they do is make people feel bad. Privilege is not a dirty word, it's an impetus to act. Some of us will use our privilege in a gentle way, others will choose to be more direct with our power. Although she grew up privileged in many ways, Jo is a great example of someone who has learned to work through the emotions that arise and move to a place where she acknowledges her privileges, and then joins together with those who don't have as much to instigate positive change.

Lesson 8: Awareness, compassion, and now action

Each of these lessons shaped my understanding of inclusion. In isolation, each one is important, but together they represent something more powerful. Inclusion isn't an end state. Inclusion is an act of doing. It doesn't happen by accident. In my experience it happens most naturally when individuals go through three steps.

1. **Awareness:** First, they seek to understand – that process can happen by reviewing data, listening to the lived experience or more broadly seeking information which informs.

2. **Compassion:** When individuals find a connection to what they have learned, and care about the issues others face, positive action becomes a more likely outcome. Without compassion, individuals often get stuck at the awareness stage.

3. **Action:** To be inclusive, you must use both the awareness and the compassion you have to take targeted action. Which means inclusion isn't about the past, it's about the future, and your ability to see, learn and act in new ways in order to include people you have yet to meet with differences you have yet to know.

Chapter 7

The Power of Relationships – Exploring Authenticity, Affinity and Bias

> 'If you really want to make a friend, go to someone's house and eat with him – the people who give you their food give you their heart.'
> Cesar Chavez[1]

In Chapter 3, I shared how my Black colleagues first compiled and then shared their experiences of systemic racism with me. It was more than fifteen years ago, and to this day, I am ashamed of my reaction. There were no stories of visible acts of aggression towards the Black community within the organisation, and in my mind, if you couldn't see it, that meant it didn't exist. If I am honest with myself, not only did I lack the basic understanding of how to spot systemic racism, I was also hesitant about the word itself. I didn't want to believe that my organisation, or anyone in it, was racist. Instead of asking my Black colleagues to help me see how racism presents in different situations, I immediately dismissed the evidence they had given me, and in doing so, I dismissed the lived experience of dozens of Black colleagues. My denial meant that I closed down the conversation and closed off the opportunity to help fix the issue. It would take me years to recover that trust.

In her thought-provoking book *Why I Am No Longer*

Talking to White People About Race, Reni Eddo-Lodge suggests that 'If all racism was as easy to spot, grasp and denounce as white extremism is, the task of the anti-racist would be simple. People feel that if a racist attack has not occurred, or the word "n—r" has not been uttered, an action can't be racist. If a black person hasn't been abused or spat at in the street, or a suited white extremist politician hasn't lamented the lack of British jobs for British workers, it's not racist'.[2]

You won't find systemic racism by searching for the presence of overt negativity – neither will you find the more subtle, but more prolific forms of sexism, homophobia and ableism. So how do we spot it?

Systemic discrimination only becomes visible when you start looking for the absence of positivity. It can be more easily found in what doesn't exist rather than in what does. To find it, you have to look for an absence of what should be there in the first place. It happens when someone is subtly excluded from day-to-day team bonding. Or when they get passed up on invites to team drinks, to a night out, or to an occasional coffee in the canteen. It happens when a line manager doesn't take the extra time to coach someone who has a performance gap. It happens when a person is consistently not considered for that stretch role or never seen as 'ready' for the next level. It happens when we seek out flaws more readily and more often than we find the words of praise. It happens when we use banter to make someone feel inferior. It happens when someone is hired and there is no effort to help them succeed. Instead, others watch and wait for them to fail. It happens when second chances are not given, and one mistake is all it takes to be overlooked for years.

It doesn't just happen to one individual. Systemic discrimination exists when our collective behaviours mean that the combined effect of this lack of positivity, lack of support and lack of second chances has disproportionate outcomes for an entire group, not just a single person.

Take mistake making, for example. Research suggests that we systematically punish women and ethnic minorities more harshly when they make a mistake. Abhishek Parajuli, a University of Oxford researcher, studies how we perceive negative information about men and women in positions of power.[3] In one experiment, Parajuli created two fictitious politicians, Susan and David. When members of the public were shown the identical and fabricated profiles of Susan and David, they both received a 60 per cent positivity rating. However, when Parajuli invented a scandal for both candidates, and then re-tested sentiment towards Susan and David, he found that David's positivity rating had increased to 70 per cent, while Susan's had stayed the same. How is it that for the same failure, positive sentiment towards the male politician increased, while positive sentiment towards the female candidate remained the same?

The punishment gap isn't just a fictitious one. It arises in the real world too. Harvard Business School researchers studied the impact gender had on a failure in the financial services industry by looking at the after-effects of being fired for misconduct. What they found was startling. Following an incident of misconduct, only 63 per cent of female advisors remained employed in the industry. Meanwhile, 76 per cent of male counterparts remained employed.[4] In the medical industry, we find a similar punishment gap. Investigations into US Medicare referral rates for doctors after they have a patient die during surgery found that referrals to female surgeons dropped by 54 per cent in the period after a patient died. When it was a male surgeon who lost a patient, the drop was only 5 per cent.[5]

These disproportionate outcomes are a clear example of systemic sexism. Whether your role in society is as a politician, a financial advisor or a surgeon, when a woman makes a mistake, the world judges her more harshly than a man in the same position. The same punishment gap exists for people of colour. In the UK, if you are Black and male, you are not only significantly more likely to be arrested than a white person, you are also more likely to be charged, and more likely to have your trial moved to a higher court for the same crime. [6]

> 'Keep your head down.' You will typically see some form of this messaging in nearly all Black families. Even a lot of white families share this message of caution with their young. The difference is that you rarely, if ever, get a second chance if you're Black. The stain of any error sticks to you. If you muck up and you're white, more often than not, you get another roll of the dice. For someone like me, there is no second throw. No reset, no forgiveness nor understanding and certainly no polite invitation to try again. Multiple attempts to offer your best are not afforded if you're Black or brown.
>
> Rob N.

Systemic racism in the workplace can be found in anything from lack of coaching to lack of opportunity, lack of investing in someone, or a lack of direct and actionable performance feedback.

> At work, I often get pulled into random forums or brainstorms for my input. I know I'm invited because there are no other Black voices – mostly, it's all white

*people. I accept that I've been asked for my 'diverse'
input (and I do actually encourage adding new seats to
the table when a group is monocultural), but when I
open my mouth, sometimes it doesn't feel like I am
treated as an equal.*

*'Oh, that's such a different way of looking at it . . .'
is the reaction I often get when I contribute something
that's not remotely controversial or fresh. When it's
followed by silence, and no sort of affirmation that my
input or idea was welcomed, that kind of comment
certifies my difference. It's othering. I am already the
only person of colour in the room and now there's a
big neon arrow pointing down at me.*

*The feeling of difference and being an outsider has
repeated throughout my career. It's easy to make someone feel that way through lack of affirmation, by always
being put last on the agenda or sometimes from the
body language in the room when you present. I respond
to this cycle by overcompensating, putting myself forward, appearing extra confident. It's exhausting.*

*I spoke in a meeting about commissioning at my last
job and the entire room, around 150 leaders, sat there
with crossed arms and cross faces. I was a junior associate presenting a piece of work fully in line with the
company's strategic direction but their body language,
and very obvious lack of wanting me to 'win' in that
situation, made me want to shrink and die.*

Sian

Many of these actions seem banal enough. It's hard to
describe any immediately negative impact or to directly link
them to racism. On their own they add up to very little. But
it isn't just one room, and one presentation with a sea of

unsmiling white faces. It's the combination of rooms, the consistent lack of a warm welcome or positivity. All told, they add up to an impenetrable barrier for people who look or act differently from those who fit seamlessly into a white normative culture.

A friend of mine describes this kind of racism as a paper cut. A single cut has a minimal effect. But thousands of tiny cuts leave you raw, sore and hesitant to put your hand back in. Daily racial cuts affect your ability to thrive. They lead you to doubt your own capability and your own self-worth. And, in my experience, they also lead most people to behave in a way that reinforces their own exclusion. When you feel excluded or on the periphery, it's very hard to behave in a way that makes you feel more included. The more you feel like an outsider, the more you act like one – thus creating a spiral of exclusion.

Relationships matter

Ask anyone how to get on in life and chances are they will tell you about two things: hard work, and the importance of strong relationships. Despite this, and the vast amount of effort that organisations have invested in diversity pro-grammes aimed at women, men are still more likely to be sponsored and coached at work than their female counter-parts.[7] Often that additional coaching is not intentional but is more a result of our comfort in engaging with members of our own sex.

Several years ago, I was discussing the talent profile and capability of senior women with a client. He was a man in his early fifties and married with children. Though he was working four days a week in London, his family lived in another country. After flying into London every Monday morning, the rest of the week he stayed in an apartment in the city. This meant he could work as late as he wanted when in London and it left him free to take clients and colleagues to dinner on a regular basis.

It was clear from our conversations that he knew his senior men better than he knew the senior women who worked for him. He understood the men's skills as well as their aspirations and ambitions. When it came to the senior women who worked for him, he was more hesitant about what they wanted and where they saw their careers going. When I asked him why he had less knowledge of the women's skills and their aspirations, his response gave me food for thought. Most of the men he worked with also worked away from their wives and children during the week, which left the men free to meet in the evening. He had been seeing them regularly out of working hours for drinks and dinner. The women were often not available to join, either because they saw evenings with family as sacred or because they were needed at home to take care of domestic duties more often than their male counterparts were. Compounding the issue was the fact that he, as a married man, did not feel comfortable having dinner alone with a woman in the way he was okay dining with a man on his team. As a result, he didn't know the senior women who reported to him in the same intimate way he knew the men.

It turns out he's not the only one. According to research from Lean In, 60 per cent of men in the US and 40 per cent of men in the UK who manage people are uncomfortable mentoring, working alone or socialising with a female colleague.[8] Male managers are also six times more likely to hesitate to have work dinners with female colleagues. This hesitation is growing in the post-#MeToo era. Men simply don't want to be put in a position where they could be accused of inappropriate behaviour. Unfortunately, when senior men hesitate to engage with women in their team, those relationships will be lacking in strength.

In today's world, the majority of those in leadership positions are likely to be white men. Those leaders don't intentionally know women less well, just as they don't mean to have less engagement with ethnic minority, lesbian, gay or other colleagues of 'difference'. But the fact remains that they don't. In a 2021 study on relationships in the workplace, 59 per cent of Black women reported never having had even one informal interaction with a senior leader.[9] Whether we mean to or not, senior leaders are disproportionately less likely to have high-affinity relationships with individuals on their team who are different from themselves.

Encyclopedia Britannica defines affinity as 'a feeling of closeness and understanding that someone has for another person because of their similar qualities, ideas, or interests'.[10] With affinity comes warmth, affection and fondness. That positivity spills out into how we feel about and how we embrace those around us. When we don't share the same background, act in the same way or like the same things, affinity isn't always easy to find. It's also something which you cannot easily fake, or pretend you feel. When we don't feel affinity for a person or a group, we have to be honest about those feelings, and know that we have more work to do in order to create a culture of fairness and to ensure our biases don't lend themselves to lesser outcomes for those groups or individuals.

The effects of minimising contact

As much as we like the idea of integration and mixing between racial groups, very few of us actually do mix. We may meet a relatively racially and ethnically diverse group of people as we go about our working day. The closer we live to a metropolitan city, the more likely that racial diversity exists. But when it comes to our dinner table, ethnic and racial diversity isn't a given. More often than not, a gap exists between the diversity of our world and the diversity of those people we welcome into our home. As a result, we 'minimise contact'.

I first heard the term 'minimising contact' in Binna Kandola's book *Racism at Work*.[11] I hadn't considered the importance of deep and meaningful friendships between racial groups and their ability to create deep and meaningful relationships at work. It's such an obvious reality. Most people I meet are extremely quick to tell me how much they love travel, how they love eating food from around the world and exploring different cultures. But those same people would be among the first to admit that when it comes to the people they invite into their homes, to their dinner tables or over for a playdate with their children, those guests look a lot like they themselves do. In the US, 68 per cent of white people have never had a Black person at their dinner table.[12]

What stops most of us from mixing and from inviting people who are racially different to our dinner tables? For some, the lack of racial integration in our schools has a lasting effect on the lack of racial integration in our adult life. If you went to a predominantly white school, your childhood friends are likely to be predominantly white. That trend often continues through to university, where white students spend time creating lasting memories, some of which are through studying, but many of which are through drinking, with other white students. As we move into the working world, we are continually drawn to those who are like us, and a continuous circle of tight-knit relationships is formed. If you're white you are less likely to have close friends who are Black, Latino/a, Indigenous or Asian. Sure, you might have one or two, but broadly speaking those relationships will be few and far between. Asian individuals are more likely to have Asians in their inner circle and Black individuals are more likely to have close Black friends. Minimising contact isn't just a white thing. The same is true for all communities.

Vulnerability and trust are interlinked. A lack of confidence and connection with people who are different from ourselves means we do not allow ourselves the same level of vulnerability. And, because the ability to be vulnerable is a key element of trust, when vulnerability is curtailed, trust is a less likely outcome, and the cycle repeats.

Who sits at our dinner table matters. Trusted relationships in our personal lives extend into the workplace and can have a profound effect on who we choose, who we rate, and who we invest in. Deep relationships are likely to create deep affinity, and as a result, deeper connections and greater positivity. Despite our best intentions, affinity creeps into workplace decisions. If we spend less time in intimate settings with people who are different from ourselves, the level and depth of affinity we have for anyone in that group is often lower. Affinity biases, or the preferences which drive us to feel deeply positive, neutral or negative towards specific groups, are incredibly common. They show up in how we are drawn towards people who look like us, act like us and come from a similar background. Stronger feelings of affinity rarely extend to people we don't know well or are less comfortable being around.

Stereotyping often plays a role in exacerbating affinity bias. Whether conscious or unconscious, when we make generalisations about any particular group and then apply those generalisations to an individual, we are guilty of stereotyping. Racial stereotyping is something most of us would like to think we don't do. But racial stereotypes are particularly prevalent and hard to combat when racial groups have limited experience of each other. The more high-intimacy contact, varied interactions and human connection you have with people in a group, the more you can see the fallacy within racial typecasts. Not all Asians are good at maths just as not all Black people are good at sport and not all Mexican Americans are field workers who have entered the country illegally.

> My workplace was doing a bit of research collecting the lived experience of people from different levels in the organisation. I had been an employee for over thirty years and was invited to be part of an exercise in collating relevant stories and lived experience. As part of that process, I was being interviewed by an eminent professor who had been brought in especially to collect those stories. It was a casual interview, over lunch. He started with an open question: 'Tell me about you.' In sharing my story, I told him I was a dad, with two kids. At which point he leaned in, interrupting me, and said, 'By the same mother?'
>
> I sat there in shock. The effect was immediate. I lost my hunger. Everything went quiet and hazy. I couldn't believe what he had asked me and I was initially confused by why the question was posed. I didn't confront him. I was literally caught in the headlights. In fact, I didn't say much from that point onwards. I don't

think the professor ever realised what he had said or the impact it had on me.

Once again, this micro-aggression had rendered the victim 'less than' and, in this case, reduced my performance through shock and my feeling of offence. Meanwhile, the perpetrator (the professor) just went about the everyday activity, almost certainly putting my silence down to my inability to articulate myself.

Rob N.

Can you imagine for a moment being Rob? Imagine what it's like to have such a blatant stereotype thrown in your face in the middle of an interview. What would you do? How would you react? And more importantly, what kind of lasting legacy would it have on your sense of self?

It's not intentional and nor is it usually even conscious, but racial stereotypes and minimised contact compound each other. When we don't have our own set of diverse and unique data points to counter a bias, we lean even more on stereotypes to fill in the blanks. It doesn't help when the racial homogeneity of the media presents a skewed perspective on the world. How can we begin to get a clear view of what it means to be Black or Asian when the key sources of information in our lives are so white?

Our reaction to transgender individuals is a good example of how, when we have limited data points or don't have trusted relationships with members of a group, bias fills in the gaps. We make predictions or assumptions about trans people based on previous 'experience' even when that experience is likely based on what we've read in the newspaper or seen on television.

Our lack of intimate knowledge of a group means that we are prone to bias. In my experience, the groups who face the most extreme and prevalent stereotypes are Black men, the trans community and Muslim individuals. Individuals in all three groups spend significant energy working to distance themselves from commonly held stereotypes.

> *When I went to pick up my paper on the day after the London Bridge attack, my local shop owner bowed his head and pointed to the front page. 'These are not Muslims,' he repeated several times. 'These are terrorists. They are not the same thing.'*
>
> *I've been getting my paper from the same corner shop for almost twenty years. I've never believed he, or his son, were anything other than smiling men, but I realised in that moment how important it was to him that I know these are the actions of terrorists, not the actions of Muslims.*
>
> Jan

Imagine feeling the need to tell the person who you see daily that the stereotype of extremist, terrorist or jihadist isn't who you are. People who are in frequently stereotyped groups have different ways to distance themselves from the stereotype. Some, like the local shop owner selling Jan her newspaper, verbalise it. Others alter their behaviour in order not to be seen as one of 'those people'.

In a series of interviews I completed to help a client understand the experience of Black colleagues, I met a young investment banker who confided in me that he never wore a coat to work, not even in winter, because of the automatic response it created in people. Instead, he wore layers of shirts under his suit which he would then remove in the bathroom once getting to the office. Can you imagine having to worry about being seen as a threat to such an extent that you cannot risk wearing a winter coat? Not only does that kind of behaviour change have physical implications (it's wet and cold in London in the winter), it also leaves an emotional scar. At what point do you start believing stereotypes as 'the truth' and allow them to limit your ambitions and your life possibilities?

> *I end up with this feeling, this niggle, that I don't belong. That despite my parents being born here, despite me being born here, I am still being tolerated to a point. I am aware of the covert way people look at me on the bus, and at the shop, making sure I pay. I have to constantly try to show that I am a good person in order to ease that feeling.*
>
> Vivienne

We can only hope to overcome the pervasive nature of these stereotypes if we first understand why they have a place in our inner mind. Stereotypes only work when we don't have many other data points to counter them. If we have minimal authentic or generally low-intimacy friendships with Black individuals, then we are more prone to bias against the Black community. Conversely, if we have highly authentic or high-intimacy relationships with Black individuals, then we can look at racial stereotypes and see them for what they are – gross generalisations which have very little to do with the person in front of us. But intimacy isn't one-sided. It takes both parties to invest in a relationship and 'diverse' people often hold back. Relationship gaps are is exacerbated when minority groups lean on the idea that 'my work will speak for itself'.

> *It's a challenge that every Black parent faces at the moment. Our kids have more opportunity than we had. Before, there was one way to success – through*

excelling at school. There was a mindset that exams were the measuring stick for success and as a result schoolwork came at the detriment to other kinds of development.

My dad was an educator. It took him a lot to accept me being Head Boy. He didn't look at it as a way to develop my leadership skills. He thought it would distract me from getting good grades. Most people of an older generation don't put stock in leadership positions at school. The net effect is that when you look across Black professionals, you will find a lot of them excelling in technical careers – as medical doctors, as lawyers, as accountants or pharmacists – but they are totally absent from other professions. That's because of uni-directional parenting.

The impact isn't just on which profession you choose, it's visible in leadership. For the first few years after graduating, kids who have been coached to excel at school do okay in the workplace. But as you get higher in an organisation you need softer skills, and those skills are not always built or encouraged.

Vince

Whether you're Black, Asian, Latino/a or in any other ethnic minority group, chances are that you don't want to be known for the colour of your skin. The same is true for women, the LGBTQ+ community, individuals with a disability and every other minority group I've ever encountered. None of us want to be defined by our difference. Instead, we want to be valued for the intelligence we possess and the quality of work we produce. Which is why so many of us double down on hard work and in doing so underestimate the weight of workplace relationships. This is further exacerbated in communities where parents actively coach their children not to be visible. 'Keep your head down.' 'Don't put your head above the parapet.' 'Don't be disruptive.' 'Get in, do a good job, and get out.' There are very good reasons for this coaching. Being noticed for the colour of your skin, for being gay or labelled as 'disabled', was once unlikely to lead to a positive outcome. And if we're being honest, even today some of those things can lead to pain or even death.

I get the desire to be judged on work. Never in my life have I wanted to be included for my boobs. But the problem with doubling down on hard work is that it doesn't take into account the role of relationships. Is anyone really judged on work alone? Relationships are, and always have been, key to success. Spending more time on increasing the quality of your work and spending less time focused on relationships has direct consequences. Relationships matter as much as, if not more than, talent, which is why the building of connected, vulnerable and high-affinity relationships between members of different diverse groups is vital to inclusion.

The role of bias

In recent years, bias has been a huge focus and a huge distraction. Unconscious bias has gone from a specialist psychology field to something commonly discussed in many large organisations. That rapid rise to consciousness, no pun intended, has meant organisations are rushing to solve their bias problems. Training has been rolled out en masse and, like any kind of training, it can range from being exceptionally poor and unengaging to being the most profound moment in someone's year or career.

My first training in bias was more than two decades ago

and it sticks out in my mind only because it was so incredibly dull. It did very little to increase my understanding of the subject and nothing at all to change my behaviour. It was a two-hour death-by-PowerPoint where the instructor read out content on slides about 'micro-inequities'. Today, a lot more awareness exists about bias, and although the training has improved significantly, very little has changed as a result. In fact, some claim the focus on bias has no sustained impact on long-term behaviours.[13] Why isn't all this focus on bias helping?

For starters, bias and the instincts which underpin our biases are almost as natural as breathing. At a base level, bias is simply preference. It's our reptilian brain's way of shortcutting and speeding up our decision-making time in order to keep us alive. Those core preferences are hardwired. They existed because thousands of years ago we were literally fighting for our lives. Daily survival required us to detect threat instantly and to put into place an immediate behaviour to alleviate that threat. The world has changed for most of us. We no longer live in caves. We no longer need groups to protect us from predatory animals, or to help us hunt for large prey. We have come a long way in our fight for our survival, but our biases, it seems, have not.

On the whole, we are drawn to people like us and are fond of people with whom we are most familiar. We seek out information and points of view which confirm our own beliefs. We judge individuals who behave in what we consider 'abnormal' or unexpected ways – assuming any individual behaviour is indicative of a wider issue. We make assumptions that past performance is an indicator of future potential.

Most of our biases follow clear logic – they exist to help us rationalise inputs and to make quick decisions meant to keep us alive. Although our environment has changed a lot since those instincts were needed for basic survival, biases still govern how we think and act. Take height bias, for example. We no longer live in a world where hunting plays a role in how we secure food, or where physical protection from wildlife or other tribes is a daily necessity. And yet, we are still drawn to tall people. Today, Fortune 500 CEOs are, on average, six feet (or 1.83 metres) tall. That is 2.5 inches taller than the average American man. A staggering 30 per cent of Fortune 500 CEOs are over six feet tall, but in comparison only 3.9 per cent of American men are that tall.[14] Height and intelligence are not related, but you're almost ten times more likely to be a Fortune 500 CEO if you're over six feet. Perhaps tall leaders were integral to survival in the dog-eat-dog world of our hunter–gatherer ancestors, but this is no longer the case. There is no modern-day need to be drawn towards the tall executive, and yet we are.

Bias is everywhere. It's in every decision we have ever made and in every future decision we will make. From our choice of real or dry shampoo, tea or coffee, a full English or no breakfast at all, we are constantly making biased decisions. Even the decision to prepare for a meeting several months in advance compared to the decision to 'wing it' is biased as it is laden with preference and personal judgement. And although skipping breakfast results in no more harm than an empty stomach, the impact of other biases is not trivial. A 2020 United Nations global study on gender social norms found that roughly half of the world's men and women feel that men make better political leaders, 41 per cent feel that men make better business executives and 40 per cent feel that men have more right to a job than women do when employment is scarce.[15] In the UK, one in four employers admit they are less likely to employ some-one with a disability.[16] Those biases, be they against women as leaders, or biases that stop someone from offering gain-ful employment to a person with a disability, have real and significant consequences.

The study of bias creates many questions. How can we differentiate biases which are helpful in a modern context and get rid of the ones that are either irrelevant or harmful? How do we learn to spot bias as it's happening? What tools do we need to harness our biases and make sure they don't have a negative impact on others?

If we don't answer these questions, we are unlikely to remove the effects of bias on the workplace. In fact, there is evidence to suggest that the more we talk about bias, but don't spend the time figuring out how to remove its effects, the more we may exacerbate it. Researchers from the Uni-versity of Washington, UCLA and UC Santa Barbara showed that the mere presence of diversity policies, diversity training and diversity awards cause white people to be less likely to believe racial discrimination exists and cause men to be less likely to believe gender discrimination exists, des-pite other data and evidence.[17] If bias programmes only teach individuals about the existence of bias, but don't cre-ate new skills and new behaviours, bias may become even more prevalent than before.

Our fear of being (seen to be) biased

If you ask most people the point-blank question 'Are you biased?', very few will admit that yes, they are indeed biased. Most responses would be 'No, of course not'. In my experience, these responses are genuine. People do not want to be biased in part because being biased feels like a direct contradiction of being nice when, in reality, being a nice person has very little to do with whether we are biased or not.

There are also a handful of people I've met who are aware that they are biased but believe the effect of their bias is minimal or that they somehow have bias 'under control'. But control is hard to achieve if we aren't consistently conscious about how our inner brain is guiding our outward behaviours.

To demonstrate the effects of bias, American television company ABC planted a hidden camera crew in a park to capture reactions of average US citizens during a midday walk through the park as they witnessed a bike being 'stolen' by a white male actor, a Black male actor and a white female actor.[18] Over the course of several days, the actors take turns stealing a planted bike by cutting through the lock in broad daylight. When questioned, each of the actors makes it very clear that the bike isn't theirs, while the hidden film crew captures the reaction of park visitors on camera and the variance in their response delivers a stark visual representation of bias in action.

When asked the direct question, 'Is that your bike?' the male white actor responds with, 'Technically, no.' The reaction he receives is mild. 'You shouldn't do that' is repeated by many passers-by. And although park walkers make it clear they don't like the fact he is stealing the bike, they do nothing about it. Dozens of people pass by but only once does anyone try to stop him.

When the same set of questions are asked of the Black male actor who is attempting to 'steal' the bike, he responds with the same 'Technically, no' as his white counterpart. The reaction he receives is noticeably different. Immediately, people begin shouting at him. Groups of people are attracted to the scene. Several people film or photograph the Black actor to take evidence to the police. 'You won't get away with this' is the sentiment he receives. Another park-goer is so angry he attempts to take the actor's tools so that he cannot steal the bike.

The response the white actor receives is not only significantly less aggressive to that of the Black actor but additionally, many people try to ensure the Black 'thief' is caught by the police and suitably punished. Not a single passer-by who interacts with the white 'thief' does anything of the sort.

When an attractive white female actor attempts to steal the bike, the response she receives is gobsmacking. In broad daylight she is seen cutting the lock off a bike which she openly tells the park-goers is not her bike. And yet, three different men, two of whom are walking with their female partners, offer to help her. The men proceed to take over the tools and to cut the lock off the bike for her or to remove the pole it is chained to. Interestingly, the women who see the female actor trying to steal the bike do try to intervene to stop her from stealing it.

Only when I saw this video on bias did my understanding of unconscious bias truly begin. The hidden film had uncovered something that is impossible to deny. The variance in the reaction of hundreds of individuals in the park, and the underlying belief systems which led them to act as they did, looked something like this:

White people are okay, even when they do bad things.
Black people steal things and should be punished.
Women need help.

These statements sound ludicrous. The statements *are* ludicrous. They are also ugly. None of us would like to admit that our biases run deep enough that we believe such racial nonsense or hold such a view of women. And yet, the actions of the hundreds of average citizens make it clear. Whether we like to admit it or not, our unconscious bias drives us to treat different people differently. These biases on race and gender play out in our everyday lives and have very real consequences for women, for the Black community and for many others.

Over the course of my work, I've discovered that fear of being seen to be biased changes people's behaviour. I often find that feedback given to ethnic minorities isn't as rich, as detailed or as corrective as it could be. Instead, performance reviews tend to be shorter, vaguer and less actionable. Sometimes the feedback is never given at all.

> *I was in a meeting recently where another ethnic minority presented and they were not prepared; they did not have the skills to present in the way they needed. Everyone talked amongst themselves about the individual's lack of capability, but no one talked to them. Don't avoid feedback. You're not supporting their growth.*
>
> *If you see a flaw, tell me. If you see I am not ready, prepare me. Be honest with me. If I am wearing the wrong thing, behaving in the wrong way, missing a skill, I want to know. Bring me into your coaching world.*
>
> *Vivienne*

People avoid constructive feedback because they want to avoid assumptions of bias (or of racism, in this case). But avoiding feedback doesn't help the person who needs to receive coaching. If no one ever tells you, you never get a chance to grow.

Bias can seem very harmless, and to some extent at an individual level, it can be. But when we layer individual biases together and look at the collective societal impact, the facts and outcomes for certain groups are clear. Bias plays a prominent role in creating and maintaining inequality. We have no hope of combatting the effects of it if we pretend it doesn't exist.

A fancy name for racism

In 2017, the BBC did a test using an identical CV, one under the name Mohamed and the other under the name Adam. Adam received three times as many offers for interviews.[19] In an experiment to test the bias against Black-sounding names in the US job market, researchers sent 5,000 fake CVs in response to live job adverts. White-sounding applicants received 1.5 times as many call-backs as visible Black American-sounding names.[20] It turns out we prefer Emily and Greg to Lekisha and Jamal. It isn't just Mohamed or Lekisha and it isn't just the UK or the US. Decades of research and dozens of studies have been done which prove name bias plays a role when applying for a job. The findings are clear: whether you live in the US, Australia,[21] Canada,[22] Scotland,[23] Germany, Norway, the Netherlands, Spain[24] or Britain, if you have an 'ethnic' sounding name, you are significantly less likely to receive a call-back or an interview during recruitment.

The impact is that candidates who don't have 'white-sounding' names have to send significantly more applications just to receive a positive response, and some go so far as to change their name in order to get a different response from recruiters and employers.

My mum is from a tiny village in Wales. I was born there, but we lived abroad in Kuwait, where my father was from. In the early 1990s, we moved back to Wales and the transition was rough for everyone. My village is a closed community and outsiders have not always been welcomed. I was three and my name was Karima Hussein. No matter how hard my parents tried, no nursery would take me until my mum decided to change my surname to her maiden name, and I became Karima Bryant. We whitewashed my identity to give me access to something as basic as education. I was ethnically ambiguous enough to pass as white, and so growing up no one really questioned my identity or my background.

My mother and father eventually divorced when I was four and a half; I didn't see my father again after he returned to the Middle East. My mum remarried and I was raised in a white, middle-class household with all sorts of privilege – including a white-sounding surname. I went to private school. I had horses and went on big holidays abroad. I didn't have any diverse friends because there wasn't anyone diverse where I was from.

When I went to university in Manchester everything changed; I felt compelled to explore my Arabic roots. Manchester was different to the little village in which I had grown up. I found friends from all different walks of life and felt the freedom to begin to craft my own identity. I decided to take my name back and once again be known as Karima Hussein. At the end of university, I was applying furiously for jobs. It was May 2010, and I hadn't had a single call-back. By November I had given up on the job search when a friend said *to me, 'It's your name, you know.' And so, I changed my surname again, removing Hussein from new applications. Almost immediately, the phone calls came pouring in. Nothing about my experience had changed. It was the same CV, except I had my British surname.*

I grew up at a time where the Middle East was under intense scrutiny. From an early age, I've had to change to fit in, leaning into the side of my identity that was the same as everyone else around me. I spent years hiding away the other 50 per cent of who I am. Eventually it takes a toll, there's a lot of internalised bias, self-loathing and shame that you are conditioned to feel. My shame also carries the weight of knowing my name was changed in order to make my life easier. In doing so, my experience has been one of privilege, access and opportunity, over hardship and inequality– all because of a name.

Karima

We call this phenomenon 'name bias', but that is just a fancy name for racism. It isn't always intentional, but it always has some level of impact. Who knows what the recruiters were thinking when they scanned Karima's CV? It's possible that they weren't even aware of why they were moving her to the 'no' pile. It's also possible that her CV was screened by an AI tool, as is the case in many large organisations. Whether the screening was done by human or technology, the dampening effect on opportunity remains the same.

When I look back at the hiring which I did in the early years of my career, I can remember being in a hurry. I can also remember purposefully prioritising candidates to call back if I knew how to pronounce their name. I wasn't being intentionally racist, and I had no desire to help or harm one candidate over another. I was driven more out of a desire to eliminate awkward conversations about name pronunciation, and a necessity to fit CV sifting and candidate screening in between meetings. But in my haste, and in my ignorance, I was being racist nonetheless.

Unintentional racism doesn't just happen in interviews. HR data often shows that ethnic minorities receive disproportionately negative outcomes when it comes to performance management and promotion. They are also less likely to be selected for talent programmes and be seen as 'high potential' in succession planning exercises. Consequently, more white individuals go on to rise into leadership and executive ranks within organisations, and in doing so, enjoy the salaries and the positions of power which result.

Investing in bias aversion tools and skills

When we know and understand the prevalence of bias, we can begin to build the set of tools and capabilities needed to counter bias and reduce the impact it has on others. Unfortunately, many bias programmes teach individuals about bias, but stop short of helping teach how you counter bias before or as it is happening. Bias removal is a bit like a diet. You can suggest that someone doesn't eat sweet things, but unless you take the ice cream from the freezer and the chocolate from the drawer, it is simply too tempting not to eat them.

In addition to acknowledging that bias exists in each of us, we need to look further and see how bias manifests in our processes and our systems, and remove it through structured change and behaviour programmes. The critical people decisions we make as employers have a direct effect on the future of the human beings we meet. When we have high affinity towards one group, or a lack of affinity towards another, the decisions we make are skewed by those biases. Organisations must have clear skill development and process redesign to remove and counter bias from key decision points such as:

- who we let in (external hiring)

- how we stretch and grow through offering opportunity (objective setting)

- who we rate and who we promote (performance ratings and promotions)

- who we see as capable of growing, leading or making it to the next level (succession and talent planning)

But bias isn't simply present in formal processes. In my experience, it's just as likely to creep into everyday informal decisions such as:

- who we trust to lead when we are away (deputising)

- who we invest time in, who we give additional support to (coaching/mentoring)

- how we react when someone makes a mistake (forgiving)

- who we believe in and who we encourage to succeed (sponsoring)

When we boil affinity down, it is the positive, yummy goodness that we feel for people we like. Bias either enhances or reduces affinity and it often plays a bigger role in decision making than we would like to admit. Whether it be stereotyping, our tendency to like people like ourselves, the way in which we associate one aspect of an employee's performance with another aspect of their performance, or how higher or lower expectations for an individual manifest in how we treat them, affinity biases have a strong effect on our workplace relationships.

Bias is natural. It's not the only reason we face the inequalities we have today, but it plays a key role in perpetuating inequality. It affects whether we invest in another human being, whether we consider them part of our crew, whether we give them the benefit of the doubt (or we constantly look for a mistake in their work), and whether we trust them for the next project, case or critical piece of client work.

Expanding our affinity and intimacy to create high-authenticity relationships

In a very powerful TED Talk on the subject of bias, Vernā Myers suggests that 'biases are the stories we make up about people before we know who they actually are'.[25] She's on to something. The less we know about a particular group, the more prone we are to negative stereotypes and the less likely we are to have high affinity for someone in that group. One of the best approaches to removing the effects of affinity bias is to create opportunities where we can get to know people from different backgrounds in an intimate and unfiltered way. When you know someone's story, you are much less likely to fabricate one based on what you've seen or heard about people like them.

Several years ago, Wall Street executive Khe Hy set out on an experiment to see just how much time he was spending with people in different 'diverse' groups. He looked back at his diary for the previous two years, tracking every meeting he attended. The result was staggering. Eighty-one per cent of the people he met were men, 19 per cent were women and not one person he met with was openly gay, lesbian or bisexual. When he looked at the meetings through the lens of race, he found that, despite being Asian American himself, a mere 3 per cent of the people he met were people of colour.[26]

The profound lesson from Hy's research wasn't the fact that he was spending more time with white heterosexual (or perhaps in-the-closet) men. The key learning is what Hy did once he realised the imbalance in how he spent his time. He used the data as a catalyst, setting a clear plan for himself to open up opportunities to others. He continuously tracked future meetings and purposefully targeted spending more time and having more authentic interactions with women and other minorities. Most importantly, he decided to play an active role in deciding how, and with whom, he spent time.

> *Invite me into your circle. Bring me into your world. When you want to get to know my life and my experience, you need to know I am looking for reciprocation. Open the doors of opportunity. Invite me to your dinner table. Invite my kids on a night away with yours.*
>
> Vivienne

If we want to create a more equal and fairer world, we must have personal understanding around how our own biases manifest, be aware of how we feel about those who are different from us, and how the strength of our relationship affects the outcomes of others. And if we are to overcome our biases and reverse the effects of systemic discrimination, we need more people to invest in high-affinity, high-intimacy relationships with people who are different. That will promote both a curiosity to explore the differences that come with diversity and the skills to be able to do it well.

> *Race was a quiet observation on my side. I was very aware that I was the only client-facing Black individual in our business. For the first five years of my career, I was the only Black woman in the building. I didn't share my observation with any of my colleagues. It just was. I accepted it. The journey to finding my voice to speak about race started with permission. When I received an email from our CEO to talk about a new focus on fairness, I sat up in my chair and remembered thinking, what does this mean for me? All of the questions that were reserved for the privacy of family and friends bubbled to the surface.*
>
> *A few weeks later, one of our senior leaders leaned over to me and said, 'Can I ask you something?' It was our first honest conversation about race. He, as a white man, wanted to know what I, as a Black woman working in media, thought about the H&M campaign which had come under fire for showing a little Black boy in a cardigan with a monkey on the front of it. All he did was ask my opinion about something on race. I've never led with my race. It was the first time in fourteen years anyone had asked my opinion on advertisements which feature or target the Black community. That honest conversation changed everything.*
>
> Caroline

Intimacy and authenticity aren't one-sided. Remember all the editing we discussed in Chapter 6? Be it the gay individual not sharing personal stories, someone trying to hide an invisible disability or a person of colour trying to check their racial identity at the white workplace door, the more we edit, the less likely we are to be authentic. And authenticity matters when it comes to meaningful relationships. It's tied to vulnerability, to truth and to trust. If we are to expand and strengthen our relationships to a point where they play a positive role in reducing inequality, everyone in the relationship must play their part.

Chapter 8

Choosing Your Role

'The world of the future is in our making.
Tomorrow is now.'
Eleanor Roosevelt[1]

When it comes to inclusion, people take a variety of roles. There are those who are blatantly racist, homophobic, sexist, ableist, ageist, and so on. Individuals in these roles actively work to block progress, create harm and withhold equality. At the other end of the spectrum are the activists who campaign to drive change and are purposeful in their intention and take an active role in agitation. They are unafraid to challenge inequality in a forceful way.

Activist
Ally or Advocate
Curious
Tolerant
Neutral
Ignorant
Apathetic
Anti or Negative
Racist / Homophobic / Sexist

If we are honest with ourselves, most of us find the groups in bold a bit distasteful – albeit for different reasons. We don't condone the behaviour of those at the hateful end of the spectrum, but we also don't particularly want to start a fight with anyone on that side. It's too risky. And, although we may support the ambition of the activists on the other end of the spectrum, the work they do, and the disruption they cause, make us uncomfortable. For all our belief in fairness and equality, feminism is still a loaded word. We don't condone racism, but most of us are not willing to be anti-racists. Activism is what other people do.

The truth is that most of us sit in the middle. We sit in the roles that are not in bold, and in those roles, we are doing very little to influence the outcome. If diversity and inclusion were a sporting match, we wouldn't even be on the pitch. Instead, we would be sitting on the sidelines watching the debate for the future play out between a small number of very vocal and opposing sides. We might cheer for our team, or hold our breath at a particularly challenging move, but generally, we sit in the warm and fuzzy bubble of naivety and neutrality. Being in the middle gives an illusion of impartiality, but impartial we are not. In our silence and inaction, we empower those who would reduce, belittle or harm others.

Inclusion is not a spectator sport. Even in our unwillingness to stand up to either unconscious bias or conscious bullying, we are unwittingly amplifying the racist, the homophobe, the misogynist or the sexist.

We all hope to find ourselves on the right side of history. We rely on the belief that our legacy of being a good person will see us through in the end. But when it comes to inclusion, hope is not enough. Hope allows us to continue to hang out in the shadows waiting for someone else to fix what is broken. It is easy to claim to be an ally; it is much harder to actually show up and do the work.

Even those of us who take a more active role towards inclusion for one group are not likely to be taking the same role for every group. Nor are we taking the same role 100 per cent of the time. We move along the spectrum of roles on any given day of the week and in the different situations in which we find ourselves. It simply isn't possible to be a perfect ally all of the time. Instead, we need the desire and the skills to recognise when we shift to a role which we didn't intend to take, and then we need to make the necessary course correction to get back to being an ally.

Allyship is not down to luck or fate. It's not a spin of the

wheel or a roll of the dice. It requires conscious consideration, follow-through, and action.

Today, we are making the collective social decisions which shape our future. We envisage diversity as a battle being fought between two ends of the spectrum, but the reality is the battle, and the culture war in which we find ourselves, will not be won or lost by the two groups at either end shouting it out. It will be won by those in the middle. The ones who today are idle, but tomorrow, if they choose to participate, will turn the tide in either direction. If they move from tolerance and curiosity, and into active allyship – however big or small the action – they have the capacity to shape the world into the kind of place we aspire for it to be. Conversely, if those in the middle slip into apathy, or worse yet, an aggressive or anti role, we have the capacity to unravel progress and perpetuate harm.

'It's just a matter of time' and 'Won't our children fix this?'

In almost every diversity workshop I run, someone will inevitably share stories about their racist grandfather, their homophobic aunt or their sexist father. Old people, it seems, are the reason these outdated views still exist. Conversely, we pin a lot of our hopes on the next generation. Won't our children fix this for us? Isn't it just a matter of time until equality works its way through the system?

Unfortunately, our children and our young people are not as open as we would like to believe. Despite young people being significantly more likely to publicly identify as LGBTQ+ than any other generation, not all young people are open to the idea of same-sex relationships or expressions of gender identity. While overall bullying of LGBTQ+ children has dropped by 55 per cent since 2012, nearly half of British lesbian, gay and bisexual pupils and 64 per cent of trans pupils are still bullied.[2] When it comes to racism, almost all British children have experienced racism at school.[3] One in four female students at mixed-sex schools have been subject to unwanted physical touching of a sexual nature while at school, and one in three teachers in mixed-sex secondary schools say they witness sexual harassment in their school on at least a weekly basis.[4] Ugly belief systems and ugly behaviours are being handed down from generation to generation.

Many believe that if we let our modern world play out, men will naturally assume more of a role in parenting, women will rise to leadership in greater numbers, and other inequalities that people of colour, gay individuals, trans individuals, or individuals with a disability face, will simply iron out over time. Unfortunately, if history is a predictor of the future, we can say with absolute assurance that we will not simply drift towards a more equal and inclusive society. The World Economic Forum measures gender parity across four dimensions: in education, in health, in political empowerment and in economic participation and opportunity. Current estimates suggest it will take 135 years, or six generations, to achieve global gender parity for women.[5]

The coronavirus pandemic was a world-changing event. For many, it catapulted forward by decades our ability to work remotely. That flexibility could, in theory, transform gender equality. In reality, Covid-19 has not changed domestic gender dynamics in a measurable way. Many men did more housework in lockdown, but from Canada to Spain, Brazil to Denmark, women, and more specifically mothers, spent significantly more time on childcare and household chores.[6]

We can hope that our children will be more open and more willing to change, but how much longer do we want to wait? Are we really willing to leave these problems for our children to fix? Should we not instead do our utmost to make the change we are capable of making now?

Personally, I don't want to pass the parcel of inequality and pin either the hope or the hard work on my children. It's up to me to take action and I am impatient for change.

Fear and laziness are not our friends

There is a deeply imbedded fear in many white individuals I meet. If I talk about race, will I say the wrong thing? Will I offend someone? Will the result be that I am labelled as racist? Our widespread lack of confidence is exacerbated by a widespread lack of knowledge. Should I say 'Black'? Or is 'Black' offensive? What's the difference between a 'person of colour' and a 'coloured person'? Our fear of saying the wrong thing stops many of us from getting out of the starting block on race. Instead, we say nothing at all.

People who can talk about subjects like race are often given labels like 'brave' and 'courageous'. We need to move away from talking about race as daring and move towards talking about race as normal, as important, and as part of what we all do. Choosing to engage on these topics is not brave – it's essential.

I'm white and I've got it wrong on race many times. In all honesty, I don't think it's possible to work in this space and at some point not put your foot in your mouth or be challenged about what you've said or how you said it. One of the more humbling lessons I learned was from my friend Michelle. It was only the third time we had met, and our friendship was building. I was enthusiastically telling her about my work when I used the word 'non-white' as a substitute for ethnic minority. As I said it, she politely set down her coffee and leaned forward, looked me straight in the eye and said, 'I wouldn't use that term if I were you.'

I could tell I had offended her and was both flustered and frustrated. I didn't immediately understand what was wrong with the term. It seemed safe enough. I could have bitten my tongue and moved on, but rather than shy away from my lack of understanding, I decided to ask, 'Why not?'

Michelle was calm but firm in her reply: 'Because you're making it about white people, as if the world is centred around them.' As she leaned back, I could tell she felt the conversation was done. But I was still confused. I knew full well that by continuing to make this an issue, I could be entering dangerous territory for the conversation and for our budding friendship. 'I still don't quite get it,' I said. Her smile wavered a bit as she calmly replied, 'Let me put it this way, let's say we were talking about women . . . Replace the term women with the term non-men. How does it feel now?'

I could feel myself physically recoiling at the concept of women as 'non-men'. Never in a million years would I call myself a non-man, nor would any woman I know. In that moment it became both clear and obvious why non-white was not okay. Defining a group by what they are not, rather than what they are, is as absurd as it is condescending.

The reason I put my cup down is because I was thinking, 'Is it worth my energy talking to this particular person?' It's a judgement you often have to make. I choose very intentionally who I challenge. The person has to be open enough and willing enough for us to have an informed conversation. If they are not, there is a potential it just ends up in an argument.

When you didn't get it, and you said you didn't, it was

*really good because we got to go to the next level. Non-
white seems like a small thing, but it's big. It's indicative
of how we centre whiteness – it happens everywhere.*

Michelle

That conversation could have been a make or break in
my friendship with Michelle. It was embarrassing to be
called out. I felt ashamed about my social ignorance, but
also my professional ignorance. How could I, a person who
works towards racial equality as part of my day job, be so
blind to the effect of my clumsy language, and to the powerful nature of white centricity?

But the reality is, there was no course at school to teach me
race relations. Not for me, and not for anyone. Like many of
my peers, I grew up in a homogeneous small-town bubble.
You could count the number of Latino/a, Black, Asian and
mixed-race kids in our town on one hand. In my first year of
high school, a new Black student joined, but he only stayed for
a few weeks. Shortly after arriving, he was chased by a group
of older local boys and held down while one of them cut off
his hair. That incident should have been a defining moment for
me. It was disturbing because I knew that physically assaulting
someone was wrong. But if I am honest with myself, it was
easy to ignore the racial implications of the event and to let it
fade into a distant memory. It was only years later that I would
think critically about what happened and understand the message being conveyed by a group of powerful white boys to a
Black newcomer in a very close-knit community.

The university I went to was significantly more accepting
and more diverse. I made close friends who were Hawaiian,
Asian and Black, but as a young white woman I was 'blind'
enough to race that I never thought to ask my friends about
their racial experiences. Like many others, I didn't 'see race'

because race did not 'apply' in my case. As well-intentioned as I was in not wanting to see race, my lack of willingness to admit it existed meant I was woefully underprepared when it came time to address racial bias and racial inequalities in my workplace.

Letting go of any ignorance is uncomfortable. But the only way we get through to the other side is to go through that discomfort. Let me be clear. If you do talk about race, you will at some point get it wrong. It is inevitable. But that fear should not hold you back. When you say or do the wrong thing, you will be corrected. It is humbling and sometimes even humiliating. In that moment it can seem like the end of the world. But the reality is you will be okay. It is an unpleasant experience, and it may hurt your feelings, but the lesson learned has the potential to make you stronger, more confident, better at engaging in race, and better at being a racial ally.

> *Several years ago, I decided I wanted to be able to talk to colleagues about race. As I began preparing for those conversations, I realised I was totally ill-equipped. There were people of colour in my life, but I had never talked to them about race. I was clumsy and worried I would cause offence. I began talking to my team, a group of HR leaders, and realised it wasn't just me. We could see the mountain, but we had no equipment to climb it.*
>
> *Curiosity and a desire to make things better was our starting point – after that came humility. The more I learned, the more I realised I didn't know. It was then I had to ask for help. Conversations about race can be quite exposing and I realised I needed skills and tools.*
>
> *Once I did get the tools, I had to go out and start talking about race. I had to start listening. I knew eventually I would put my foot in my mouth, and I did. I*

made a very big mistake. When I was corrected, I was mortified. I had never meant to get it wrong, but I was forgiven. In fact, the team who gave me the feedback offered a reverse mentor who began to challenge some of the systemic pieces which at first I couldn't see.

Sarah U.

Psychologist John Amaechi talks about 'embracing the wince'. He suggests that if, in your efforts to engage in topics of race, or the particular issues faced by the Black community in your organisation or society, you do or say something that doesn't land quite right, don't forget about it – learn from it. The only way to move forward is to choose to learn new behaviours. That will require making mistakes and letting go of your ego when you do. There will never be a version of you that doesn't have blind spots, but the probability that your blind spots are negatively affecting others will diminish as you learn.

You're being tested. You have to be prepared to accept that, whether intentional or not, you may have profoundly wronged others. It's unsettling. The conscious part of us has to begin to question the unconscious. To meet people, to hear their story, and to confront your own soul is a disturbing experience. It's a struggle to embrace, but it's exhilarating.

Jan

Embracing the wince doesn't mean we should be lazy. I often hear people complaining about how language has changed so quickly that it's 'hard to know what the right thing to say is'. I am not sure language is changing that fast. Many of the terms which are not acceptable today have not been acceptable for a long time and many, quite frankly, have never been acceptable.

Words that are offensive, rude or used to degrade or humiliate simply should not be used. Ever. But other phrases and words are less clear. So how do we find out what's right and what's wrong in terms of diversity vocabulary? First, if we have an idea that a phrase is not acceptable, we must take the time to find out why. The word 'coloured' is a good example. Most people I meet have some sort of peripheral awareness that 'coloured' is not an acceptable term to use, but very few people I've met can explain why, and almost no one has done their homework to find out.

When you know the term is potentially offensive but aren't willing to educate yourself, you send a signal that you are lazy when it comes to race. It only takes a moment. A quick online search will get you a long way to understanding that 'coloured' was central to legally enshrined racism. It was used to divide places you could not go, the access you did not have, the pro-tection you did not enjoy – based purely on the melanin in your skin. Coloured was used to segregate and denigrate for almost a century. How can a word which was a key pillar of systematic racial oppression be okay? It carries the weight of the sins that racism, bigotry and white supremacy gave life to.

Although many people are well meaning when they use the term coloured, what they signify in using it is that they don't understand racial history. Their ignorance is a signal of privilege. Those who clumsily use the word are those who didn't need to know it, because 'coloured' never applied to their family, to their history or to their lived experience.

If coloured is inappropriate and person of colour doesn't always resonate, what should we call someone? When it comes to discussing race, there is no perfect answer to what the 'right' term is. No one label is going to fit everyone, nor should it. I recommend starting with wide terms like ethnic minority or person of colour, and then getting more granular as you get to know someone. The individual may tell you those terms don't fit, but they won't be offended. You can then ask how they do identify, which opens up a richer conversation. When you hear someone describe themselves it will give you a good indicator as to how they see their racial identity. They may self-refer as an Indian man, an Asian woman, a woman of colour, a Black mum, mixed race, of mixed heritage, Puerto Rican, Mexican, Latina, French Cambodian or simply as American or British. Self-identity allows someone to express their sense of self, which is why I use inoffensive terms and then listen and am ready to adjust.

The more you talk about race, the more you begin to pick up on how people refer to themselves and become better at mirroring their language. It takes patience and practice as well as a willingness to be corrected when you get it wrong.

It's not what you say, it's how you say it. There are plenty of moments in life when we don't know what the right thing to say is. Take the example of talking to a colleague after they have been off work due to a death in the family. How do we know how to behave? Are we brave and do we say, 'I'm really sorry for your loss'? What if they don't want any mention of it in case they're just holding it together and are avoiding bursting into tears? And if we don't say anything, will they wonder, 'Why aren't people showing that they care? Someone close to me has just died!'

This is emotional intelligence. We will fail to use the right pronoun. We will fail to pronounce someone's name correctly. Approach it with humility. Ask – is this okay? Let them know they can tell you they don't wish to answer if the question is too intrusive. If someone doesn't want to talk, we need to know that this is not a rejection. If the response to your questions is 'I would rather not talk about this', that's okay. You don't need to run away. Respectful curiosity is the key.

Suran

It also takes an element of personal judgement to choose the best term. On a number of occasions, I've met a few people of colour who don't mind the term non-white, but now that I have interrogated the term, I won't use it. It doesn't sit right with me, even if it does seem okay to the person I am speaking to.

We should know why coloured is not acceptable just as we should understand the history and the implication of other phrases. 'Eenie meenie minie moe' should not be taught to children – not with any lyrics. 'The rule of thumb' has an association with the ability to beat your wife with an implement, as long as it is no wider than the width of your thumb. Whether that association is correct or not, it is important to understand the context of the words we choose.

Language is important, and words do matter. They have the potential to lift and the potential to crush. There are consequences when we use words like 'unhinged', 'crazy' or 'nuts' – just as there are consequences when we call woman a 'nag', say she's 'frigid', 'ditzy' or 'hormonal' or say a father or a man is 'useless'. The more we choose to be knowledgeable about language and aim for words that lift, the more powerful we become.

The power of allyship

Diversity networks are everywhere. Women's networks. LGBTQ+ networks. Race networks. Disability networks.

Parenting networks. There is a network for almost everyone. They were created to give women and other minority groups a safe place to discuss the challenges they face. Diversity groups do a lot of good. They promote visible role models. They can create strong alignment and energy to back diversity ambitions. They allow for vulnerable conversations, where you can talk about your experiences with others like you and where you can let down your guard. That can often make life feel less lonely and less isolated.

> *I want to feel seen, heard and understood. My black-ness is part of who I am, but it's not all that defines me. Being believed, being heard and being listened to are incredibly important. As a Black woman, I have to self-advocate a lot. No one is going to do it for me. But when I do this and show my ambition, it's not always well received.*
>
> *Psychological safety is critical. You cannot find a resolution to the problems we face without it. I enter so many spaces where I don't feel safe – where I am the only Black woman, Black person, or even person of colour. But when I am in a room with others like me, it's so affirming. That's why Black spaces feel so good.*
>
> Michelle

But a diversity approach which puts all the (diverse) eggs in one basket has some fundamental flaws. When we over-emphasise the need for minorities to have safe spaces, and we focus on what we can do to help them achieve or change, we underestimate three important facts:

1. Putting minorities in a room does very little to bring the majority along on the journey, and the

sense of secrecy can lead to increased frustration and pushback from those who are not allowed in the room.

2. People in the minority group don't need to be 'fixed'. Programmes aimed only at minorities are often based on flawed assumptions.

3. Those with the power to change are not in the room. No matter how inspired or courageous people feel when they are in the room with others like themselves, when they leave the room, the world outside still hasn't changed. If minorities could fix inequality, they would have done it a long time ago.

This is where allies play a critical role. The sheer fact that we are not in the minority means that we hold a unique level of power to drive change. Every single one of us, regardless of which diversity group we are in, or not in, has the potential to be an ally to someone else. If we are the able-bodied person, we can be an ally to those with a disability – finding ways to adjust, include and make the world accessible. If we don't happen to be a parent or carer, we can still be an ally and support members of the team who are, and understand the unique needs they have. If we are white, or even a light-skinned ethnic minority, we can be an ally for those who have darker skin.

It's only when the majority, those who do not have to experience the daily challenges which arise from being different, choose to take an active role and play a part that meaningful change begins to happen.

Chapter 9

Allyship in Action

*'But we must accept one central truth and
responsibility as participants in a democracy:
Freedom is not a state; it is an act. It is not some
enchanted garden perched high on a distant
plateau where we can finally sit down and
rest. Freedom is the continuous action we all
must take, and each generation must do its part
to create an even more fair, more just society.'*
John Lewis

Many of you reading this book may aspire to be an ally. Claiming to be one is easy, but the simple truth of the matter is that there is no such thing as a passive ally. You are not an ally if you're not taking action. If we are to move the dial on inclusion, and on better, more equitable outcomes for diverse groups, more allies need to show up in meaningful ways. Which leads us to what is perhaps the most critical question of this book: which actions can I take to create meaningful and inclusive outcomes?

I often get asked by clients for a checklist which defines 'good' allyship. It's something I am always loath to do, for a number of reasons. There is no singular answer as to what an ally should do. How can there be? First, every situation and every person you encounter is different. Second, when we condense complex and emotive areas like diversity into a list of five or ten things, they can become meaningless. Any list worth the paper it's written on would need to be detailed and comprehensive, otherwise it risks being inaccurate or trite. Finally, and perhaps most importantly, checklists by their very nature also assume that once you complete the list, tick, you're done. But inclusion isn't ever 'done'. Our society is evolving and the actions we need to take to create an inclusive society are evolving too.

This chapter is not a checklist for allyship. Instead, I have created a series of prompts and principles to help as a guide as you find your own path forward. It's intended to help you test actions and create new habits. By all means use it to get started, but do not be limited by it. Add to it. Adjust it. Build your own. If we each grow our capability and our appetite for change, together we redefine what is possible.

It's important to recognise that being an ally isn't a fixed role. It isn't as if some people are allies and others never get to play that role. It's dynamic, which means that sometimes we will be the ally, and other times we will be in need of allyship. That's because all of us will be in the majority group on some aspect of diversity. In that instance, we are part of the group who hold the social power and have the platform, and the actions we take will have a significant impact on the inclusion of other people. But we all also experience what it's like to be different. Whether it be mental ill health, physical disability, age, race, religious beliefs, sex, gender identity, sexual orientation, or something entirely different, every single one of us will also be in a minority group of some kind. In our minority moment, we don't have the same platform and we may well need someone to listen, to understand, to give a damn, and to take action both for and with us.

Allyship isn't fixed. It isn't singular. And it isn't a solo role. Ally or receiver, we are all in this together.

Universal principles of allyship

Some behaviours and actions are unique to the group for which you want to be an ally, but there are quite a few foundational basics which apply no matter which group you are trying to include. You should recognise each one from your journey through the book, but below are a few questions to help guide you towards effective allyship. These questions, and the behaviours that underpin the answers to them, are not limited to the four primary areas of focus in this book. Whether the person you are trying to include is Jewish, is autistic, speaks English as a second language, or comes from a lower socioeconomic background, these principles can be applied to create inclusion for any group or individual.

How can you move beyond 'nice'?
Nice is not enough. In fact, nice is often irrelevant and it may lead you down a path of neutrality or apathy if you aren't careful. You can have a greater impact by being less nice. Being a decent person is a great starting point, but we need more than that. Challenge yourself to move out of the space of nice and to take on some of the grittier aspects of inclusion, which may require you to cause discomfort or even upset as you challenge and reconfigure the world.

What role will you choose? Is there a gap between your aspiration and your action?

Most of us have a desire to be better, to do better, but it's more comfortable to take a passive role. How active are you really? And are you taking the same role for every group? If you make a conscious choice about what role you want to take, you are much more likely to achieve your ambition. Some days you'll miss the mark – you're human. Getting it right all of the time isn't possible, which is why it's so important to develop an ability to catch yourself when the gap happens, and then to take the necessary steps to get back to where you aspire to be.

What will it take to get comfortable talking about the uncomfortable?

Whether it's race, gender, sex, sexual orientation, disability, mental health, religion or any other aspect of diversity, you cannot change anything which you are afraid to talk about. You may worry about saying the wrong thing, but in my experience, the person of colour, the transgender person, the gay person, or anyone else you are trying to engage, isn't usually worried about you saying the wrong thing. They are much more likely to be worried that nothing will change. You will inevitably get it wrong and are likely to be course-corrected, but allyship isn't about you. It's about the power you wield to change things for others. Don't let your fear of saying the wrong thing stop you from being part of that change. Go on. Fall flat on your face. It's embarrassing when you get that 'do better' nudge, but dust yourself off and try again. I can assure you that you will be better for the experience.

How can you acknowledge difference without overdoing it?

Difference is powerful, but it doesn't have to define us. Teach kids that noticing difference is okay. If your child points out that lady with 'chocolate' skin or the man with one leg, don't pretend they didn't say it. Acknowledge it. Celebrate it. My daughter once pointed out a man with facial disfigurement standing next to us in an airport queue by loudly saying, 'Mummy, that man has a purple face.' Instead of dismissing or being embarrassed by her remark, I acknowledged it with a positive response: 'He does indeed, and isn't it beautiful.' It wasn't a perfect response, and I won't pretend it wasn't extremely uncomfortable in that moment. But the man's reaction is something I will never forget. He simply turned to my daughter and me with a beaming smile and said, 'Thank you.' Seeing difference is not the problem; it's what we do once we see it that counts.

How can you make time to become better educated and to hear the lived experience of others?

You don't have to have all the answers, but you do have to start somewhere. Seek out spaces and places where allies are welcomed and immerse yourself. Even if you have limited time, there are options to build your knowledge. Read. Listen. Do some online research from more than one source. Listen to a podcast. Watch a documentary that relates to an unfamiliar group. Take the extra hour to be in the room for Pride, for International Women's Day, for Diwali, for Eid or for other inclusion activities. Each of these will increase your knowledge and your understanding. Chances are that people who are different from you are experiencing the world differently. The more you can find ways to listen to those experiences, the better prepared you will be to take inclusive action. I don't know anyone who isn't busy, but if you want to grow your skills in this space you have to make inclusion learning a priority.

How can you intervene when you know things are not right?

We have all been there. It's the moment where we wince, and we try to hide when racism, homophobia or sexism rear up and make themselves visible. These moments can be threatening if we are on the receiving end. Even if we are not the intended recipient, being in the vicinity is extremely uncomfortable. As a consequence, very few of us speak up and speak out. Taking action isn't always easy. Very few of us are able to intervene in the moment. Often, it's only when we walk away and are in a safer space we reflect and realise that we wish we had acted differently. You don't miss the opportunity if you don't speak up in the exact moment. Sometimes it takes distance from the situation to work up the nerve, and find the words, to intervene responsibly and with integrity. The more you do it, the easier it becomes. Speaking out can feel risky, but the reality is that the more people speak up, and the more allies call out inappropriate behaviour, the more we create a collective energy to stop these negative things from happening.

Where can you use the power of your voice to call out things which others cannot, without fear of consequence?

Unfortunately, when a white person calls out everyday racism, or the lack of ethnicity at a decision-making table, people are likely to take more notice than when a person of colour does the same. Similarly, if a man calls out when women are being spoken over, or a mate is making offhand remarks about women, men are more likely to stand up and listen. Allies need to call out behaviours which aren't helping and take some of the risk away from those who are on the receiving end of the behaviour in the first place. When British cricketer Azeem Rafiq shared his stories of racism within the game, many people were quick to question why he had not spoken out at the time. The truth is, he wasn't in a position of power to call things out. And when he did, his voice was not recognised. White people can call out racial inequality without the fear of being labelled as an 'angry' person or seen as someone pulling out the so-called race card. When those not in a minority group call things out, their voice is not only more likely to be heard, but their feedback is also more likely to be actioned.

What's your role when someone suggests the 'race card', 'gender card' or any other 'card' is being pulled?

When someone suggests the race card has been pulled, it automatically neutralises the truth – overlaying it with an assumption that the ethnic minority is out 'to get us' or that they have some hidden agenda. In effect, the pre-emptive mention of the race card minimises the voice of the person in the minority, suggesting that their story is untrue, blown out of proportion and that they unnecessarily added race in, when it played no role. This is a great example of gaslighting. The same reaction often happens with women who raise issues of sexism, or LGBTQ+ individuals who raise issues of homophobia or transphobia. We make an assumption that they are 'weaponising' their diversity status. In my experience, any mention of a 'card' throws an organisation (and the individuals within it) into defence mode. Rather than seeking to find out if race, gender, disability, sexual orientation or any aspect of diversity did have a role to play, people start worrying about being sued and get both defensive and legalistic. Instead of going into defence mode, when an accusation that an individual is using their minority status to seek favour is made, we should look closely and keep an open mind, seeking first to understand the experiences of all involved and the motives of the person suggesting its use in the first place.

How can you avoid action which attempts to 'fix' minority groups?

One of the most common workplace diversity interventions are training or leadership development courses aimed at teaching minority groups how to 'network', how to 'lean in', how to 'navigate' their career. While all of these can be useful interventions, they don't take into consideration one important truth. If the end result of the programme is that our minority groups behave more like the rest of the organisation, we iron out the diversity, and the diversity of thought, which we were seeking in the first place. Targeted skill programmes are important, but only if they are created with conscious consideration. We must spend as much, or perhaps even more, time working to fix the organisational culture. To achieve inclusion, we need to create an environment where people who are different, people who look different, and people who think or act differently, are not only welcomed, they are thriving.

How can you better engage in the messy side of inclusion?

Violence, hatred and anger are off-putting. But they are real, and they won't go away on their own. Challenge yourself to talk about these issues – with your partner, with your friends, and yes, even with your children. If you own or support workplace inclusion initiatives, challenge yourself to be less clinical in the scope and to bring in these tough and off-putting aspects of our society. If we all take an active role in rooting them out, we are much more likely to succeed than if we overlook these issues, or pretend they do not exist. Conversations may seem like a drop in the ocean, but we cannot fix the issues we face if we pretend that they aren't happening. When we talk about the messy stuff, we encourage others to engage and to speak up, and in my experience, those conversations eventually lead to people making more empathetic choices in future.

What does it mean to act with substance?

Performative allyship helps no one. Blacking out your social media feed, painting a rainbow or espousing your sadness at a particular incident are examples of that surface-level allyship. They could have a positive effect if they are backed up by continuous efforts. But if done in a one-off manner, they are just that – a performance. Ask yourself, is what I am doing aimed at making change? Or am I trying to make myself feel better? Don't misunderstand me, the size of an intervention isn't what makes something performative. Small interventions can matter, but they must have substance. Even something as simple as engaging a neighbour or a friend in a meaningful conversation helps, especially if it increases their

understanding, reduces negative behaviour, or makes someone feel included.

How can you dedicate the time it takes to build trust?

Conversations and interventions cannot be one-off. If we
want to partner together to solve inequality, we have to
build authentic relationships which last over time, and be
in it for the long haul. You cannot simply engage one week
and then disappear for the next fifty-one. Trust isn't freely
given in many cases, because there was a consequence to
being overly trusting in the past. Disclosure and vulnerability are something you earn only with time and commitment.
If you were inclined to support racial equality after the
Black Lives Matter movement erupted in the summer of
2020, ask yourself: Where am I now? Am I still supporting,
learning, engaging and actively working to reduce racial
inequality? Or was I only there when everyone was expect-
ing me to be?

What's your role in creating psychological safety?

Individuals edit in order to blend in and 'get on'. The more
you have to worry about how someone will react to your
sexual orientation, your gender identity, your skin colour,
your cultural norms, or any other thing that makes you
'different', the more time and energy is spent in the process of covering up who you really are. As an ally, you can
shortcut the need to cover or edit by signalling that it's
okay for someone to be themselves and in turn by creating
a culture where others are welcoming of that difference.
Signalling looks different for each group. Racial signalling

might include welcoming cultural norms and lessening the impact of dominant white societies on music, clothing and behaviours. Signalling for lesbian, gay or bisexual individuals might be as simple as using the word 'partner' instead of an assumed heterosexual wife/girlfriend or husband/boyfriend when asking about someone's home life. Disability signalling includes sharing your awareness of adjustments – and working together to create an environment where people are not only no longer hiding their disability, but are actively sharing their story and their unique needs.

How can you expand who is at your dinner table and within your trusted circle?

There is no better way to build trust than to break bread together. If you have a diverse working life, but those who are trusted enough to be at your dinner table look a lot like you, it's time to expand who you bring into your inner circle, who you are vulnerable with, and to whom you extend trust. If you don't have any close friends who are gay, who are trans, who are Black, go and find places in your community where you can meet people from those groups. Even in largely homogenous communities, people of difference exist; you may just need to take a bit more effort to be in the same places they are, or to create an environment where they feel safe to be open about who they are or who they love. If you already have people in your network, but they sit on the periphery of your friend set, invest more time in getting to know them. Prioritise that coffee with a work colleague. Decide to talk to someone different from yourself at a parents' evening or beside the football pitch. Opportunities to step closer abound if you are willing to look for them.

Where can you bring people in and ensure their voice is heard?

We all hold some element of power. Whether our power be that we are one of the 'in' mothers in the neighbourhood coffee scene, we lead a team at work, design products to take to market, or volunteer for a local sporting club, all of us have a chance to see who is invited to the table and who is not. Next time you are in that position, ask yourself: who is missing from this conversation? What are the implications when we don't include the inputs and perspectives of diverse groups in our thinking? Diversity is not relevant all the time, but there are moments when it is fundamental to success.

How well are you embracing data and seeking proportional outcomes?

All things being equal, we would expect both those in the majority and those who are 'diverse' to achieve proportionate outcomes in life. Whether we are looking at school (test results, selection for head of year or head of school) or the workplace (recruiting, promotion, selection for talent programmes, the outcomes of grievance and harassment claims, the impact of organisational design changes or the attrition in an organisation), we should expect proportionality in outcomes for every group. If they are not happening, we need to find out why. If people of colour make up 20 per cent of an organisational level, logic says that 20 per cent of all performance-rating categories (top, middle and bottom) and 20 per cent of all promotions from that level should be attained by people of colour. That may not be exactly the case every year, but if you find that results are continuously skewed in a way that favours the majority, it's time to do something about it. If outcomes are not proportional, we need to seek out the answers as to why not and build in safe-guards to drive proportional change. Data is an excellent tool to help root out inequality.

How can you lean into the fact that you are biased (we all are), and then work to build capability and control to reduce the effects of your bias on others?

Chapter 4 posed the fundamental question regarding diversity gaps in our organisations: 'Is it that we are biased? Or are they not good enough?' If we assume that the answer is both, then we can assume responsibility for our part. You are biased, but you can change. Why not invest in building your bias-aversion toolkit and skillset? From offline recruitment exercises to see what more a candidate can do beyond good interviewing and good storytelling, to thinking about who deputises for you when you're away and how you can challenge yourself to choose someone who thinks differently from you, to questioning why you feel more positive affinity for certain members of the team, there are dozens of ways to combat bias in everyday life and in important decision-making moments.

Where can you find the connections, the overlaps and the intersections?

The challenges we face are not mutually exclusive. We cannot focus on women and omit the unique challenges that women of colour, gay women, trans women, women with a disability or older or younger women face. The world is far too interconnected for that kind of siloed thinking. Not only are we more effective at delivering inclusion when we 'connect the dots', we are better for it. Trans men, for example, are redefining masculinity. They are not bound by the same social models that most of us were sheep-dipped in. That freedom means trans men are creating something different, new and untethered from societal expectations. We can all learn and benefit from that innovation. Our social hierarchy suggests men are at the top and that women are 'less than'. That unseen and unspoken power structure doesn't simply affect women, it affects anyone who challenges that hierarchy – that includes lesbian, gay and trans individuals.

How can you prepare for pushback?

Pushback is inevitable in the inclusion space. Not everyone is cheering for team equality and many people have personal belief systems which may mean they don't want to see you succeed. If you encounter someone on the racist, homophobic, transphobic or sexist end of the spectrum, understand the difference between their agenda and yours. Their aim is to put down, squash or hold back equality. As an ally, you aren't trying to squash anyone, but you also cannot tolerate negative, rude or malicious behaviour. If the negativity you are receiving is too much, don't be afraid to call in reinforcements. When I announced I was writing this book, I picked up a Twitter troll within minutes of my first social media post. After three or four very negative and direct tweets in my direction, an ally of mine stepped in and said, 'I've got this. Concentrate on your book.' She took the heat away from me and engaged with the person who wanted to send me a constant stream of negativity. It was exactly what I needed in that moment.

Allyship isn't fixed or binary

Like many things in our world, we have a tendency to over-simplify the concept of allyship. Many people would argue that you either are an ally, or you're not. But allyship is not singular and the truth isn't that binary. Allies aren't just white people or heterosexual people. Allies aren't just men or those without a disability. Every single person has the potential to be an ally to someone else, or to a group to which they do not belong. We also have the potential to be the one in receipt of allyship.

Allyship is also multi-dimensional. You can be an active ally to the LGBTQ+ community because of your awareness and understanding, and at the same time you can be totally ignorant to disability, lacking any knowledge of the adjustments needed to make the world a fairer, more accessible place for individuals with a disability.

It's good to ask yourself where you sit on the ally spectrum outlined in Chapter 8 for different groups. If my own journey is anything to go by, I suspect the role you are taking is different for different groups. Being completely honest with myself, my own allyship has grown through the writing of this book. In particular, it has helped me develop my ability to support the transgender and non-binary communities. Just the simple act of writing my thoughts down in a way that is clear enough for others to follow has required me to grow and engage in a different and deeper way.

Once you have a clear view as to where you are, setting an ambition as to where you want to be is a great next step. Then comes the process of educating yourself as to what the specific needs are for that group. The following sections are examples of strong allyship in action for (cis) men and women, the trans community, lesbian gay and bisexual individuals, and people of colour.

Allyship for women *and* for men

The #HeForShe movement created awareness of the actions which men could take to create a more inclusive world for women. But what about #SheForHe actions? What role do women play in making the world a better place for men? And for that matter, what role do cisgender individuals play in helping the transgender and gender non-conforming community find their path to a successful and happy life?

Gender allyship is multi-dimensional. Here are a few ideas on how you can be an ally with impact in the gender space.

Aim for equals and partners. Act with respect

In an attempt to be more inclusive of girls and women in the mountain biking community, a New Zealand adventure park changed the name of a particular bike trail from 'Bro-Zone' to 'O-Zone'.[1] The heat the park owners received for the change in name was immense, with people making comments such as 'Glad I identify as a tree', or suggesting that maybe the track should be renamed 'Ho Zone' to include the women who were clearly offended by not being included. I don't condone their behaviour or even like their choice of words, but I can see why some people might be frustrated. Broadly speaking, we are often most frustrated with change when the change seems irrelevant, and names and words often don't seem that big a deal. But it's not the effect of omitting one woman that is the problem, just as it's not the singular effect when one person calls a woman catty, bossy or abrupt. It's the collective reduction, exclusion and dismissal of women, or any other group for that matter, which we have to watch out for. When trans individuals are asking for recognition and respect, it's not okay to start suggesting that someone can 'identify as a tree'. We should take note when women are omitted or disparaged just as we should take note when male-bashing is present. Not everyone is trying to 'mansplain' just as all fathers are not 'useless'. That kind of flippant hostility has no role in a modern and decent world. Enough is enough.

Embrace equal laundry

Domestic and social roles fall heavily on women and girls. If men and boys aren't doing their part, they are perpetuating the idea that parenting, laundry and running the household is 'women's work'. Finding the right balance in sharing domestic chores and rearing children is important for everyone, and in my experience, it leads to happier relationships. If imbalance is something which you have noticed in your relationship, try writing down all the mental and physical labour needed to run your home (and, if you are parents, to raise your children). Then, work with your partner to divvy up the work proportionally. Laundry and domestic duties may seem like a dull part of allyship, but it's pivotal to creating a world where girls and women are equals and partners, who receive equal rights, equal voice, equal opportunity, equal pay and equal respect.

Be honest about the pervasive nature of men's violence against women and girls

Rape, abuse and unwanted touching are still horrifically commonplace. Those issues don't go away until we decide to ensure they go away and take the necessary corrective actions. We need to reframe this kind of violence and misogyny, and make sure that it's no longer seen as a 'women's issue'. It's everyone's issue, and one in which men play a vital role. We need more men to talk to their friends, to call out what's not okay. Whether it's subtle misogyny like a suggestion that someone 'runs like a girl', or something as invasive and life-altering as a sexual assault, it needs to be reputationally expensive not to call that kind of behaviour out.

Embrace new kinds of leadership

I often hear that part of the problem is that women (and other minorities) don't want to rise to leadership positions. When women bow out of leadership pipelines, it is seen as an example of women having 'a lack of ambition'. But is it really true that women don't want to be leaders? Or do they not want to lead in the same way as the current leadership? In my experience, more women fall into the latter category, and many men do too. Taking the time to understand why the current model of leadership is off-putting to many is important. If we want diversity of thinking, we need women to be successful in leading in the way they want to lead, not trying to reshape women to fit into a male model of leadership. This freedom to redesign leadership is also likely to inspire men who think and behave differently to stay in your organisation.

Be part of a culture which encourages boys and men to express their feelings

Expressions like 'be a man' and 'man up' have no place in a modern world. They may seem harmless, but they reduce the likelihood of healthy emotions and physical connections, which are basic human needs – regardless of sex. It doesn't matter who you are, we all deserve to live in a world where feelings are not bottled up and human touch is not curbed for fear of ridicule. Boys and men are no exception.

Reduce your role in perpetuating useless gender norms

Whether the assumption is that women are 'better' at parenting, or men are not 'allowed' to have long hair, rigid and unhelpful gender norms are abundant in our society. Do your part to challenge and eliminate them where you can. No more birthday parties with mermaids vs. pirates. No more making fun of your son who enjoys playing dress-up. No more telling girls to find something more appropriate to do when they want to have a go at boxing, rugby or other contact sports, and no more assertions that a girl who is good at sport is a 'tomboy'. Let go of the gender-based assumptions as to what makes a boy a boy and a girl a girl. Challenge yourself to look deeper at gender norms and make a conscious choice as to whether or not you feel they add value in the modern world. If they do, by all means embrace them. But if not, play your part in relegating those norms to a thing of the past.

Help men redefine success

Men's perceived success is still tied to how much they earn and what role they have at work. Just as we need more women in technology, sales, science and leadership positions, we have a dearth of men in human resources, marketing, nursing, teaching and other service-oriented professions. Any gender skew is harmful. We need men to be allowed to choose any profession, or any level in a profession, which is suitable for their passions and their skills without fear of social judgement. That includes being an at-home dad.

Support *everyone* in becoming active parents

Formal flexible-working programmes are almost entirely dominated by working mothers who need predictable flexible working patterns to allow for daily caring. Whether they are a parent or someone who just wants to go to the gym at a decent time of the day, we need more men to choose agile and part-time working schedules. When men choose a life outside of work, they will not only invest in their own happiness, but those men will also bring a new perspective to the organisational culture. We also need men to feel they can participate in those formal programmes without judgement. We all play a role in removing the stigma of men who take on a more primary role in caring. Whether it's as simple as asking our local café or pub to install baby changing facilities in both toilets, or inviting men along to children and parents' groups, a little goes a long way.

Resist the temptation to divide boys and girls, men and women, when it isn't necessary

Whether it's to create teams for a quiz, getting together for a parents' night at the pub, or to create groups for a PE lesson, separating based on sex is fast and easy. It's also lazy and harmful. Use that division only when it's necessary, not as a default.

The trans ally

The divisive nature of the trans debate may scare you from playing your part, but if there were more individuals involved who were seeking calm, thoughtful and collective conversations about how we can create a world that works for trans and cis individuals alike, everyone would benefit. If you choose to be a trans ally, you may find the following actions a helpful start.

Expand your understanding of sex and gender

When someone tells you it's the way boys 'are', or that girls are simply more 'natural' at something, do your own research. Explore what has been proven to be nature and what we know is largely due to the social environment in which children are raised. The more we allow freedom of expression and break free of preconceived ideas around gender, the healthier our world will be for every person – regardless of their gender identity.

Be open to gender exploration

Don't be afraid if your child comes home from school and asks to be referred to as 'they'. Children try on all sorts of things and chances are your child is trying on being inclusive. Listen and support. Find out why they feel it's important to use different pronouns. It may be due to a personal sex and gender disconnect, but it may also be a simple desire to be inclusive. It's easy to disregard playing with pronouns as 'millennial identity politics' but our children are exploring new boundaries with sex and gender. Not all of that exploration is going to lead to them being transgender. And if does, it's not something we should fight tooth and nail to avoid. Children need our unconditional love and support.

Seek out real trans voices

Balance what you read in the media and watch on TV with listening to real trans individuals about their experience. The average trans person isn't wealthy. They aren't famous. They are ordinary individuals experiencing genuine challenges and looking for basic human rights. If you don't know anyone who is trans, most trans-focused charities have dozens of stories from individuals you can listen to online. If TV is easier for you, look for programmes which don't over-sensationalise or dramatise the trans experience.

Understand what trans individuals are asking for

Contrary to how it is often portrayed in the media, trans individuals aren't looking to 'trans' others or to reduce women's rights. In my experience, trans people are focused on a few basic needs: to be respected and treated with dignity, to have access to healthcare – including support with mental health and medical transitioning if it's right for them – protection against discrimination in employment, protection against physical and emotional violence, and to be loved and accepted by others.

Explore your emotions – if you feel uncomfortable or negative towards the trans community, work on letting go

For some, the existence of the trans community can feel like a threat. Rather than reject how you feel about transgender individuals, try to pause and be honest about how you feel and why you feel it. Are you feeling triggered or threatened? Are those feelings based in logic and fact, or are they driven by something else? Do you want to feel differently? If so, how can you build a path towards that place? Spend some time reading to build your knowledge. If a quiet corner and a thoughtful book works for you, I recommend *The Transgender Issue: An Argument for Justice* by Shon Faye. If you find documentaries more accessible, try *Disclosure* on Netflix.

Listen and be respectful

Whether it's listening to the pronouns which someone uses to describe themselves, or listening to how someone self-identifies (e.g. 'I am non-binary', 'I identify as gender neutral', 'as a trans woman', 'as someone who is genderqueer'), when you listen and you mirror your language, you start in a position of respect. You won't get it right all of the time and you will make a mistake with language and pronouns, but your efforts won't go unnoticed. In case it's not clear, suggesting that someone can identify as a 'tree' or as a 'penguin' is not respectful, it's degrading.

Understand the concerns of cisgender people and help by balancing emotion and fact

Cis women have real worries about safety and about the erosion of women's rights. It's important we listen to and understand those worries. But it's also important that we challenge stereotypes and balance those emotions with facts. Trans rights don't inherently counter (cis) women's rights – though there are areas like sporting competitions where we need to balance fairness and inclusion. When we recognise the need to be more thoughtful and more nuanced, we all can play a role in crafting solutions that are more likely to work for more people. It may not be possible for everyone to agree on a way forward, but it's important we don't let the concerns of a few people negatively affect the basic rights of the trans community.

When you become an ally of transgender or gender non-conforming people, your actions matter. You will be playing a part in making society a better, safer place for transgender people and for all people, trans or not, who do not conform to historic gender expectations.

Lesbian, gay, bisexual and queer allyship

The lesbian, gay, bisexual and queer community have been galvanising heterosexual allies to drive change for decades. Votes for gay rights across the world would not have been possible without the role that allies played, and without the clear request that the queer community made. In the Western world, acceptance of gay, lesbian and bisexual individuals has been (for the most part) on a linear and positive trajectory for decades. It has not been without setbacks, and we are by no means 'done', but the role of allies has been most clearly laid out in this space. If you aim to be an ally, here are a few things you might want to know.

Coming out takes time and energy – simple actions make it easier for gay, lesbian, bisexual (and trans) people to be themselves

The experience lesbian, gay and bisexual friends and colleagues have is different. That experience can range from wonderful inclusive moments, to slightly awkward hesitations, to negative or even aggressive or violent reactions to their sexual orientation. This range of reactions is something the LGBQT+* community knows all too well. The simple fact is that heterosexual people don't have to come out about their sexual orientation, ever. Individuals who have alignment between sex and gender, or who don't feel a sense of conflict in their gender identity, don't have to come out, ever. If you want to be inclusive, take it one step further and take actions to make the never-ending coming-out journey simple, smooth and more welcomed. Whether it be changes in your language or other visible symbols of allyship, by signalling your support you make it easier for someone to decide to be themselves around you.

Don't hide behind your acronyms

Learn how to say lesbian, gay, bisexual and queer without blushing, rather than always referring to sexual orientation as an acronym. LGBQT+ can be used when frequently referencing groups of individuals, but part of making sexual orientation a relevant and normal part of everyday life means we must learn how to say terms like lesbian, gay and bisexual with confidence.

---

* In this section, you will note that many allyship actions for lesbian, gay and bisexual individuals are relevant to trans individuals too.

Be clear on why who you love is as relevant in the boardroom as it is in the bedroom and use your knowledge to educate others

One of the most common questions I encounter in my line of work is 'why does sexual orientation have anything to do with the workplace?' Many see sexual orientation as more of a bedroom issue than a boardroom issue. If you have not given much thought as to how experiences differ, sexual orientation can appear to be a matter which is only relevant to physical intimacy, and well, to the bedroom. But the more you understand about the lesbian, gay, bisexual or queer experience, the more you can see that who you love is a fundamental piece of who you are. Heterosexual individuals live almost all of their lives outside of the bedroom, and the same is true for any lesbian, gay or bisexual person. Who you love is relevant to the experiences of every day – from shopping, to eating out, walking to school, conversations at work, and everything in between; who you love is a foundational part of one's life. Try to uncouple it and you uncouple an important piece of your own identity. Try to hide it, and you end up shaving off part of who you are in many everyday interactions. If you're struggling to understand why who you love is relevant, try an experiment in limiting information about your home life to those you meet. Whether it is responding to the question from a colleague on Monday morning about what you got up to at the weekend, answering the salesperson's query about your husband or children, sharing your holiday plans with a friend, or the need to pause a meeting in order to tell someone at home you're running late, consider the adjustments you would have to make in order not to disclose the sex of your partner.

Ask about someone's personal life

Many heterosexual people hesitate to ask if someone has a partner because they don't want to be seen as suggesting someone is gay. When you let the worry of offending someone overrule your behaviour you create fewer chances to get to know colleagues who may be gay, lesbian or bisexual. You don't have to single out anyone in the process. Try using the word partner instead of husband, wife, boyfriend and girlfriend. You can use it with everyone. It's a great starting signal that you are accepting of the gay community. When someone does disclose that they are in a same-sex relationship, show the same curiosity and respect you would if their partner was heterosexual.

Understand that 'Pride' is not just a party

Pride Month is an important moment in the LGBTQ+ calendar to celebrate and to galvanise around the challenges the community still face. If we make Pride just a celebration, we lose sight of the fact that violence and homophobia are still real threats. And, while we have achieved big wins in some places, we have a long way to go to achieve universal gay rights. If you attend a Pride march or activity, by all means enjoy it – just make sure you challenge yourself to understand how the LGBQT+ community needs you to show up the rest of the year.

Be mindful of the geographic disparity and the reality faced around the world by many who are LBGTQ+

If you're heterosexual, it's likely you've never given much thought about the map of where it is safe to be open about who you love, or about your gender identity. Not only is holiday planning considerably different when you're gay or trans, working in a global and interconnected organisation can also be a challenge. A work newsletter in Toronto or a social media post in London can accidentally put a colleague in danger in Moscow or Dubai. Conscious consideration must be paid to both the physical safety and mental support of LGBTQ+ individuals working across international boundaries.

Let go of preconceived ideas about bisexuality

Bisexual and pansexual people happen to love people who may be of the same or opposite sex, but they, like you, love people for who they are. Being bisexual is not youthful experimentation which will eventually end. Bisexual individuals are not 'indecisive', nor does being bisexual make someone more or less likely to be promiscuous or unfaithful than heterosexual, lesbian or gay people. These preconceived ideas are as trite as they are harmful.

Becoming a race ally

White allies can be powerful agents of change for racial inclusion. But not all race allies are white. We need allyship between and within ethnic groups. Whether it's Mexican individuals who are allies to Black individuals or Asian individuals who are allies to Indigenous or Native groups, or lighter-skinned mixed-race individuals who are allies to darker-skinned individuals, allyship is an option for everyone.

Stop pretending not to see skin colour

As an ally, you need to see colour. You need to see the beauty and difference within it, but also see the effects which having lighter or darker skin can have on life opportunities and outcomes. Instead of focusing on not seeing it, focus on what you do when you see black and brown skin.

Learn to talk about race, ethnicity and culture – expect to be course corrected

Without a doubt, the most common concern I get from white people about racial equality is that they will say or do the wrong thing. Chances are, you will. But put yourself in the shoes of the person of colour for a moment. When we wallow in worry, we focus on how we feel, rather than how the other person needs us to show up.

Be thoughtful when lumping everyone 'of colour' into one amorphous group

Sometimes it's necessary to talk broadly about experiences of 'ethnic minorities' or 'people of colour'. You will have noticed I use both terms throughout the book. Using wide and inoffensive terms like these can be helpful, but whenever and wherever possible, we need to leave these broad categories and be more specific. Not everyone with brown or black skin experiences the world the same, just as not every woman experiences the world the same. The experiences of Black, Asian, Latino, Latina, Native American, First Nations, Indigenous, Māori, mixed-race and mixed-heritage individuals vary greatly between and within groups. The more specific you can be, the more accurate the support you provide will also be.

Don't avoid honest or tough feedback

A few times in my diversity journey, I've noticed a tendency to avoid important constructive feedback when the recipient is a person of colour. Instead of getting the important course correction and the necessary coaching, people avoid tough conversations for fear of being seen as a racist. Whether you're a line manager, a teacher or a friend, the result is the same. The important coaching moments are skipped, and the individual doesn't get the same chance to grow. Sometimes it means they end up with critical gaps in behaviour or skills which they don't know they need to correct, but that are glaringly obvious to others. Being an ally is not about being soft. It also includes being firm and fair. Honest coaching and feedback are needed for everyone, regardless of their skin colour, to learn and to grow.

Understand the exhaustion and trauma caused by racism

Reliving experiences of racism is traumatic and triggering – even if you are not the one who experienced them in the first place. While forwarding a video or asking a colleague to relive or speak about a racist incident may feel like the right thing to do, there is a fine balance between exploring the truth and extending the trauma. You may find it helpful to check in first as to whether a person feels comfortable speaking about a particular issue.

Know that racism plays out differently for the Black community

Colourism, or the racial discrimination within a single racial group that is based upon skin tone, is present in all ethnic minority communities. It doesn't matter where you are from, the darker your skin, the worse off your life chances. The prevalence of 'white is better' or 'lighter is better' attitudes are just one reason why anti-blackness is so prevalent in our society.

Challenge racial stereotypes

Racial stereotypes have a stranglehold on our society in part because most people have highly homogeneous friend sets. When you lack deep, meaningful and trusted relationships with many people from different racial or ethnic backgrounds, you rely heavily on assumptions and stereotypes to fill in the gaps. All of us can do better at challenging when those stereotypes are present. It is not probable or even logical that 'everyone' from any racial group behaves in a particular way. Recognising when our brain makes those associations and assumptions, and limiting their ability to affect our judgement, is critical to reducing racial bias.

Be anti-racist

Racial divisions have been visible for centuries, but the events of 2020 created a fundamental shift in expectations. It's no longer enough to say 'I am not racist' and ignore that divide. Each of us, no matter the colour of our skin, is urgently being asked to be anti-racist and take an active role in dismantling racism. Anti-racists don't try to explain away racist behaviours or to ignore them; they intervene. Next time your neighbour or friend makes a quip about 'those people', don't be complicit in the casual racism. Ask which people they are referring to, and what their intent is in sharing the remark. Next time you recruit for a role and the shortlist is all white, stop the process, and restart the search with more openness and more intent. It's possible that no person of colour was qualified, but not probable. What's more likely is that you have work to do to expand your networks and the people you invite into your recruiting process.

Appreciate, don't appropriate

Ethnic, cultural and religious diversity is part of what makes living on this earth exciting. The sheer scale of difference and variety between human beings is both educational and exhilarating. From food to clothing, hairstyles, festivals and rituals, it can be a uniquely wonderful experience when you dive into the rich tapestry of difference in this space. But there is a line between appreciation and appropriation. Blacking your face, or any other part of your body, for fancy dress is not okay. Nor is dressing up as someone from another culture, in costume or caricature, or using a cultural or religious symbol as an item of fashion. It's not the same as participating in traditional and thoughtful local ceremonies or sharing in cultural exchange. If you're not sure if what you're doing is right, find out.

There is no such thing as a perfect ally – keep going and keep growing

You don't become a perfect ally overnight. It's okay to get some of this wrong – I certainly did, and I still do. We are all imperfect. It's inevitable that our versions of allyship will also be imperfect. But that doesn't mean they won't create a positive impact for others, and it doesn't mean we won't do better next time. In the words of Maya Angelou, 'Do the best you can until you know better. Then when you know better, do better.'[2]

Chapter 10

Hope, Heroes and the Bonus of Bravery

'Real change, enduring change,
happens one step at a time.'
Ruth Bader Ginsburg[1]

In many great stories the ending is the part where the hero saves the day – but usually only after an epic adventure, after a series of twists and turns, after enduring defeat and then arising to be the hero we know they can be. In this book, and in the story of real life, you are the hero.

Being the hero might seem like a daunting task. But being a hero isn't just about big, bold moves. There are many ways to use your sphere of influence to drive change. We must each find our own path to inclusion and embrace our kind of action. Each of us has the potential to use our influence to shape the world around us. Just as activism ranges from flag waving and street marching to quiet challenge in private spaces, allyship spans an entire spectrum of activity. There are literally hundreds of thousands of actions that will make a difference – what is important is that you choose a role and choose a set of actions which are right for you.

What you do and how you use your power depends on your context. As a parent, you have the potential to be the domestic hero. You have influence over how your children are raised. You play a key role in developing both inclusive mindsets and inclusive skills in your child. Even little things such as who comes over for a playdate, the clothing or toys you provide, or making sure your son and daughter both get to play sport, make a difference.

As an educator, you have influence over how you build inclusion in the classroom, how you pair children together, which content you highlight or what stories you tell. You also have influence as to how you build diversity into your core curriculum and inclusion into daily classroom habits and behaviours. How are you creating teams? Where is difference highlighted and explored? How are wider classroom activities underpinning your inclusive ambitions as an educator? What skills are we building to help pupils unpick the complex social issues they will face as adults?

If the workplace is your sphere, you can show up as an ally in a multitude of ways: through who you hire, how you run a meeting, how you treat a customer, who you deputise to while you are away, who you give the stretch assignment to, who you take the time to coach and mentor, or to whom you give a second chance. It doesn't matter if you're the CEO or the shop floor assistant – look around and see what needs changing, and then play your part to make that change happen.

Like any hero's path, the road towards equality isn't always straightforward, and it certainly isn't easy. I suspect some of you may have reached the end of this book and feel that being inclusive sounds like hard work. Maybe a few will have given up halfway, so if you made it this far, you've already invested a good chunk of your time, and I thank you for sticking with it.

The reality is that if we are to create a more equal, fairer and decent world, it will require work and it will carry some level of risk. That risk is why some people choose to keep their head down and not engage on this stuff. They believe that too much can go wrong if you are actively engaged. But inaction and ignorance are not valid strategies. And, in my experience, taking a passive role doesn't negate the risk; it only postpones the inevitable. Diversity isn't going away. Neither is the need to navigate difference or rising societal expectations that we do better and work to evolve our society.

The more you learn, listen and collaboratively engage in this space, the less risk you face. That's not to say that you won't encounter setbacks along the way, or that you won't get called out. In all probability, you will. But being open to adjustments, and willing to partner to drive change, means those adjustments are likely to be less jarring and less public.

Social change requires lifting up the rocks of humanity and looking at what's hiding beneath. The things that crawl out may surprise you. Some may be frightening to encounter, but others may delight you with their beauty. That's because tackling inequality isn't only risky, it's also hugely rewarding.

There are dozens upon dozens of studies that prove increased diversity and increased inclusion make strong financial sense. The benefits of diversity tend to fall into one of the following categories: enhanced market performance; better reputation and marketplace brand; improved innovation and team performance; better employee engagement and retention.[2] The plethora of research which supports the business case for diversity is interesting, but let's face it, enhancing your return on invested profit isn't what makes most of us jump out of bed in the morning. Humans simply don't work that way.

People decide to take action because they believe the world can be better than it is today, and because they want to do something about it. The real reward is more intrinsic. It's what I like to call the business case of bravery. When an individual (or an organisation) decides to play a part in creating a fairer, more balanced world, you get a bravery bonus.

That bonus is made up of a whole host of good things from which all parties gain. Because allyship isn't one-sided, it's reciprocal.

Being an ally requires interrogation of your own beliefs. Knowing oneself, and knowing what you stand for, is a deeply affirming process. Allyship requires us to see the world through someone else's eyes and to have compassion for what they experience. That may even include leaning into the potential shame, self-hatred and diminished self-belief that the world places on people who are 'different'. Allyship requires the courage to challenge the status quo. Sometimes that challenge is easy, and other times it requires standing up in such a way that we take either social or physical risks in doing so. Those courageous moments are often some of the most rewarding.

Those in receipt of allyship get the benefits which additional support, coaching and mentorship bring. We get access to new platforms and new opportunities. But we also benefit on an emotional level. We get the freedom to be honest about what the world throws at us. We get the power of telling our truth, and not going it alone. And if those negative emotions from others have permeated inside, tainting self-worth and self-belief, inclusion can form part of the process of replacing them with pride and self-love.

Whether you're the ally or the one receiving allyship, the process of inclusion requires giving. It requires being more open, more vulnerable and more connected. It requires working together in such a way that, as a result, you are rewarded with deeper mutual respect and deeper trust. Being on the receiving end of that kind of positivity and intimacy feels good.

As adults, we don't often talk about our basic need for human connection, though most of us know it's fundamental to positive growth and development from the moment we are born. Trust. Intimacy. Love. They are all necessary elements to positive human development. We spend a lot of time worrying about their presence for children, but we don't often consider them as a necessity for adults. Unfortunately, they can be patchy in the relationships we develop later in life; whether it's because of busy lives, the reduction of our interactions to fleeting moments over technology, or because of our own emotional baggage, loneliness is very real. For me, allyship is the antithesis of loneliness. It's such a connecting and rewarding process; the more you do it, the more you get in return.

We started this journey talking about the enormity of the challenges we face. I won't pretend they aren't colossal in scale. Whether we are talking about hunger, climate change-related disasters, the trauma of war, the growing number of refugees, inequality or the political divides over human rights – it's easy to feel impotent or insignificant in the face of such widespread challenges.

Instead of despair, I urge you to choose hope, and then to combine it with action. We may not have the power to stop war, but we are not powerless. Nor are we alone.

A single action, no matter how bold, won't change the collective nature of racism, homophobia, transphobia or sexism. But everyday actions are not insignificant. They matter. They matter because life isn't lived at the collective level. It's lived at the individual level, where everyday actions (including the imperfect ones) make the difference between inclusion or exclusion, joy or pain, opportunity or disadvantage. They also matter because little things become big things and the combined power of individual action is awe-inspiring.

Our world is not only brutal and beautiful, it's also magical and malleable. If we work together, with clear intention and follow-through, we can shape it into one we all want to be part of.

Glossary

Language is a vital part of human connection. Without it, we lack the basic tools to communicate, to hear and be heard. In this glossary, you will find a list of commonly used, misunderstood and confused words which crop up in the diversity space, with an emphasis on those that are particularly relevant to sexual orientation, gender identity, sex, race and ethnicity.

It's important to note that while a glossary of language can guide you, language is often defined by situation and context. There are terms which are clearly offensive and degrading. I would never advise using those. But even terms which are not degrading may not fit. For example, when I am working with or talking to someone in the US about race and ethnicity, I start with the term person of colour, and then get as specific as I can. In the UK, I start with the term ethnic minority and then do the same detailed adjustment to my language. There are moments when neither of those terms work. Individuals often guide me if a term doesn't fit how they see themselves. When they do, I listen, and I adjust. I encourage you to do the same.

Language is constantly evolving, but that evolution is neither swift nor finite. Finding confident grounding in what to say and why to say it requires both curiosity and situational awareness.

African American: An inoffensive term which until recently was regularly used to describe Black Americans. The move away from African American has come from many in the Black community who have been born and raised in America and have little to no cultural connection with the continent of Africa, or any of the countries within it. Today a more commonly used term is Black American.

Androgynous: Those who have a combination of both male and female characteristics, or an absence of both. Androgyny can refer to personality traits (someone who behaves in a way associated with both male and female gender traits), physical features (such as face shape or body shape), or sexual organs (someone who has both male and female reproductive organs – also often called a hermaphrodite).

Asexual: An individual who lacks sexual attraction to others.

Asian: An umbrella term used to describe anyone of Asian heritage. The racial grouping of 'Asian' represents individuals with roots from forty-eight different countries. Culturally speaking, there is huge variance between East Asian countries such as China, Japan and Taiwan, and South Asian countries such as India, Pakistan and Sri Lanka, and countries like Saudi Arabia, Iraq, Oman and Yemen. Asia is geographically and culturally diverse, and the individuals with an ethnic heritage from a continent of 4.4 billion people are no exception. Within the US, Asian Americans are the fastest-growing ethnic minority group, growing from 10.4 million individuals in 2010 to 18.9 million in 2019.[1] In England and Wales, Asians are the largest ethnic minority group, making up 9.3 per cent of the population.[2]

BAME or BME: Black Asian and Minority Ethnic (BAME) is a term used in the England and Wales census. While the term itself does not have an offensive history, it has been most widely used by the UK government to group together people from Africa, the Caribbean, the Middle East and Asia to compare census data. While it is helpful to have standard terms to measure progress, using BAME as a way to describe people is flawed for a number of reasons: 1) Most people don't identify as 'BAME' or 'BME', which makes it off-putting when you ask someone about their experience as a 'BAME'. 2) It groups together such a large set of individuals the grouping becomes almost meaningless. Individuals in the BAME category make up 9.9 million or 18.3 per cent of the population of England and Wales, but in the context of the wider world, BAME-heritage countries represent a stagger-ing 6.6 billion people living on earth. 3) It hides the important detail and context about the way the world is experienced differently for different ethnic groups – which is why I avoid using the term BAME unless I am referring to census data, and even then, I break down the sub-categories where pos-sible to get specific and detailed.

BIPOC: Black, Indigenous or person of colour. See 'person of colour' on page 323 for more details.

Bisexual: A person who is attracted to individuals of the same or opposite sex.

Black: A term used to describe individuals of African or Caribbean heritage. Although originally Black was a negative term created to describe individuals with African features and darker skin colour, today the term is widely used with pride. It has been reclaimed by the Black community world-wide. Across England and Wales, 4 per cent (roughly 2.2 million) of the population are Black,[3] and in the US 13 per cent (4.3 million) of the population are Black.[4] But the country with the world's largest Black population outside of any country in Africa is Brazil, where 7 per cent (15 million) of the population are Black.[5] You may have noticed that in this book, I have capitalised the word Black when referring to its use in racial, cultural and ethnic terms. There is some debate among journalists and writers as to why Black is capitalised but not white. It was the *Columbia Journalism Review*'s focus on Black referring to a sense of identity and community which turned the tide for me as an author.[6] The only groups who seek to use 'white' to refer to a sense of identity are those which have white supremacy as their core purpose – which is why I do not capitalise the word white when referring to race.

Brown: A term used most by people of colour, and in my experience by Asian, lighter-skinned Black individuals and individuals of mixed heritage to suggest racial inclusion. Using the term brown signifies that if we are going to call people by the colour of our skin, we should do it universally, as opposed to calling some groups by ethnic heritage and others by skin colour.

Cancel culture: A culture where it's common to withdraw support for an individual or organisation when they say or do something which is deemed offensive. Cancelling or boycotting someone is often done in a very public way with very little chance for someone to explain or argue their case, which is part of the reason why such a backlash against cancelling exists. Behaviours which are unacceptable should be called out, but often a deeper exploration and thoughtful discussion with an individual nets a more positive response than a knee-jerk social-media-led reaction – especially when the situation requires nuanced understanding.

Cis or cisgender: A term to describe someone whose gender matches their birth sex. Cis is a Latin prefix which translates to 'on this side of' – meaning cis people feel an alignment of gender and sex. Trans, on the other hand, translates to 'on the other side of'. A woman who is cisgendered is a cis woman and a man is a cis man.

Coloured: A negative term in many countries of the world – especially within former British colonies. The term is considered highly offensive due to historic laws and treatment of 'coloured' individuals in a degrading and demeaning way. Coloured should not be used when describing racial groups, with the exception of South Africa where the word coloured does not have the same negative legacy. Instead, it describes those of mixed racial heritage and is one of four key racial groups protected by post-apartheid laws.[7]

Colourism: A specific form of racism based on the colour or shade of one's skin. The darker your skin tone, the more likely you are to experience the negative effects of colourism. The lighter your skin, the more likely you are to experience the positive effects. Colourism, which is sometimes called 'shadeism', is based on your proximity to whiteness and is present all around the world. Like racist behaviours, colourist behaviours are not limited to groups outside of the one being targeted. Colourism also exists between people of the same racial grouping. Like other forms of racism, some people who are colourist are not always aware of their behaviour, or of the negative consequences which it drives. Others are very much aware of their actions and do so intentionally.

Ethnic minority: An umbrella term used to describe individuals of colour. In the UK, that encompasses four key groups: Black, Asian, Mixed Heritage and Other (including Arab or any other group not listed), but the groups that make up the 'ethnic minority' in each country in the world are slightly different. In the US, Hispanics and Latinos/Latinas are the largest ethnic minority groups, followed by Black Americans. But there are several other less talked-about ethnic minority groups including Native Americans, Asian Americans, Alaska Natives, Native Hawaiians and Pacific Islanders. In this book, I use the term ethnic minority and person of colour interchangeably. They are imperfect descriptions, but they are inoffensive, and, more importantly, they open a conversation. If someone tells me they don't feel like an ethnic minority, or a person of colour, it allows me to ask how they identify and to get more specific and more personal. It's worth noting that there are many countries in the world where, proportionally speaking, white individuals make up the 'ethnic minority'. It would not be an appropriate term to use in those countries when referring to people of colour.

Ethnicity: A set of cultural, geographical and social norms. Often used interchangeably with race, but it is not the same thing. Ethnicity is a culmination of cultural attributes including elements of one's ancestry, heritage and geographical roots. Ethnicity is a blend of where you come from and how you act – not how you look. For example, the breadth of cultural and social norms between Cameroon, South Africa, Libya and Jamaica is far-reaching. Daily life experiences between all four countries are almost impossible to compare, which means that although individuals from those countries could be considered racially similar, the same could not be said about ethnicity.

Intersex people: Individuals who have a discrepancy between internal reproductive organs, external genitalia or other sexual characteristics. Intersex conditions are sometimes referred to as disorders of sexual development or DSDs. Some are visible at birth, such as ambiguous genitalia, but others are not understood until later in life when, for example, the slurry of hormones at puberty do not match external genitalia. Data suggests that approximately 1.7 per cent of the population are born with intersex traits – which is approximately the same percentage of people who are born with red hair.[8] Many people confuse being trans with being intersex. They are not the same thing.[9] While there is no exact, internationally agreed definition of intersex, intersex is an umbrella term used to describe individuals who are born with reproductive or sexual anatomy or physical characteristics that do not fit the typical definitions of male or female. In comparison, transgender individuals are likely to be born with physical attributes that match typical male and female attributes, but their gender identity is different from the sex they were assigned at birth.

Gender: A social construct driven by local culture and often expressed in binary terms of masculinity and femininity. Gender is often assumed from the assigned sex at birth and varies greatly based upon location and the period of time in history.

Gender coding: Assigning traits of behaviours as permanently and/or exclusively male or female.

Gender identity: A person's own sense of gender. It can match a person's assigned sex at birth, or it can differ.

(Gender) Non-binary: A person who does not subscribe to conventional gender distinctions but identifies with neither, both or a combination of male and female genders. Non-binary individuals also sometimes use the term to express a lack of identity with conventional gender distinctions. Some individuals prefer the term non-binary and others genderqueer. The distinction between the two is often one of individual preference. It's worth noting that the trans community is in the midst of exploring and defining terminology. This exploration is only made possible by societal openness and the result is that new understanding and more nuanced language is emerging as individuals explore what fits and feels right.

Gender fluid: A person who does not see themselves as having a fixed gender. A gender-fluid individual's gender identity fluctuates, and their expression of gender (what they wear or how they look) does too.

Gender expression: The way in which an individual expresses their gender identity, typically through how they look, what they wear or the way in which they behave.

Heterosexual: A person who is attracted to others of the opposite sex.

Heteronormative: A state where everything and everyone is assumed heterosexual until proven otherwise. Or, where

heterosexuality is considered 'normal' and any other relationship model 'abnormal'.

Homosexual: A person who is attracted to those of the
same sex.

Latino/a/x: A term used to describe a person of Latin
American origin or descent. Latinx is a gender-neutral term
more commonly used with younger generations, and Latino
and Latina are more likely to be used by older generations.

LGBTQ+: LGB or lesbian, gay and bisexual refers to one's
sexual orientation and who you love. T, which stands for
transgender, refers to one's gender identity. While lesbian,
gay, bisexual and transgender (LGBT) are often pulled into
one group, they are fundamentally different elements of
diversity. Q stands for queer and questioning. The + refers to
the fact that sexual preference and gender identity are complex and personal in nature. At times in this book, you will
see I have separated LGB and Q from T. My intention is not
to exclude trans individuals from lesbian, gay and bisexual
communities. They are a part of the LGBTQ+ community
and there are clear moments when that alignment makes
sense. However, my aim is to help each reader gain better
understanding and empathy, and better preparation for
action to support both the gay and the trans communities.
To do that, you have to understand how gender plays out for
everyone – cisgender and trans alike – and how sexual orientation is different from gender identity.

Majority/minority group: Minority refers to the group of
individuals who, based on their diverse characteristic, are
either fewer in number or fewer in power than the majority

population. There are, for example, more than a hundred countries in the world where women outnumber men, but in those instances, women still remain the minority in power.[10]

Mixed/mixed race/mixed heritage/multiracial: In this context, 'mixed' includes anyone who has a mixed ethnic background, or a mixed ethnic and white background. Individuals of mixed race can often feel they are part of many, or none, of the races they represent. The census category of 'Mixed or Multiple Ethnic Groups' is the fastest-growing category of individuals in England and Wales – today, one in six ethnic minorities are mixed race.[11] Population projections suggest they will be the largest ethnic minority group in twenty-five years. In the US, the term multiracial is used. Between 2010 and 2020, Americans with a multiracial identity grew by 276 per cent, and the figure now stands at 34 million people, or one in ten.[12]

Pansexual: Those who are attracted to all sexes and genders. Pansexuality is similar to bisexuality, but purposefully includes the trans community. That does not mean that bisexual individuals are not open to relationships with transgender individuals. It simply means the term pansexual was created in order to decisively signal trans inclusion.

Performative allyship: Actions which are taken in order to further one's personal profile or benefit, rather than to benefit the group or cause at hand. Performative allyship is a type of surface-level activism.

Person of colour (POC) or woman of colour: An inoffensive American term which is used to describe any ethnic minority. In this book I use person of colour interchangeably with ethnic minority.

Queer: An umbrella term used to describe those not on the heterosexual side of the spectrum. This term was once used as an insult to show someone's difference from the 'norm' but has been reclaimed in recent decades by the LGBTQ+ community and reshaped to positively embrace difference. Words like queer are both painful and empowering. I use the term queer with respect and with the intention of empowerment for the LGBTQ+ community.

Questioning: Someone who is unsure about or exploring their sexual orientation and/or gender identity.

Race: A grouping based on physical characteristics such as skin colour, facial or body structures. Race is often intermixed with ethnicity, but they are not the same. Race is a recent social construct which appears to have emerged in the seventeenth century with European imperialism and colonisation.[13] To make matters more complex, race is also not a fixed construct. Like gender, race is both how you see yourself and how others see you. Even if you don't feel you belong to a certain group, if you have the physical characteristics of a group, others may see you in that group. For example, you may consider yourself mixed race, but to someone else, you simply appear Asian or Black.

Sex: A classification assigned at birth relating to genitalia and reproductive functions. Sex is currently derived from your hormones, your chromosomes and your genitalia.

Sexual orientation: Sexual orientation is a spectrum which describes our attraction to others. We often picture one end of the spectrum being those of us who love someone of the opposite sex (heterosexual), the other end being those of us who are homosexual, gay or lesbian (those who love someone of the same sex), and somewhere in the middle lies the bisexual, who can love someone of the same or opposite sex. While these are common plots on the sexual-orientation continuum, there are others which, although used less often, are important to understand: pansexual (those who are attracted to all genders – like bisexual, but pansexual purposefully includes the trans community), asexual (those who lack sexual attraction to others), fluid (those whose sexual orientation has changed or is changing), queer (an umbrella term used to describe those not on the heterosexual side of the spectrum) and questioning (someone who is unsure or exploring their sexual orientation).

Snowflake: A derogatory term used to suggest someone is overly emotional, easily offended, and/or unable to deal with opposing opinions. The term has risen to prominence in the last decade and is often used to call out what is seen as hypersensitivity of the younger generations. Today, the term is very popular with tabloids and media which play to the incendiary nature of the diversity debate, and enjoy pitting left against right, young against old, and so on. The challenge with the use of the term snowflake is that it's a 'handcuff insult' – any reply, retort or response to being called a snowflake generally plays to the original insinuation, thus proving you are indeed a 'snowflake'.[14]

TERF or trans-exclusionary radical feminist: An acronym or term used to describe individuals who are behaving in a way which excludes transgender women from women's rights. The slang term has been at the centre of many heated arguments between cis women and trans women, and indeed between cis women and other cis women.

Transgender or trans: Transgender is both the umbrella term which describes those whose gender does not match the sex they were assigned at birth, and also describes the community of individuals who have chosen to live in alignment with the gender they feel they are. On one hand, it can encompass the entire gender non-binary and gender-fluid space. And, on the other hand, it can very specifically describe someone who has transitioned. In the latter context, it refers to someone whose gender does not match the sex they were assigned at birth. Trans people may use a wide variety of terms to describe themselves, including transgender, transsexual, trans woman, trans man or genderqueer. When used more widely as an umbrella term, trans can also encompass categories such as non-gendered, agender, genderless, crossdresser, gender fluid, gender non-binary, third gender, bigender and more.

Trans community: The broad community of transgender individuals as described under the transgender umbrella above.

Transsexual: A term used in some instances to describe a person whose gender does not match the sex they were assigned at birth (transgender) but more commonly used in the trans community to describe an individual who has undergone gender reassignment either through surgery or hormone replacement. I don't personally use this term as none of the trans individuals I've met refer to themselves as transsexual.

Trans man: An individual assigned female at birth but who has a gender identity, and a sense of self, which is male.

Trans woman: An individual assigned male at birth but who has a gender identity, and a sense of self, which is female.

Transitioning: When an individual decides to transition from living as the gender which matches the sex they were assigned at birth, to living in alignment with their gender identity, this process is called transitioning. Not all transgender individuals go through a transition. More importantly, not all transitions are visible. While reasons to transition are personal, as more trans individuals become visible, there is a higher proportion of people choosing to make a visible transition than ever before. Transitions are varied. For some, a transition may be an internal change in how one views or accepts oneself. For others, a transition may be expressed through a choice of clothing or choice of partner. And for others still, a transition may include hormones or even surgery.

Acknowledgements

It takes a village.

Writing a book is a herculean effort. Some do it fast, and others take years. All told, it took me more than five years from first pen on paper to publication. Along the way, I found endless support and encouragement, and I had thousands of thought-provoking conversations. And so it's with great pleasure that I give special thanks to a number of people.

At the top of that list is my husband, Anthony. You encouraged me (and challenged me) and then championed me. I would never have done this without your support.

Nor could I have done it without Diane and Suran, who both were there from the beginning, who read and re-read, who talked through every painstaking element and coached me through every emotional wobble... all the while refraining from judgement and helping me move each version to a better place. I am lucky to call you both friends.

To those who contributed their lived experience to make this book more meaningful and true to life, thank you for your willingness to go with me to those uncomfortable (and sometimes beautiful) spaces and to allow others to experience the world in new ways:

Alicia, Ally, Anthony, Ayla, Caroline F., Chris, Elly,
Glen, Hannah, Izzy, Jack, Jake, James, Jan, Jo, John,
Katy, Karima, Marlise, Michelle, Niran, Patrick,
Philippa, Rob C., Rob N., Sarah D., Sarah U., Shipra,
Sian, Sophie, Suran, Tim, Tolu, Vince, Vinod, Vivienne

Thank you to the early readers (Sarah L., Louise, Katy, Alicia, Yolande, Jane and Izzy) who saw the book with all its flaws but gave advice instead of giving up, and the final readers (Caroline W., Marlise, Leonora and the Unbound editorial team) who helped me put on the final coat of editorial polish.

And finally, a special thank you to Glen for making concepts in the book come to life through your talent and your dynamic illustrations.

Endnotes

Foreword

1 Billie Jean King, 'Tennis legend Billie Jean King on Title IX: "You can never understand inclusion until you've been excluded"', The ReCount, 2022, therecount.com/watch/tennis-legend-billie-jean-king/2645879590
2 Johanna Kassel, 'Armstrong accused of "serial cheating"', *Financial Times*, 2012, www.ft.com/content/d6a1960a-12fa-11e2-ac28-00144 feabdco
3 Chris Chase, 'Recap: Lance Armstrong with Oprah Winfrey Part II', *USA Today Sports*, 2013, eu.usatoday.com/story/gameon/2013/01/18/ lance-armstrong-and-oprah-winfrey-ii-live-updates/1846823/

Introduction

1 European Commission, Directorate-General for Research and Innovation, 'She Figures 2021: gender in research and innovation: statistics and indicators', EU Publications Office, 2021, data.europa.eu/doi/10. 2777/06090
2 Sirena Bergman, 'Business Leaders More Likely to be Called Stephen Than to be a Woman', *Independent*, 2019, www.independent.co.uk/ life-style/ceo-women-business-sexism-ftse-100-a9073391.html
3 Emma Hinchliffe, 'The number of women running Fortune 500 companies reaches a record high', *Fortune*, 2022, fortune.com/2022/05/23/ female-ceos-fortune-500-2022-women-record-high-karen-lynch-sarah-nash/

4 Helene Wolf, 'FAIR SHARE Monitor 2020 – What we found', Fair-share, 2020, fairsharewl.org/more-women-in-leadership-positions/

5 'Proportion of women parliamentarians worldwide reaches "all-time high"', United Nations, 2021, news.un.org/en/story/2021/03/1086582

6 'List of elected and appointed female heads of state and government', Wikipedia, 2022, en.wikipedia.org/wiki/List_of_elected_and_appointed_female_heads_of_state_and_government

7 Adia Harvey-Wingfield, 'Women are advancing in the workplace, but women of colour still lag behind', Brookings University, 2020, www.brookings.edu/essay/women-are-advancing-in-the-workplace-but-women-of-color-still-lag-behind/

8 Hannah Summers, 'Black women in the UK four times more likely to die in pregnancy or childbirth', *Guardian,* 2021, www.theguardian.com/global-development/2021/jan/15/black-women-in-the-uk-four-times-more-likely-to-die-in-pregnancy-or-childbirth

9 'Working Together to Reduce Black Maternal Mortality', Centers for Disease Control and Prevention, 2022, www.cdc.gov/healthequity/features/maternal-mortality/index.html

10 Ephrat Livni, 'Only six countries worldwide have equal legal rights for women and men', Quartz at Work, 2019, qz.com/work/1561077/world-bank-women-have-equal-legal-rights-in-just-6-countries/

11 Hannah Ritchie, Max Roser and Esteban Ortiz-Ospina, 'Male vs Female Suicide Rate 2017', Our World in Data, 2017, ourworldindata.org/suicide

12 Connor Ibbetson, 'How many people don't have a best friend?', You-Gov, 2019, yougov.co.uk/topics/lifestyle/articles-reports/2019/09/25/quarter-britons-dont-have-best-friend

13 Jane Wharton, 'Countries around the world where the punishment for being gay is death', *Metro,* 2019, metro.co.uk/2019/04/04/countries-around-world-penalty-gay-death-9114133/

14 'The countries where gay marriage is legal', *The Week,* 2019, www.theweek.co.uk/lgbt-rights/97859/countries-where-gay-marriage-is-legal

15 Matt Lavietes and Elliott Ramos, 'Nearly 240 anti-LGBTQ bills filed in 2022 so far, most of them targeting trans people', NBC News, 2022, www.nbcnews.com/nbc-out/out-politics-and-policy/nearly-240-anti-lgbtq-bills-filed-2022-far-targeting-trans-people-rcna20418

16 'Accelerating Acceptance 2019', Gay and Lesbian Alliance Against Defamation (GLAAD), 2018, www.glaad.org/publications/series/accelerating-acceptance

17 Rachel Savage, 'Rising populism stokes homophobic hate speech across Europe – rights group', Reuters, 2020, www.reuters.com/article/us-europe-lgbt-rights-trfn-idUSKBN1ZY0X3

18 'Ethnic group, England and Wales: Census', Office for National Statistics, 2023, www.ons.gov.uk/peoplepopulationandcommunity/culturalidentity/ethnicity/bulletins/ethnicgroupenglandandwales/census2021

19 Nicholas Jones, Rachel Marks, Roberto Ramirez and Merarys Rios-Vargas, 'Improved Race and Ethnicity Measures Reveal US Population Is Much More Multiracial', Census Bureau, 2021, www.census.gov/library/stories/2021/08/improved-race-ethnicity-measures-reveal-united-states-population-much-more-multiracial.html#:~:text=In%202020%2C%20the%20Black%20or,million%20and%2012.6%25%20in%202010

20 'Nearly all FTSE 100 companies have met the Parker Review's "One before 2021" target to improve ethnic diversity of FTSE 100 boards', Ernst & Young, 2022, www.ey.com/en_uk/news/2022/03/nearly-all-ftse-100-companies-have-met-the-parker-review-s-one-before-2021-target-to-improve-ethnic-diversity-of-ftse-100-boards

21 Delphine Strauss, 'Black representation at top of FTSE 100 companies falls to zero', *Financial Times*, 2021, www.ft.com/content/a80c0b94-43d7-4594-a6ae-65cc9b4952e4

22 Abbianca Makoni, 'The Fortune 500 List Has A "Record Number" of Black CEOs – But There Are Still Only 6 Of Them', People of Colour in Tech, 2022, peopleofcolorintech.com/front/the-fortune-500-list-has-a-record-number-of-black-ceos-but-theres-still-only-6-of-them/

23 Ruchir Sharma, 'The billionaire boom: how the super-rich soaked up Covid cash', *Financial Times*, 2021, www.ft.com/content/747a76dd-f018-4d0d-a9f3-4069bf2f5a93

24 'The Employment Situation – June 2022', Bureau of Labor Statistics (US Dept. of Labor), 2022, www.bls.gov/news.release/pdf/empsit.pdf

25 Clare Lally, 'Impact of COVID-19 on different ethnic minority groups', UK Parliament, 2020, post.parliament.uk/impact-of-covid-19-on-different-ethnic-minority-groups/

Chapter 1

1   Afua Hirsch, 'The case for British slavery reparations can no longer be brushed aside', *Guardian*, 2020, www.theguardian.com/commentis free/2020/jul/09/british-slavery-reparations-economy-compensation

2   Jessica Stoller-Conrad, 'Why Did Western Europe Dominate the Globe?', Caltech, 2015, www.caltech.edu/about/news/why-did-western-europe-dominate-globe-47696#:~:text=Although%20Europe%20represents%20only%20about,percent%20of%20the%20entire%20world

3   'List of Largest Empires', Wikipedia, 2022, en.wikipedia.org/wiki/List_of_largest_empires

4   New World Encyclopedia contributors, 'Quit India Movement', *New World Encyclopedia*, 2019, www.newworldencyclopedia.org/p/index.php?title=Quit_India_Movement&oldid=1020900

5   Diarmaid Ferriter, 'Inglorious Empire: What the British Did to India (Book Review)', *Irish Times*, 2017, www.irishtimes.com/culture/books/inglorious-empire-what-the-british-did-to-india-1.2981299#:~:text=Up%20to%2035%20million%20died,a%20%E2%80%9C British%20colonial%20holocaust%E2%80%9D

6   The Editors of Encyclopedia Britannica, 'Indian Removal Act', *Encyclopedia Britannica*, 2022, www.britannica.com/topic/Indian-Removal-Act

7   'Indian Act', *The Canadian Encyclopedia*, 2020, www.thecanadianencyclopedia.ca/en/article/indian-act

8   Eric Hanson, Daniel P. Games and Alexa Manuel, 'The Residential School System', Indigenous Foundations, First Nations and Indigenous Studies, University of British Columbia, 2020, indigenousfoundations.arts.ubc.ca/residential-school-system-2020/

9   'The Sixties Scoop', Indian Residential School History and Dialogue Centre, irshdc.ubc.ca/learn/the-child-welfare-system-and-the-sixties-scoop/

10   'Honouring the Truth, Reconciling for the Future (Summary of the Final Report of the Truth and Reconciliation Commission of Canada)', Truth and Reconciliation Commission of Canada, p1, 2015, publications.gc.ca/collections/collection_2015/trc/IR4-7-2015-eng.pdf

11   Amanda Robinson, 'Turtle Island', *The Canadian Encyclopedia*, 2018, www.thecanadianencyclopedia.ca/en/article/turtle-island

12   Melvin I. Urofsky, 'Jim Crow law', *Encyclopedia Britannica*, 2021, www.britannica.com/event/Jim-Crow-law

13 'Brown vs Board of Education', History.com, 2022, www.history.com/
   topics/black-history/brown-v-board-of-education-of-topeka

14 Keith Lowe, 'Five times immigration changed the UK', BBC, 2020,
   www.bbc.com/news/uk-politics-51134644

15 David Olusoga, '"London is the place for me": David Olusoga on the
   Windrush generation', History Extra, 2018, www.historyextra.com/
   period/20th-century/london-is-the-place-for-me-david-olusoga-
   on-the-windrush-generation/

16 '1968 Race Relations Act', UK Parliamentary Archives, 1968, www.
   parliament.uk/about/living-heritage/transformingsociety/private-
   lives/relationships/collections1/1968-race-relations/1968-race-
   relations-act/

17 Tracy Jan, 'Redlining was banned 50 years ago. It's still hurting minorities today', *Washington Post,* 2018, www.washingtonpost.com/news/
   wonk/wp/2018/03/28/redlining-was-banned-50-years-ago-its-still-hurting-
   minorities-today/

18 Jeff Henderson and Valerie Karn, 'Race, Class and the Allocation of
   Public Housing in Britain', *Urban Studies*, vol. 21, no. 2, pp. 115–128,
   1984, journals.sagepub.com/doi/10.1080/00420988420080281

19 'Financial Inclusion and Ethnicity: An Agenda for Research and Policy
   Action', Runnymede Trust, Appendix 4: *Risk and Redlining – US and
   Netherlands,* 2008, assets.website-files.com/61488f992b58e687f1108
   c7c/617be008ff72b2243a23e88b_FinancialInclusion-2008.pdf

20 Brenda Richardson, 'Redlining's Legacy of Inequality: Low Ownership
   Rates, Less Equity For Black Households', *Forbes*, 2020, www.forbes.
   com/sites/brendarichardson/2020/06/11/redlinings-legacy-of-ine
   quality-low-homeownership-rates-less-equity-for-black-households/?
   sh=7dcdb51d2a7c

21 UK Parliament Lords Discussion, 25 November 1981, vol 425, cc769-
   78, api.parliament.uk/historic-hansard/lords/1981/nov/25/the-scarman-
   report

22 Sir William Macpherson of Cluny, Advised by Tom Cook, the Right
   Reverend Dr John Sentamu and Dr Richard Stone, 'The Stephen Lawrence Inquiry', Publishing.Gov.UK, 1999, assets.publishing.service.
   gov.uk/government/uploads/system/uploads/attachment_data/
   file/277111/4262.pdf

23 'Race & Justice News: White Supremacists in Law Enforcement, Germany's Approach', The Sentencing Project, 2021, www.sentencingproject.

org/news/race-justice-news-white-supremacists-in-law-enforce
ment-germanys-approach/

24 'France: Class Action Lawsuit against Ethnic Profiling', Human
Rights Watch, 2021, www.hrw.org/news/2021/07/22/france-class-action-
lawsuit-against-ethnic-profiling

25 Hilary Osborne, 'Financial inequality: the ethnicity gap in pay, wealth
and property', *Guardian*, 2020, www.theguardian.com/money/2020/
jun/20/financial-inequality-the-ethnicity-gap-in-pay-wealth-and-
property

26 Nadine White, 'Ethnic minority unemployment 70% higher than white
joblessness for past 20 years', *Independent*, 2021, www.independent.
co.uk/news/uk/home-news/ethnic-minority-unnemployment-labour-
disparity-b1950050.html

27 'Unemployment', Annual Population Survey, Gov.uk, 2021, www.
ethnicity-facts-figures.service.gov.uk/work-pay-and-benefits/unemploy
ment-and-economic-inactivity/unemployment/latest

28 'Household income', Family Resources Survey, Gov.uk, 2022, www.
ethnicity-facts-figures.service.gov.uk/work-pay-and-benefits/pay-and-
income/household-income/latest

29 Jonnelle Marte, 'Gap in US Black and white unemployment rates is
widest in five years', Reuters, 2020, www.reuters.com/article/us-usa-
economy-unemployment-race-idUSKBN2431X7

30 Kriston McIntosh, Emily Moss, Ryan Nunn and Jay Shambaugh,
'Examining the Black-white wealth gap', Brookings Institution, 2020,
brookings.edu/blog/up-front/2020/02/27/examining-the-black-white-
wealth-gap/

31 Amy Scott, 'Black applicants are more likely to be denied mortgages,
study finds', Marketplace, 2020, www.marketplace.org/2020/06/26/
black-applicants-more-likely-be-denied-mortgages/

32 Ishaan Tharoor, 'The dark side of Winston Churchill's legacy no one
should forget', *Washington Post*, 2015, www.washingtonpost.com/news/
worldviews/wp/2015/02/03/the-dark-side-of-winston-churchills-legacy-
no-one-should-forget/

33 Pamela Parkes, 'Who was Edward Colston and why is Bristol divided
by his legacy?', BBC, 2020, www.bbc.com/news/uk-england-bristol-
42404825

34 'The Sexual Offenses Act 1967', Parliamentary Archives HL/PO/PU/
1/1967/c60, 1967, www.parliament.uk/about/living-heritage/transfor

mingsociety/private-lives/relationships/collections1/sexual-offences-act-1967/sexual-offences-act-1967/

35 Peter Tatchell, 'Don't fall for the myth that it's 50 years since we decriminalised homosexuality', *Guardian*, 2017, www.theguardian.com/commentisfree/2017/may/23/fifty-years-gay-liberation-uk-barely-four-1967-act

36 Harvey Day, 'Section 28: What was it and how did it affect LGBT+ people?', BBC, 2019, www.bbc.co.uk/bbcthree/article/caccob40-c3a4-473b-86cc-11863c0b3f30

37 Kit Bradshaw, 'Military marks 20 years since homosexuality ban was lifted', Sky News, 2020, news.sky.com/story/military-marks-20-years-since-homosexuality-ban-was-lifted-11906701

38 Peter Coulter, 'Same-sex marriage now legal in Northern Ireland', BBC, 2020, www.bbc.co.uk/news/uk-northern-ireland-51086276

39 Jeffrey M. Jones, 'LGBT Identification in US Ticks Up to 7.1%', Gallup, 2022, news.gallup.com/poll/389792/lgbt-identification-ticks-up.aspx

40 Niall McCarthy, 'Europe's LGBT population mapped', Statista, 2016, www.statista.com/chart/6466/europes-lgbt-population-mapped/

41 Heather Carrick, 'Census 2021: how many LGBT+ people are in England and Wales? Gender and sexual orientation data explained', National World, 2023, www.nationalworld.com/news/uk/census-2021-results-lgbt-people-england-and-wales-gender-sexual-orientation-data-3977619

42 Will Dahlgreen and Anna Elizabeth Shakespeare, '1 in 2 young people say they are not 100% heterosexual', YouGov, 2015, yougov.co.uk/topics/lifestyle/articles-reports/2015/08/16/half-young-not-heterosexual

43 'New GLAAD study reveals twenty percent of millennials identify as LGBTQ', Gay and Lesbian Alliance Against Defamation (GLAAD), 2017, www.glaad.org/blog/new-glaad-study-reveals-twenty-percent-millennials-identify-lgbtq

44 Colin Poitros, 'The "Global Closet" is Huge – Vast Majority of World's Lesbian, Gay, Bisexual Population Hide Orientation, YSPH Study Finds', Yale School of Medicine, 2019, medicine.yale.edu/news-article/the-global-closet-is-hugevast-majority-of-worlds-lesbian-gay-bisexual-population-hide-orientation-ysph-study-finds/

45 'Raiders' Carl Nassib becomes first active NFL player to come out as gay', *Guardian*, 2021, www.theguardian.com/sport/2021/jun/21/nfl-raiders-carl-nassib-comes-out-as-gay

46   Zoe Applegate and Martin Barber, 'Justin Fashanu: 30 years since foot-
     baller came out', BBC, 2020, www.bbc.com/news/uk-england-norfolk-
     54617759

47   'LGBTQ+ facts and figures', Stonewall, 2016, www.stonewall.org.uk/
     media/lgbt-facts-and-figures

48   Daniel Villarreal, '40 out LGBTQ participants in the 2019 Women's
     World Cup', Outsports, 2019, www.outsports.com/2019/6/11/18660
     301/out-gay-lesbian-bi-2019-women-world-cup-soccer

49   Josh Jackman, 'Half of LGBT+ people stay in the closet at work, study
     reveals', PinkNews, 2018, www.pinknews.co.uk/2018/06/27/half-of-
     lgbt-people-stay-in-the-closet-at-work-study-reveals/

50   Isabelle Collins, 'Young, keen, LGBTQ+ and proud . . . and going back
     in the closet to start their careers', HRZone, 2021, www.hrzone.com/
     talent/retention/young-keen-lgbtq-and-proud-and-going-back-
     in-the-closet-to-start-their-careers

51   Josh Jackman, 'Lloyd's first openly bisexual CEO on receiving abuse:
     "You should die"', PinkNews, 2018, www.pinknews.co.uk/2018/
     10/08/bisexual-lloyds-first-ceo-abuse-die/

52   'LGBTQ+ facts and figures', Stonewall, 2016, www.stonewall.org.uk/
     media/lgbt-facts-and-figures

53   Crispin Blunt, 'Britain has the most gay parliament in the world – use
     it as a force for good', *New York Times*, 2021, www.thetimes.co.uk/
     article/britain-has-most-gay-parliament-in-the-world-use-it-as-
     force-for-good-Owcgczznk

54   'National Data', Out for America, 2022, outforamerica.org/

55   The Reality Check Team, 'Homosexuality: The countries where it is
     illegal to be gay', BBC, 2021, www.bbc.co.uk/news/world-43822234

56   'No Support – Russia's "Gay Propaganda" Law Imperils LGBT
     Youth', Human Rights Watch, 2018, www.hrw.org/report/2018/12/12/
     no-support/russias-gay-propaganda-law-imperils-lgbt-youth

57   Lucy Ash, 'Inside Poland's "LGBT-free zones"', BBC, 2020, www.bbc.
     co.uk/news/stories-54191344

58   Yvette Tan, 'Brunei implements stoning to death under anti-LGBT
     laws', BBC, 2019, www.bbc.co.uk/news/world-asia-47769964

59   David Pegg, Hilary Osborne and Caelainn Barr, 'Sultan of Brunei, who
     passed anti-LGBT laws, owns slew of luxury UK properties', *Guardian*,
     2019, www.theguardian.com/world/2019/apr/14/sultan-of-brunei-
     hassanal-bolkiah-uk-properties

60 Richard Dahl, 'Understanding Florida's "Don't Say Gay" Bill', FindLaw, 2022, www.findlaw.com/legalblogs/law-and-life/understanding-floridas-dont-say-gay-bill/

61 'Legislation Affecting LGBTQ Rights Across the Country', American Civil Liberties Union, 2022, www.aclu.org/legislation-affecting-lgbtq-rights-across-country

Chapter 2

1 Gloria Steinem interview with Graeme Green, 'A Word With Gloria Steinem', *New Internationalist*, 2016, newint.org/columns/finally/2016/05/01/interview-gloria-steinem

2 Dr Anne Fausto-Sterling, 'The Five Sexes: Why Male and Female are not Enough', *New York Academy of Sciences*, vol. 33, 1993, www.researchgate.net/publication/239657377_The_Five_Sexes_Why_Male_and_Female_are_not_Enough

3 Susan Donaldson James, 'You Got the Luck of the Irish: You're a Redhead!', ABC, 2014, abcnews.go.com/Health/redheads-irish-share-lucky-traits/story?id=22916335

4 Vasanti Jadva, Melissa Hines and Susan Golombok, 'Infants' preferences for toys, colors, and shapes: sex differences and similarities', *Archives of Sexual Behavior*, vol. 39, no. 6, pp. 1261–1273, 2010, doi.org/10.1007/s10508-010-9618-z

5 Vanessa LoBue and Judy DeLoache, 'Pretty in pink: The early development of gender-stereotyped colour preferences', *British Journal of Developmental Psychology*, vol. 29, 2011, www.researchgate.net/publication/51578057_Pretty_in_pink_The_early_development_of_gender-stereotyped_colour_preferences

6 Dora Vanette, 'How Pink and Blue Became Gendered Colors', A Women's Thing, 2020, awomensthing.org/blog/pink-and-blue/

7 Olivia Petter, 'John Lewis Gender Neutral Clothing Labels Faces Public Backlash', *Independent*, 2017, www.independent.co.uk/life-style/fashion/john-lewis-gender-neutral-clothing-labels-response-sex-boys-girls-men-women-a7928006.html

8 'Guidelines for Psychological Practice with Boys and Men', American Psychological Association, 2018, www.apa.org/about/policy/boys-men-practice-guidelines.pdf

9   Christopher Mims, 'Strange but True: Testosterone Alone Does Not Cause Violence', *Scientific American*, 2007, www.scientificamerican.com/article/strange-but-true-testosterone-alone-doesnt-cause-violence/

10   Dov Cohen, Richard E. Nisbett, Brian F. Bowdle and Norbert Schwarz, 'Insult, aggression, and the southern culture of honor: An "experimental ethnography"', *Journal of Personality and Social Psychology*, vol. 70, no. 5, pp. 945–960, 1996, doi.org/10.1037/0022-3514.70.5.945

11   Yin Wu, Christoph Eisenegger, Niro Sivanathan, Molly J. Crockett and Luke Clark, 'The role of social status and testosterone in human conspicuous consumption', *Scientific Reports*, vol. 7, no. 1, 11803, 2017, www.ncbi.nlm.nih.gov/pmc/articles/PMC5603597/

12   Louise Cowie, 'Why are only one in 10 nurses men?', BBC, 2019, www.bbc.co.uk/news/uk-scotland-48125231

13   Laura FitzPatrick, 'Male teachers ruling out primary school jobs because they fear being viewed with suspicion', *Telegraph*, 2019, www.telegraph.co.uk/news/2019/01/13/male-primary-teachers-speak-fears-perceived-suspicious-working/

14   Graeme Paton, 'Teaching in primary schools "still seen as a woman's job"', *Telegraph*, 2013, www.telegraph.co.uk/education/educationnews/9849976/Teaching-in-primary-schools-still-seen-as-a-womans-job.html

15   Martin Daubney, 'No, men are not all potential paedophiles', *Telegraph*, 2014, www.telegraph.co.uk/men/thinking-man/10669864/No-men-are-not-all-potential-paedophiles.html

16   Leah Montebello, 'Less than two per cent of eligible parents use Shared Parental Leave', *City AM*, 2021, www.cityam.com/less-than-two-per-cent-of-eligible-parents-use-shared-parental-leave/

17   Ben Houghton, 'Uptake of paternity leave drops to 10-year low, report finds', *People Management*, 2021, www.peoplemanagement.co.uk/article/1747262/uptake-of-paternity-leave-drops-to-ten-year-low#gref

18   'Shared Parental Leave: Where Are We Now?', My Family Care, 2016, www.myfamilycare.co.uk/resources/white-papers/shared-parental-leave-where-are-we-now/

19   Miranda Larbi, 'A third of Brits think mum should stay at home to look after children', *Metro*, 2018, metro.co.uk/2018/07/10/third-brits-think-mum-stay-home-look-children-7698041/

20   Ryan Kh, 'The Stigma Surrounding Stay at Home Fathers', The Good Men Project, 2019, goodmenproject.com/parenting/the-stigma-surrounding-stay-at-home-fathers/

21 'Shared Parental Leave: Where Are We Now?', My Family Care, 2016, www.myfamilycare.co.uk/resources/white-papers/shared-parental-leave-where-are-we-now/

22 David M. Mayer, 'How Men Get Penalized for Straying from Masculine Norms', *Harvard Business Review*, 2018, hbr.org/2018/10/how-men-get-penalized-for-straying-from-masculine-norms

23 Rachel Emma Silverman, 'Gender Bias at Work Turns Up in Feedback', *Wall Street Journal*, 2015, www.wsj.com/articles/gender-bias-at-work-turns-up-in-feedback-1443600759

24 Marie Evertsson and Katarina Boye, 'The Transition to Parenthood and the Division of Parental Leave in Different-Sex and Female Same-Sex Couples in Sweden', *European Sociological Review*, vol. 34, no. 5, pp. 471–485, 2018, academic.oup.com/esr/article/34/5/471/5056857

25 Gayle Markovitz, 'Why are women more depressed than men?', World Economic Forum, 2020, www.weforum.org/agenda/2020/03/are-women-less-happy-than-men/

26 Global Burden of Disease Collaborative Network, 'Global Burden of Disease Study 2017 (GBD 2017) Results', Institute for Health Metrics and Evaluation (IHME), Our World in Data, 2018, ourworldindata.org/suicide#suicide-by-gender

27 Kate Devlin, 'Men "twice as likely as women to become alcoholics"', *Telegraph*, 2009, www.telegraph.co.uk/news/health/news/4337549/Men-twice-as-likely-as-women-to-become-alcoholics.html

28 'Alcohol – Key Facts', World Health Organization, 2022, www.who.int/news-room/fact-sheets/detail/alcohol#:~:targetText=Overall%20 5.1%20%25%20of%20the%20global,total%20deaths%20are%20 alcohol%2Dattributable

29 Hannah Ritchie and Max Roser, 'Drug Use', Our World in Data, 2019, ourworldindata.org/drug-use

30 Peter Baker, 'Going for bloke: Gambling as a men's health issue', Royal Society for Public Health, 2021, www.rsph.org.uk/about-us/news/going-for-bloke-gambling-as-a-men-s-health-issue.html

31 F. Perry Wilson, '"Sex Addiction" in 10% of US Men, 7% of Women?', Medscape, 2018, www.medscape.com/viewarticle/904398

32 Jason S. Carroll, Dean M. Busby, Brian J. Willoughby and Cameron C. Brown, 'The Porn Gap: Differences in Men's and Women's Pornography Patterns in Couple Relationships', *Journal of Couple & Relationship Therapy*, vol. 16, no. 2, pp. 146–163, 2016, DOI: 10.1080/15332691.

2016.1238796, www.tandfonline.com/doi/abs/10.1080/15332691.201
6.1238796

33 Jeffrey D. Sachs, 'Addiction and Unhappiness in America', World Happiness Report, Chapter 7, 2019, worldhappiness.report/ed/2019/
addiction-and-unhappiness-in-america/

34 'Sex Ratio of Prisoners Across the World: Taking Gender Seriously',
AcrossWalls.org, 2010, www.acrosswalls.org/sex-ratio-prisoners-across-
world/

35 'Frequently Asked Questions about Transgender People', TransEquality,
2016, transequality.org/issues/resources/frequently-asked-questions-
about-transgender-people

36 The Lancet, 'Transgender rights critical for the health of 25 million
transgender people worldwide', ScienceDaily, 2016, www.sciencedaily.
com/releases/2016/06/160617082306.htm

37 'Trans People in the UK', UK Government Equalities Office, 2018,
assets.publishing.service.gov.uk/government/uploads/system/uploads/
attachment_data/file/721642/GEO-LGBT-factsheet.pdf

38 Liam Knox, 'Media's "detransition" narrative is fueling misconcep-
tions, trans advocates say', NBC News, 2019, www.nbcnews.com/
feature/nbc-out/media-s-detransition-narrative-fueling-misconceptions-
trans-advocates-say-n1102686

39 'Seven Things About Transgender People That You Didn't Know',
Human Rights Campaign, www.hrc.org/resources/seven-things-about-
transgender-people-that-you-didnt-know

40 Qalonymos ben Qalonymos, 'On Becoming a Woman', first published
in *Even Bohan (Touchstone)*, 1322, translated by Peter Cole in *The
Dream of the Poem: Hebrew Poetry from Muslim and Christian Spain,
950–1492*, Princeton University Press, Princeton, 2007, pp. 285–6

41 'Two-spirit', Wikipedia, 2022, en.wikipedia.org/wiki/Two-spirit

42 'Elagabalus', Wikipedia, 2022, en.wikipedia.org/wiki/Elagabalus#
cite_note-dio-history-lxxx-16-41

43 'Gender Recognition Act 2004', Legislation.gov.uk, 2004, www.legis-
lation.gov.uk/ukpga/2004/7/contents

44 'LGBTQ+ facts and figures', Stonewall, 2016, www.stonewall.org.uk/
media/lgbt-facts-and-figures

45 Movement Advancement Project, 'A Broken Bargain for Transgender
Workers', National Center for Transgender Equality, Human Rights

Campaign and Center for American Progress, 2013, www.lgbtmap.org/transgender-workers

46 'State Equality Index 2021 – Employment', Human Rights Campaign, 2022, www.hrc.org/resources/state-equality-index

47 Rachel Muller-Heyndyk, 'Transphobia rife among UK employers', *HR Magazine*, 2018, www.hrmagazine.co.uk/content/news/transphobia-rife-among-uk-employers

48 Jody L. Herman, Andrew R. Flores and Kathryn K. O'Neill, 'How Many Adults and Youth Identify as Transgender in the United States', Williams Institute UCLA, 2022, williamsinstitute.law.ucla.edu/publications/trans-adults-united-states/

49 'Accelerating Acceptance 2017', Gay and Lesbian Alliance Against Defamation (GLAAD), 2017, www.glaad.org/files/aa/2017_GLAAD_Accelerating_Acceptance.pdf

50 'Overview: Gender dysphoria', NHS, 2020, www.nhs.uk/conditions/Gender-dysphoria/

51 Chantal M. Wiepjes, Nienke M. Nota, et al., 'The Amsterdam Cohort of Gender Dysphoria Study (1972–2015): Trends in Prevalence, Treatment, and Regrets', *Journal of Sexual Medicine*, vol. 15, pp. 582–590, 2018, www.jsm.jsexmed.org/article/S1743-6095(18)30057-2/fulltext#sec3.3

52 J. L. Turban, S. S. Loo, A. N. Almazan and A. S. Keuroghlian, 'Factors Leading to "Detransition" Among Transgender and Gender Diverse People in the United States: A Mixed-Methods Analysis', *LGBT Health*, vol. 8, no. 4, pp. 273–280, 2021, www.ncbi.nlm.nih.gov/pmc/articles/PMC8213007/

53 Ibid.

Chapter 3

1 Oscar Wilde, *The Importance of Being Earnest*, Act 1, p. 6, 1895, www.shmoop.com/importance-of-being-earnest/act-i-full-text-6.html

2 Manuel V. Gómez and Cristina Delgado, 'The gender no-pay gap: Women in Spain do twice as much unpaid work as men', *El País*, 2018, english.elpais.com/elpais/2018/02/13/inenglish/1518514387_016558.html

3 Arundhati Chakravarty, 'Explained: How to measure unpaid care work and address its inequalities', *Indian Express*, 2021, indianexpress.com/article/explained/explained-how-to-measure-unpaid-care-work-and-address-its-inequalities-7297857/

4 'Women shoulder the responsibility of "unpaid work"', Office for National Statistics, 2016, www.ons.gov.uk/employmentandlabourmarket/peopleinwork/earningsandworkinghours/articles/womenshoulderthereesponsibilityofunpaidwork/2016-11-10

5 Evrim Altintas and Oriel Sullivan, 'Fifty years of change updated: Cross-national gender convergence in housework', *Demographic Research Journal*, vol. 35, no. 16, pp. 455–470, 2016, www.demographic-research.org/volumes/vol35/16/

6 Gaby Hinsliff, 'The coronavirus backlash: how the pandemic is destroying women's rights', *Guardian*, 2020, www.theguardian.com/lifeandstyle/2020/jun/23/the-coronavirus-backlash-how-the-pandemic-is-destroying-womens-rights

7 Maya Oppenheim, 'Mothers doing extra 31 hours more housework each week than before coronavirus chaos, study finds', *Independent*, 2020, www.independent.co.uk/news/uk/home-news/coronavirus-housework-housework-school-closures-a9532646.html

8 Daniela Del Boca, Noemi Oggero, Paola Profeta, Maria Cristina Rossi and Claudia Villosio, 'Women's Working Behavior and Household Division of Labor During the two Waves of COVID-19 in Italy', Collegio Carlo Alberto, 2021, www.carloalberto.org/wp-content/uploads/2021/04/2nd-report-final-march-2021.pdf

9 Tiffany Dufu, 'I Was the Family Micromanager – Here's How I Learned to Let Go', *Good Housekeeping*, 2017, www.goodhousekeeping.com/life/parenting/a42864/tiffany-dufu-drop-the-ball/

10 Kim Parker, Juliana Menasce Horowitz and Renee Stepler, 'On Gender Differences, No Consensus on Nature vs. Nurture', Pew Research Center, 2017, www.pewresearch.org/social-trends/2017/12/05/on-gender-differences-no-consensus-on-nature-vs-nurture/

11 'Work Is Not to Blame for Women's Lack of Free Time; Time-pressure Is Often Self-imposed, According to Real Simple/Families and Work Institute Survey', PR Newswire (provided by Real Simple), 2012, www.prnewswire.com/news-releases/work-is-not-to-blame-for-womens-lack-of-free-time-time-pressure-is-often-self-imposed-according-to-real-simplefamilies-and-work-institute-survey-141774143.html

12 Emma Knights, 'Women in School Governance', National Governance Association, 2021, www.nga.org.uk/News/Blog/November-2021/Gender-on-governing-boards.aspx

13 'Women in the Workplace 2021', McKinsey & Company in partnership with Lean In 2021, www.mckinsey.com/featured-insights/diversity-and-inclusion/women-in-the-workplace?cid=eml-web

14 'Violence against women – key facts', World Health Organization, 2021, www.who.int/news-room/fact-sheets/detail/violence-against-women

15 'Percentage of women who have been victims of at least one form of sexual abuse or assault in public and semi-public places in France in 2017*', Statista, 2021, www.statista.com/statistics/938653/women-victims-of-sexual-assault-in-public-places-in-france/

16 Alan Travis, 'One in five women have been sexually assaulted, analysis finds', Guardian, 2018, www.theguardian.com/uk-news/2018/feb/08/sexual-assault-women-crime-survey-england-wales-ons-police-figures

17 Dalvin Brown, '19 million tweets later: A look at #MeToo a year after the hashtag went viral', USA Today, 2018, eu.usatoday.com/story/news/2018/10/13/metoo-impact-hashtag-made-online/1633570002/

18 'A place for survivors to share their stories', Everyone's Invited, 2022, www.everyonesinvited.uk/

19 Agnes C. Poirier, 'Camille Kouchner's Familia Grande: "I knew my stepfather's games ... but with my brother, too?"', Guardian, 2022, www.theguardian.com/books/2022/may/14/camille-kouchner-familia-grande-olivier-duhamel-abuse-interview

20 Meaghan Beatley, 'The shocking rape trial that galvanised Spain's feminists – and the far right', Guardian, 2019, www.theguardian.com/world/2019/apr/23/wolf-pack-case-spain-feminism-far-right-vox

21 'Swedish court clears "bottle sex" men of rape', Local, 2013, www.thelocal.se/20130515/47920/

22 'Violent sexual crimes recorded in the EU', Eurostat, 2017, ec.europa.eu/eurostat/web/products-eurostat-news/-/edn-20171123-1

23 'Violence against women: an EU-wide survey – Results at a glance', European Union Agency for Fundamental Rights, 2014, fra.europa.eu/sites/default/files/fra-2014-vaw-survey-at-a-glance-oct14_en.pdf

24 Sam Jones, 'Spanish court lifts "wolf pack" convictions from sexual abuse to rape', Guardian, 2019, amp.theguardian.com/world/2019/jun/21/spanish-supreme-court-finds-wolf-pack-men-guilty-of-rape

25 David Lisak, Lori Gardinier, Sarah C. Nicksa and Ashley M. Cote, 'False Allegations of Sexual Assaut: An Analysis of Ten Years of Reported Cases', *Violence Against Women*, vol. 16, no. 12, pp. 1318–1334, 2010, DOI: 10.1177/1077801210387747

26 'Section II, Crime Index Offenses Reported: Crime Index Total', 1996, ucr.fbi.gov/crime-in-the-u.s/1996/96sec2.pdf

27 Gideon Skinner, 'The Perils of Perception 2018', IPSOS, 2018, www.ipsos.com/en-uk/perils-perception-2018

28 'Transcript: Donald Trump's Taped Comments About Women', *New York Times*, 2016, www.nytimes.com/2016/10/08/us/donald-trump-tape-transcript.html

29 'Violence against women – key facts', World Health Organization, 2021, www.who.int/news-room/fact-sheets/detail/violence-against-women

30 Public Leaders Network, 'One woman dead every three days: domestic abuse in numbers', *Guardian*, 2017, www.theguardian.com/public-leaders-network/2017/dec/14/domestic-abuse-violence-women-femicide-review-refuge-cuts-in-numbers

31 '2020 Gender Social Norms Index (GSNI)', Human Development Reports, 2020, hdr.undp.org/content/2020-gender-social-norms-index-gsni

32 Georgia Aspinall, 'We're Not Panicking, We're Reacting. We're Not Hysterical, We're Angry', 2021, *Grazia*, graziadaily.co.uk/life/in-the-news/sarah-everard-reactions-response/

33 Jameela Jamil, 'Men's Violence Against Women with Dr. Jackson Katz', iWeigh with Jameela Jamil, 2021, podcasts.apple.com/us/podcast/mens-violence-against-women-with-dr-jackson-katz/id14988 55031?i=1000525960121

34 @Lenniesaurus, 2022, twitter.com/lenniesaurus/status/150638326921 8168837

35 Anna Codrea-Rado, 'Diane Abbott Receives Half Of All The Online Abuse Sent To Female Politicians', *Grazia*, 2017, graziadaily.co.uk/life/real-life/diane-abbott-receives-half-online-abuse-sent-female-politicians/

36 @ejrainfordbrent, 2021, twitter.com/ejrainfordbrent/status/146105804 6650691584?ref_src=twsrc-Etfw

37 Sam Cabral, 'Covid "hate crimes" against Asian Americans on rise', BBC, 2021, www.bbc.com/news/world-us-canada-56218684

38 Michelle Moore, *Real Wins: Race, Leadership and How to Redefine Success*, John Murray Press, London, 2021, pp. 107–109

Chapter 4

1   Reni Eddo-Lodge, *Why I'm No Longer Talking to White People About Race*, Bloomsbury Publishing, London, 2017, p. 213
2   Associated Press, 'Nobel laureate on "girls" in labs: "You fall in love with them, they fall in love with you, and when you criticize them, they cry"', *Business Insider*, 2015, www.businessinsider.com/nobel-laureate-on-girls-in-labs-you-fall-in-love-with-them-they-fall-in-love-with-you-and-when-you-criticize-them-they-cry-2015-6
3   'More than 12M "Me Too" Facebook posts, comments, reactions in 24 hours', CBS, 2017, www.cbsnews.com/news/metoo-more-than-12-million-facebook-posts-comments-reactions-24-hours/
4   Madison Marriage, 'Men Only: Inside the charity fundraiser where hostesses are put on show', *Financial Times*, 2018, www.ft.com/content/075d679e-0033-11e8-9650-9c0ad2d7c5b5
5   John Glenday, 'F1 bans grid girls: "the custom does not resonate with our brand values"', *The Drum*, 2018, www.thedrum.com/news/2018/02/01/f1-bans-grid-girls-the-custom-does-not-resonate-with-our-brand-values
6   'Transphobia', Merriam-Webster, 2022, www.merriam-webster.com/dictionary/transphobia
7   Madeleine Carlisle, 'Anti-Trans Violence and Rhetoric Reached Record Highs Across America in 2021', *Time*, 2021, time.com/6131444/2021-anti-trans-violence/
8   'LGBT in Britain – Hate Crime and Discrimination', Stonewall/YouGov, 2017, www.stonewall.org.uk/system/files/lgbt_in_britain_hate_crime.pdf
9   'A long way to go for LGBTI equality', European Union Agency for Fundamental Rights/Publications Office for the European Union, 2020, fra.europa.eu/sites/default/files/fra_uploads/fra-2020-lgbti-equality_en.pdf
10 'Victims or Villains: Examining Ten Years of Transgender Images on Television', Gay and Lesbian Alliance Against Defamation (GLAAD), 2013, www.glaad.org/publications/victims-or-villains-examining-ten-years-transgender-images-television

11 Julien Sauvalle, 'Andreja Pejic Makes Vogue History', *Out Magazine* 2015, www.out.com/truman-says/2015/4/21/andreja-pejic-first-trans gender-model-appear-vogue

12 'Politically correct', Merriam-Webster, 2022, www.merriam-webster. com/dictionary/politically%20correct

13 Katie Razzall, 'Maureen Lipman: Cancel culture could wipe out comedy', BBC, 2021, www.bbc.com/news/entertainment-arts-59703257

14 Ben Rumsby, 'Racist and sexist jokes trigger walkout at football awards ceremony', *Telegraph*, 2022, www.telegraph.co.uk/football/2022/05/09/ racist-sexist-jokes-mar-scottish-football-awards-ceremony-honoured/?onwardjourney=584162_v2

15 Brian Lee, 'The Importance of a Good Sense Of Humor & How to Build It', Life Hack, 2022, www.lifehack.org/584343/having-sense-humor-worse-than-being-boring

16 James Damore, 'Google's Ideological Echo Chamber', Document Cloud, 2017, www.documentcloud.org/documents/3914586-Googles-Ideological-Echo-Chamber.html

17 Clive Coleman, 'Maya Forstater: Woman loses tribunal over transgender tweets', BBC, 2019, www.bbc.com/news/uk-50858919

18 Doug Faulkner, 'Maya Forstater: Woman wins tribunal appeal over transgender tweets', BBC, 2021, www.bbc.com/news/uk-57426579

19 'People of colour seem to be superglued to the floor', BBC, 2019, www.bbc.com/news/business-50656176

20 Palash Ghosh, 'There Are No Black CEOs In Any Of Britain's 100 Largest Companies', *Forbes*, 2021, www.forbes.com/sites/palashghosh/2021/02/03/there-are-no-black-ceos-in-any-of-britains-100-largest-companies/?sh=ad927e72d8e7

21 Rob Moss, 'FTSE 100: Proportion of white male leaders is increasing', *Personnel Today*, 2021, www.personneltoday.com/hr/green-park-business-leaders-index-2021-ftse-100-diversity-inclusion/

22 Richard L. Zweigenhaft, 'Diversity Among Fortune 500 CEOs from 2000 to 2020: White Women, Hi-Tech South Asians, and Economically Privileged Multilingual Immigrants from Around the World', University of California Santa Cruz, 2021, whorulesamerica.ucsc.edu/power/diversity_update_2020.html

23 Phil Wahba, 'The number of black CEOs in the Fortune 500 remains very low', Fortune, 2020, fortune.com/2020/06/01/black-ceos-fortune-500-2020-african-american-business-leaders/

24 'Sea-change in UK boardrooms as women make up nearly 40% of FTSE 100 top table roles', Gov.uk, 2022, www.gov.uk/government/news/sea-change-in-uk-boardrooms-as-women-make-up-nearly-40-of-ftse-100-top-table-roles

25 'The Gender Pay Gap Is Widening In FTSE 100 Boardrooms', *CEO Today,* 2022, www.ceotodaymagazine.com/2022/07/the-gender-pay-gap-is-widening-in-ftse-100-boardrooms/

26 Katharina Buchholz, 'How has the number of female CEOs in Fortune 500 companies changed over the last 20 years?' World Economic Forum, 2022, www.weforum.org/agenda/2022/03/ceos-fortune-500-companies-female

27 Indya Clayton, 'New statistics from ONS show changes in UK population's sexual orientation', *Oxford Mail Online,* 2021, www.oxfordmail.co.uk/news/19333008.new-statistics-ons-show-changes-uk-populations-sexual-orientation/

28 Suki Sandhu, 'Where are all the LGBTQ+ CEOs, and what needs to change to make work more diverse?', *Stylist,* 2021, www.stylist.co.uk/life/careers/being-lgbt-at-work/475945

29 Jeffrey M. Jones, 'LGBT Identification in U.S. Ticks Up to 7.1%', *Gallup News,* 2022, news.gallup.com/poll/389792/lgbt-identification-ticks-up.aspx

30 Jim Probasco, 'Top LGBTQ+ CEOs', Investopedia, 2022, www.investopedia.com/top-lgbtq-ceos-5323561

31 'Do LGBT+ Directors Count in Fortune 500 Companies?', Out Leadership, 2017, outleadership.com/insights/do-lgbt-directors-count-in-fortune-500-companies/

32 'nTIDE June 2022 Jobs Report: Employment reaches all-time high for people with disabilities', Kessler Foundation and the University of New Hampshire, 2022, kesslerfoundation.org/press-release/ntide-june-2022-jobs-report-employment-reaches-all-time-high-people-disabilities

33 'Disability and employment, UK: 2019', Office for National Statistics, 2019, www.ons.gov.uk/peoplepopulationandcommunity/healthandsocialcare/disability/bulletins/disabilityandemploymentuk/2019

34 David Baboolall (they/them), Sarah Greenberg (she/her), Maurice Obeid (he/him) and Jill Zucker (she/her), 'Being transgender at work', McKinsey Quarterly, 2021, www.mckinsey.com/featured-insights/diversity-and-inclusion/being-transgender-at-work

35 'National LGBT Survey: Summary report', Gov.uk, 2019, www.gov. uk/government/publications/national-lgbt-survey-summary-report/ national-lgbt-survey-summary-report

36 Simon Hattenstone, 'Twitter has enabled people to behave in a way they wouldn't face to face', *Guardian*, 2013, www.theguardian.com/ lifeandstyle/2013/aug/04/caroline-criado-perez-twitter-rape-threats

37 'Hate speech vs. free speech: the UK laws', *The Week*, 2020, www. theweek.co.uk/97552/hate-speech-vs-free-speech-the-uk-laws

Chapter 5

1 Tara Westover, *Educated*, Random House, London, 2018, Author's Note, p. xii

2 Siobhan Fenton, 'Number of countries criminalising sex between lesbian and bisexual women increasing, human rights lawyers warn', *Independent*, 2016, www.independent.co.uk/news/world/number-of-countries-criminalising-sex-between-lesbian-and-bisexual-women-growing-human-rights-lawyers-warn-a7029301.html

3 A. Rampullo, C. Castiglione, O. Licciardello and V. Scolla, 'Prejudice Toward Gay Men and Lesbians in Relation to Cross- group Friendship and Gender', *Procedia – Social and Behavioral Sciences*, vol. 84, pp. 308–313, 2013, www.sciencedirect.com/science/article/pii/S1877042813016248

4 Emily Halnon, 'Men often use homophobic tweets to protect masculinity, study finds', Phys.org, 2019, phys.org/news/2019-04-men-homophobic-tweets-masculinity-article.html

5 Jeffrey M. Jones, 'LGBT Identification in U.S. Ticks Up to 7.1%', Gallup, 2022, news.gallup.com/poll/389792/lgbt-identification-ticks-up.aspx

6 Bloomberg, '"Fair and Lovely" cream rebranded "Glow and Lovely"', *Hindustan Times*, 2020, www.hindustantimes.com/world-news/fair-lovely-cream-rebranded-glow-lovely/story-enetD67c8mNeOFHMlcgMTP.html

7 E. J. Dickson, 'The dangerous rise of vaginal lightening', *Vox*, 2018, www.vox.com/the-goods/2018/12/6/18127154/vaginal-bleaching-lightening-creams

8   Nora Gonzalez, 'How Did the Rainbow Flag Become a Symbol of LGBTQ Pride?', *Encyclopedia Britannica*, 2022, www.britannica. com/story/how-did-the-rainbow-flag-become-a-symbol-of-lgbt-pride

9   'More young people in the UK identify as LGB, ONS finds', BBC, 2017, www.bbc.com/news/uk-41498713

10 'UK Black Pride', Wikipedia, 2022, en.wikipedia.org/wiki/Black_pride

11 'Sylvia Rivera', Wikipedia, 2022, en.wikipedia.org/wiki/Sylvia_Rivera

12 'Marsha P. Johnson', Wikipedia, 2022, en.wikipedia.org/wiki/Marsha_P._Johnson

13 William Yardley, 'Storme Delarverie, early leader in the gay rights movement, dies at 93', *New York Times*, 2014, www.nytimes.com/2014/05/30/nyregion/storme-delarverie-early-leader-in-the-gay-rights-movement-dies-at-93.html

14 Haroon Siddique, 'Stonewall is at centre of a toxic debate on trans rights and gender identity', *Guardian*, 2021, www.theguardian. com/society/2021/jun/05/stonewall-trans-debate-toxic-gender-identity

15 Logan Graves, 'A Look at Transphobia Within the LGBTQ community', Victoria Institute, 2018, victoryinstitute.org/a-look-at-transphobia-within-the-lgbtq-community/

16 'Overview – Phobias', NHS, 2018, www.nhs.uk/mental-health/conditions/phobias/overview/

17 Roisin O'Connor, 'JK Rowling reveals sexual abuse and domestic violence in open letter defending transgender comments', *Independent*, 2020, www.independent.co.uk/arts-entertainment/books/news/jk-rowling-transgender-letter-twitter-trans-people-a9559346.html

18 Katy Steinmetz, 'Why LGBT Advocates Say Bathroom "Predators" Argument Is a Red Herring', *Time*, 2016, time.com/4314896/transgender-bathroom-bill-male-predators-argument/

19 Amira Hasenbush, Andrew R. Flores and Jody L. Herman, 'Gender Identity Nondiscrimination Laws in Public Accommodations: a Review of Evidence Regarding Safety and Privacy in Public Restrooms', Locker Rooms, and Changing Rooms', *Sexuality Research and Social Policy*, vol. 16, pp. 70–83, 2019, doi.org/10.1007/s13178-018-0335-z

20 'Statement of Anti-Sexual Assault & Domestic Violence Organizations in Support of Equal Access for the Transgender Community', National

Alliance to End Sexual Violence, 2016, endsexualviolence.org/wp-content/uploads/2017/09/STATEMENT-OF-ANTI-SEXUAL-ASSAULT-AND-DOMESTIC-VIOLENCE-ORGANIZATIONS-IN-SUPPORT-OF-EQUAL-ACCESS-FOR-THE-TRANSGENDER-COMMUNITY.pdf

21 Jody L. Herman, 'Gendered Restrooms and Minority Stress', Williams Institute UCLA, 2013, williamsinstitute.law.ucla.edu/publications/gendered-restrooms-minority-stress/

22 'Transgender teens with restricted bathroom access at higher risk of sexual assault', Harvard School of Public Health, 2019, www.hsph.harvard.edu/news/hsph-in-the-news/transgender-teens-restricted-bathroom-access-sexual-assault/

23 Peter Walker, 'Popularity of tomboys is encouraging girls to swap gender, says NHS psychologist', *Telegraph*, 2017, www.telegraph.co.uk/science/2017/05/08/popularity-tomboys-encouraging-girls-swap-gender-says-nhs-psychologist/

24 Hannah Barnes, 'The crisis at the Tavistock's child gender clinic', BBC, 2021, www.bbc.com/news/uk-56539466

25 Shon Faye, *The Transgender Issue: An Argument for Justice*, Penguin Books, London, 2021, p. 19

26 'School Report: The experiences of lesbian, gay, bi and trans young people in Britain's schools in 2017', Stonewall, 2017, www.stonewall.org.uk/system/files/the_school_report_2017.pdf

27 Alexandra Brecht, Sascha Bos, Laura Ries, Sibylle Winter and Claudia Calvano, 'Assessment of Psychological Distress and Peer Relations among Trans Adolescents – An Examination of the Use of Gender Norms and Parent-Child Congruence of the YSR-R/CBCL-R among a Treatment-Seeking Sample', *Children*, vol. 8, no. 10, p. 864, 2021, doi.org/10.3390/children8100864

28 German Lopez, 'Myth #7: Children aren't old enough to know their gender identity', *Vox*, 2018, www.vox.com/identities/2016/5/13/17938118/transgender-children-transitioning-parenting

29 'Treatment – Gender dysphoria', NHS, 2020, www.nhs.uk/conditions/gender-dysphoria/

30 Priyanka Boghani, 'When Transgender Kids Transition, Medical Risks are Both Known and Unknown', PBS, 2015, https://www.pbs.org/wgbh/frontline/article/when-transgender-kids-transition-medical-risks-are-both-known-and-unknown/

Chapter 6

1 Tejvan Pettinger, 'Eleanor Roosevelt Biography', www.biographyon line.net, 2009, www.biographyonline.net/politicians/american/eleanor-roosevelt.html

2 Pamela Duncan and Matty Edwards, 'Huge effect of ethnicity on life chances revealed in official UK figures', *Guardian,* 2017, www.the-guardian.com/world/2017/oct/10/huge-effect-of-ethnicity-on-life-chances-revealed-in-official-uk-figures

3 Lance Hannon, Rober DeFina and Sarah Bruch, 'The Relationship Between Skin Tone and School Suspension for African Americans', *Race and Social Problems,* vol. 5, pp. 281–295, 2013, doi.org/10.1007/s12552-013-9104-z

4 Aly Yale, 'Black Homeowners Denied Mortgages More Than Twice As Often As White Counterparts, Report Finds', *Forbes,* 2018, www.forbes.com/sites/alyyale/2018/05/07/mortgage-loan-denials-more-common-with-minorities-new-report-shows/?sh=718016e5509a

5 Emma Kasprzak, 'Why are black mothers at more risk of dying?', BBC, 2019, www.bbc.com/news/uk-england-47115305

6 Catarina Saraiva and Matthew Boesler, 'Black Unemployment Rate Rises While White Joblessness Falls', Bloomberg, 2020, www.bloomberg.com/news/articles/2020-06-05/black-unemployment-rate-rises-while-white-joblessness-falls#xj4y7vzkg

7 Annalisa Merelli, 'The darker your skin the more likely you'll end up in an American jail', Quartz, 2019, qz.com/1724590/colorism-influences-probability-of-going-to-jail-new-study-finds/

8 Marco Ziegler and Christine Rauh, 'Visible Growth; Invisible Fears – Getting to Equal 2020: Pride', Accenture, 2020, www.accenture.com/_acnmedia/Thought-Leadership-Assets/PDF-3/Accenture-GTE-Pride-2020.pdf

9 'Uncovering talent: a new model of inclusion', Deloitte, 2019, www2.deloitte.com/content/dam/Deloitte/us/Documents/about-deloitte/us-about-deloitte-uncovering-talent-a-new-model-of-inclusion.pdf

10 'Why Diversity and Inclusion Matter (Quick Take)', Catalyst, 2020, www.catalyst.org/research/why-diversity-and-inclusion-matter/

11 Sebastian Bailey, 'Why Diversity Can Be Bad For Business (And Inclusion Is The Answer)', *Forbes,* 2014, www.forbes.com/sites/sebastianbai

ley/2014/05/20/why-we-should-prioritize-the-i-in-d-and-i/?sh=
825a46600d47

12   Karolina M. Lukasik, Otto Waris, Anna Soveri, Minna Lehtonen and
Matti Laine, 'The Relationship of Anxiety and Stress With Working
Memory Performance in a Large Non-depressed Sample', *Frontiers in
Psychology*, Sec. Cognition, 2019, doi.org/10.3389/fpsyg.2019.00004

13   'meritocracy (n.)', Online Etymology Dictionary, 2020, www.etymon
line.com/word/meritocracy

14   Michael Young, *The Rise of the Meritocracy (Classics in Organization
and Management Series)*, Taylor & Francis, New York, 1994

15   'Merit', Merriam-Webster, 2022, www.merriam-webster.com/
dictionary/merit

Chapter 7

1   Cesar Chavez, 'Education of the Heart: Cesar Chavez in his own words',
Cesar E. Chavez Foundation, ufw.org/research/history/education-
heart-cesar-chavez-words/

2   Reni Eddo-Lodge, *Why I'm No Longer Talking to White People About
Race*, Bloomsbury Publishing, London, 2017, p. 63

3   Abhishek Parajuli, 'The punishment gap', YouTube, TEDxLondon,
2019, www.youtube.com/watch?v=aoRCtfpSi9c

4   Mark L. Egan, Gregor Matvos and Amit Seru, 'When Harry Fired Sally:
The Double Standard in Punishing Misconduct', National Bureau of
Economic Research, 2017, http://www.nber.org/papers/w23242

5   Julia Belluz, 'Women surgeons are punished more than men for the exact
same mistakes, study finds', *Vox*, 2017, www.vox.com/science-and-
health/2017/11/23/16686532/surgeon-mistakes-gender-wage-gap

6   Noah Uhrig, 'Black, Asian and Minority Ethnic disproportionality in
the Criminal Justice System in England and Wales', UK Ministry of
Justice, 2016, assets.publishing.service.gov.uk/government/uploads/
system/uploads/attachment_data/file/639261/bame-disproportional
ity-in-the-cjs.pdf

7   Herminia Ibarra, Nancy M. Carter and Christine Silva, 'Why Men Still
Get More Promotions Than Women', *Harvard Business Review*, 2010,
hbr.org/2010/09/why-men-still-get-more-promotions-than-women

8 'Men, commit to mentor women. Not harassing women is not enough.' Lean In and SurveyMonkey survey, 2019, leanin.org/mentor-her#!

9 Christine Carter, 'Only 1 in 3 Managers Check Their Black Female Employees' Well-Being, New Study Shows', *Forbes*, 2021, www.forbes. com/sites/christinecarter/2021/02/23/only-1-in-3-managers-check-in-on-black-women-according-to-latest-state-of-black-women-in-corporate-america-report/?sh=726f846a24f0

10 'Affinity', *Encyclopedia Britannica*, 2022, www.britannica.com/ dictionary/affinity

11 Binna Kandola, *Racism at Work: The Danger of Indifference*, Pearn Kandola Publishing, Kidlington, 2018, p. 40

12 Kandola, *Racism at Work,* p. 40

13 Siobhan Palmer, 'Unconscious bias training "has no sustained impact" on behaviour, says report', *People Management*, 2019, www. peoplemanagement.co.uk/article/1742749/unconscious-bias-train ing-has-no-sustained-impact-on-behaviour

14 Bisi Daniels, 'Why many CEOs are tall people? The height of the mat-ter, By Bisi Daniels', *Premium Times*, 2016, www.premiumtimesng. com/entertainment/naija-fashion/203429-many-ceos-tall-people-height-matter-bisi-daniels.html

15 '2020 Gender Social Norms Index (GSNI)', Human Development Reports, 2020, hdr.undp.org/content/2020-gender-social-norms-index-gsni

16 Emily Burt, 'One in four UK employers would not hire someone with a disability', *People Management*, 2019, www.peoplemanagement. co.uk/article/1744755/one-four-uk-employers-would-not-hire-some one-with-disability

17 Rachel Thomas, 'How diversity branding hurts diversity', UX Collect-ive, 2017, uxdesign.cc/how-diversity-branding-hurts-diversity-66816 cbd2d67

18 'What Would You Do? Bike Theft (White Guy, Black Guy, Pretty Girl)', YouTube, 2020, www.youtube.com/watch?v=ge7i6oGuNRg

19 Zack Adesina and Oana Marocico, 'Is it easier to get a job if you're Adam or Mohamed?', BBC, 2017, www.bbc.co.uk/news/uk-england-london-38751307

20 David R. Francis, 'Employers' Replies to Racial Names', *The Digest*, National Bureau of Economic Research, no. 9, 2003, www.nber.org/ digest/sep03/employers-replies-racial-names

21 Ana Isabel Alonsagay, 'Changing your name when looking for work: should you do it?', Upskilled, www.upskilled.edu.au/skillstalk/changing-your-name-when-looking-for-work

22 Truc Nguyen, 'What's in a name? We talk to experts about racial bias in hiring and how to work to change it', CBC, 2018, www.cbc.ca/life/culture/what-s-in-a-name-we-talk-to-experts-about-racial-bias-in-hiring-and-how-to-work-to-change-it-1.4822467

23 Amit Katwala, 'Is your name ruining your life?', *Wired*, 2021, www.wired.co.uk/article/name-discrimination

24 'Growth, Equal Opportunities, Migration and Markets (GEMM) Project – Policy Briefs in Focus', 2020, gemm2020.eu/wp-content/uploads/2018/11/GEMM_Project_Policy_Briefs_lq.pdf

25 Vernā Myers, 'How to overcome our biases? Walk boldly toward them', YouTube, TEDxBeaconStreet, 2014, www.ted.com/talks/verna_myers_how_to_overcome_our_biases_walk_boldly_toward_them?language=en

26 Khe Hy, 'Identity, Privilege, and Subconscious Bias (and Bros)', Rad Reads, 2016, radreads.co/identity-privilege-and-subconscious-bias-and-bros-dd890e9cf2c7/#.ta35ai2vy

Chapter 8

1 Madeline Branch, '10 Inspiring Eleanor Roosevelt Quotes', United Nations Foundation, 2015, unfoundation.org/blog/post/10-inspiring-eleanor-roosevelt-quotes/

2 'School Report: The experiences of lesbian, gay, bi and trans young people in Britain's schools in 2017', Stonewall, 2017, www.stonewall.org.uk/system/files/the_school_report_2017.pdf

3 Natalie Marchant, 'Study: Almost all Black British children have experienced racism at school', World Economic Forum, 2020, www.weforum.org/agenda/2020/11/racism-united-kingdom-schools-black-children-inequality/

4 '"It's just everywhere": A study on sexism in schools – and how we tackle it', UK Feminista and the National Education Union, 2017, ukfeminista.org.uk/wp-content/uploads/2017/12/Report-Its-just-everywhere.pdf

5 'Global Gender Gap Report 2021', World Economic Forum, 2021, www.weforum.org/reports/global-gender-gap-report-2021/digest

6 Laura M. Giurge, Ashley V. Whillans and Ayse Yemiscigil, 'A multi-country perspective on gender differences in time use during COVID-19', *Proceedings of the National Academy of Sciences* (PNAS), 2021, doi. org/10.1073/pnas.2018494118

Chapter 9

1 James Smurthwaite, 'Christchurch Adventure Park "Bro Zone" Renamed "O-Zone" Following Social Media Backlash', PinkBike, 2021, www.pinkbike.com/news/christchurch-adventure-park-bro-zone-renamed-o-zone-following-social-media-backlash.html

2 Megan Angelo, '16 Unforgettable Things Maya Angelou Wrote and Said', *Glamour*, 2014, www.glamour.com/story/maya-angelou-quotes

Chapter 10

1 *RBG*, produced and directed by Betsy West and Julie Cohen, CNN Films, Storyville Films, Participant Media, 2018

2 'Diversity Matters', Catalyst, 2014, www.catalyst.org/research/infographic-diversity-matters/

Glossary

1 Abby Budiman and Neil G. Ruiz, 'Asian Americans are the fastest-growing racial or ethnic group in the U.S.', Pew Research Centre, 2021, www.pewresearch.org/fact-tank/2021/04/09/asian-americans-are-the-fastest-growing-racial-or-ethnic-group-in-the-u-s/

2 'Ethnic group, England and Wales: Census', Office for National Statistics, 2023, www.ons.gov.uk/peoplepopulationandcommunity/culturalidentity/ethnicity/bulletins/ethnicgroupenglandandwales/census2021

3 Ibid.

4 Nicholas Jones, Rachel Marks, Roberto Ramirez and Merarys Rios-Vargas, 'Improved Race and Ethnicity Measures Reveal U.S. Population Is Much More Multiracial', Census.gov, 2021, www.census.gov/library/stories/2021/08/improved-race-ethnicity-measures-reveal-united-states-population-much-more-multiracial.html

5 'Brazil 2010 census shows changing race balance', BBC, 2011, www.bbc.com/news/world-latin-america-15766840

6 Mike Laws, 'Why we capitalize "Black" (and not "white")', *Columbia Journalism Review*, 2020, www.cjr.org/analysis/capital-b-black-styleguide.php

7 'Coloured', Wikipedia, 2022, en.wikipedia.org/wiki/Coloureds

8 Dr Anne Fausto-Sterling, 'The Five Sexes: Why Male and Female are not Enough', *New York Academy of Sciences*, vol. 33, 1993, www.researchgate.net/publication/239657377_The_Five_Sexes_Why_Male_and_Female_are_not_Enough

9 'Frequently Asked Questions about Transgender People', TransEquality.org, 2016, transequality.org/issues/resources/frequently-asked-questions-about-transgender-people

10 John Misachi, '10 Countries Where Women Far Outnumber Men', World Atlas, 2021, www.worldatlas.com/articles/10-countries-where-women-far-outnumber-men.html

11 'Population of England and Wales', Office for National Statistics, 2018, www.ethnicity-facts-figures.service.gov.uk/uk-population-by-ethnicity/national-and-regional-populations/population-of-england-and-wales/latest

12 Nicholas Jones et al., 'Improved Race and Ethnicity Measures'.

13 Peter Wade, Yasuko I. Takezawa and Audrey Smedley, 'Race', *Encyclopedia Britannica*, 2020, www.britannica.com/topic/race-human

14 Rebecca Nicholson, '"Poor little snowflake" – the defining insult of 2016', *Guardian*, 2016, www.theguardian.com/science/2016/nov/28/snowflake-insult-disdain-young-people

Index

Page numbers in bold type refer to entries in the Glossary at the end of the book.

A Note on the Author

Suzy was born in the Pacific Northwest of the United States. During the formative years of her life, she and her family lived on a farm with no access to running water or electricity. Despite her remote upbringing, Suzy was drawn to travelling and keen to explore the wider world. After university, she joined a global management consulting firm, which broadened her reach and enhanced her understanding of people, culture and change. In 2004, Suzy moved to London, where she currently resides with her partner and two children.

Today, Suzy works with senior leaders across the public, private, education and third sectors to solve some of the most complex social issues of our time. She is a specialist in inclusion and diversity, and is widely recognised for her pragmatic and thoughtful approach to what is often emotive and messy. In addition to her client work, Suzy holds a variety of board-level roles, including being a non-executive director for the UK government and a board trustee for the Women's Sport Trust.

Mind the Inclusion Gap, her first book, summarises decades of learning about inclusion, and is part of her personal mission to create a more equitable and fairer society by helping others gain the confidence and knowledge they need to take impactful action.

Unbound is the world's first crowdfunding publisher, established in 2011.

We believe that wonderful things can happen when you clear a path for people who share a passion. That's why we've built a platform that brings together readers and authors to crowdfund books they believe in – and give fresh ideas that don't fit the traditional mould the chance they deserve.

This book is in your hands because readers made it possible. Everyone who pledged their support is listed below. Join them by visiting unbound.com and supporting a book today.

Lee Abbott
Postdoc Academy
Kate Adams
Fabian Adams-Sandiford
Cecil Adjalo

Improper Agency
Tunji Akintokun
Parbej Ali
Mark Allan
Ian Allott

Nicola Alloway
Michael Ambjorn
Ismail Amla
Maria Andersson
Robert Anderton
Jill Angelo
Sue Anstiss
Angela Arnold
Adrian Ashton
Fleur Ashworth
Mary Assad
Kelly Averis
Marta Balbous
Anna Bancroft
Ruth Banks
Nicola Bannock
Emily Barnes
Katie Barton
Val Bayliss-Brideaux
James Beck
Lorna Benton
Myles Berry
Ruth Berry
Scott Berry
Andy Berschauer
Philippa Bird
Vinod Birdi
Mettie Bishop Burris
Hannah Blackmore
Richard Bon
Jo Bostock
Victoria Bracken
Tom Bridgman

Daniel Brown
BT Group
Jamie Cadenas
Alicia Campbell-Hill
Ali Carroll
Peter Carroll
David Champeaux
Clear Channel
Martin Chapman
Heather Chen
Catherine Cheng
Joanne Chu
Denise Clarke
Clear Channel Team
Isabel Cleofe
Valerie Cleofe
James Conway
Michelle Coomber
Rebecca Cotter
Louise Coyne
Brian Crozier
Emily Csizmazia
Alison Cupito
Sue Daley
Lisette Danesi
Jane Dawson-Howe
Claire Day
Richard Day
Sue Day
Stijn De Vriendt
Richard Dear
Lieve Debeerst
Carmella Delargy

Beatrice Devillon-Cohen

Jess Dibble

Richard Dixon

Nadia Donnelly

Simon Donovan

Paul Driver

Samantha Edgar

Greg Eisenhauer

Stephanie Eitel

Dr. Sebastiaan
   Eldritch-Böersen

Rasha ElKhalili

Lorena Escudero Sánchez

Sarah Evans

Claire Ewing

Chris Ferris

Daniele Fiandaca

Gemma Field

Angus Findlay

James Fitzsimmons

Alison Forward

Ben Foulkes

Kelise Franclemont

Lorena Franco

Mark Frey

Michael Fuller

A Gardner

Chris Garrison

Fiona Gibson

Rachel Gilley

Melissa Gittens

Tim Glasby

Philip Godson

Charlotte Gogstad

Jan Gooding

Jan Gower

Kelly Craig Graham

Lj Gray

Camilla Green

Leigh Greenwood

Katy Guest

Shipra Gupta & Naresh
   Grandhi

Joanna Hammond

Rachael Hampton

Kate Hannon

Julie Harris

Renee Hartnett

Barbara Harvey

Raisa Hassan

Kim Hay

Paula Hegarty

Timm Heinrich von Bargen

Jo Henderson

Wenmei Hill

Anyi Hobson

Sarah Hogan

Mamiko Hogwood

Ayla Holdom

Paula Homan

Jessica Hooper

Sally Horrox

Nicole Horst

Sophie Houstoun-Boswall

Tess Howard

Katie and Duncan Hubber

Harriet Hughes
Colin Hunter
Jane Hunter
Aoife Hurley
Chris Hurst
Hugh Ind
Michael Inpong
Marc Andreu Iranzo
Sonnet Ireland
Daniel Jackson
Lorna Jackson
Jo James
Martine Janssen Groesbeek
Claire Jenkins
Steve Joy
Adam Kelly
Khalil Khabibullin
Ameel Khan
Dan Kieran
Jonathan Kirwan
Lisa Klancke Espinosa
Tania Koppens
Emma Lawrence
Peter Levy
Sarah Levy
Anastasia Lewis
Helis Lipping
Lara Longhurst
Roland Lyle
Aisha Lysejko
Ewan Mackay
Ellie Mackin Roberts
John Macleod

Rosie MacRae
Catt** Makin
Harry Malcolm
John Maskell
Sarah Maskell MBE
Sean Tobias May
John McArdle
Hazel McCarthy
James McCarthy
Tom McLaughlan
Justine McNeil
Kirstin McNeil
Eimear Meredith-Jones
Helen Merriott
Jo Millar
John Mitchinson
Annie Moyer
Orville Mullings
Lucy Murdoch
Sharon Murray
Carlo Navato
Simon Negus
Rob Neil
John New
Jodi Nichols
Brent Norberg
Kathy Norberg
Clare Norman
Jeremy Oates
Ronan O'Brien
Jenny O'Gorman
Noel O'Mahony
Brendan O'Dwyer

Cara O'Leary
Heidi O'Leary
Izzy Obeng
Kory Onaga
Samantha Owo
Priya Pallan
Joanne Palmer
Kristin Para
Tammy Parlour
Tracy Pennington
Lizzie Penny
Noel Penzer
Femke Perry
Natalie Phillips
Elaine Pinter
Justin Pollard
Janet Pope
Adam Powell
Jane Powell
Claire Ramage
Amanda Ramsay
Karen Willow Reddy
Allan Reid
Emily Reiter Sparks
Julie Renard
Sarah Reynolds
Louisa Richards
Eleanor Roderick
Jay Roff
Nancy Rowe
Ajoy Roy-Chowdhury
Lisa Rull
Shannon Rush-Call

Nicola Rushton
Olivier Sabella
John Sanders
Bernice Sargent
Johanna Scheer
Kim Seath
Dumisani Senda
Gillian Sephton
Paul and Muireann Sheahan
Melissa Shepherd
Laura Siddall
Richard Simpson
Claire Sinclair
Martina Skripova
Caitlin Slatter
Dixie Smith
Lori Smith
Surinder Sond
Tim Spencer
Diane E. Stephen
Jack Stevenson
Fiona Stewart
Phil Swallow
Paula Sweetman
Tasha Tarusova
The Equal Group
David Thomlinson
Nik Thompson
Abi Tierney
Kate Tilbury
Ally Tomlins
Sally Trompeter
Action Tutoring

Anoop Unadkat
Kerri Urquhart
Mikael Valot
Abigail Vaughan
Michaela von Bargen
Jonathan Waeland
Peter Webb
Geoff Weeks
Keith Wellington
Carla Welsh
AnnaLisa Wesley
Heather & Jevin West
Lou Whitaker

Annabelle White
Christine White
Kelly Widelska
Leann Wilkins
Jessica Williams
Sophie Willis
Marlise Wilson
Sally Windle
Catriona Wolfenden
James Woods
Claire Yates-Waller
Lucie Young
Kerstin Zumstein